Teacher Education

TEACHER EDUCATION

THIRD EDITION

RADHA MOHAN
Former Principal
Rajalakshmi College of Education
Thandalam, Chennai

T.V. SOMASHEKAR
Assistant Professor
Department of Education
Regional Institute of Education (NCERT)
Mysuru, Karnataka

PHI Learning Private Limited
Delhi-110092
2026

*In fond memory of **Shri Asoke K. Ghosh** (October 1942–February 2024), Founder Chairman and Managing Director of PHI Learning, whose vision endlessly inspires.*

The Legacy Continues....

Published by Pushpita Ghosh, PHI Learning Private Limited, Rimjhim House, 111, Patparganj Industrial Estate, Delhi-110092 and Gopsons Printers Pvt. Ltd., A-14, Sector-60, Noida, Gautambudh Nagar, Noida, Uttar Pradesh-201301.

₹695.00

Teacher Education, Third Edition
Radha Mohan and T.V. Somashekar

ISBN-978-93-5443-981-0 (Print Book)
ISBN-978-93-5443-932-2 (e-Book)

To

my mother,
Late Mrs. Kalpagam Subrahmanyam
with gratitude
for encouraging me to follow my dreams

Contents

PART VIII: WAY FORWARD

Preface

The Third Edition of *Teacher Education* addresses the urgent need for a transformative approach to teacher preparation. It offers valuable insights, practical recommendations, and varied perspectives to tackle current challenges and shape the future of education. The COVID-19 pandemic has underscored the importance of adopting innovative, technology-driven solutions in teacher training. As schools navigate these complexities, this edition emphasises the dual necessity of critically assessing the current state of teacher preparation and presenting forward-thinking strategies to revolutionise the field, ensuring a strong and adaptable education system for the future. The updated NCTE (National Council for Teacher Education) Regulations, shaped by the recommendations of the Justice Verma Commission along with the introduction of National Education Policy 2020 has led to several structural changes in teacher education. The NCTE has introduced diverse teacher education programs, including the 2-year B.Ed./M.Ed., 4-year B.A./B.Sc.–B.Ed., 3-year B.Ed. (Part-time), and 3-year integrated B.Ed./M.Ed. Positioning teacher education at the nexus between schools and universities will involve significant changes in the theory and practice of both pedagogy, subject content and assessment techniques.

Highlights of this Edition

The book in its third edition, is structured into eight comprehensive parts, designed to provide an in-depth understanding of teacher education:

Part I Reflections on Teacher Education
Part II Process and Practice
Part III Stages and Phases
Part IV Methods and Techniques—General and Modern
Part V Performance and Evaluation
Part VI Professional Practice and Ethics

Part VII Research and Action
Part VIII Way Forward

Each chapter delves into fundamental concepts and practical applications, integrating the vision of NEP-2020 and NCTE's commitment to preparing competent teachers for a rapidly evolving world. This edition specifically addresses the demands of the 21st century, with substantial updates to Chapters 1, 5, 6, 8, 10, 11, 13, 14, and 17.

Key Updates in the Third Edition

The present edition includes updates in the following chapters:

Chapter 1—Stakeholders: Introduces NCTE objectives and the two-year B.Ed. curriculum, with insights into NEP-2020's perspective on teacher education. The updated reference section includes direct links to key NCTE guidelines for further exploration.

Chapter 5—Practice Teaching: Discusses practice teaching as envisioned by the NCTE, supported by web links for exploring diverse teaching methods. A sample evaluation tool is included as Appendix 1.

Chapter 6—Pre-Service Teacher Education: Features updated recommendations from the Justice Verma Committee (2012) and NCTE Regulations (2014). The shift to an intensive two-year B.Ed. program is outlined, with a focus on school-based activities. Table 6.1 highlights these reforms, alongside NEP-2020 policy perspectives.

Chapter 8—In-Service Teacher Education: Revisits the significance of in-service training based on NCFTE 2009–2010. Updates include Samagra Shiksha components and strategies for designing effective training programs for teachers.

Chapter 10—Modern Techniques in Use in Teacher Education: Explores emerging classroom technologies like smartphones, tablets, and e-readers, with an emphasis on TPACK (Technological Pedagogical Content Knowledge). The interplay of technology, pedagogy, and content is modern teaching is depicted diagrammatically.

Chapter 11—Evaluation in Teacher Education: Expands on the role of stakeholders and introduces the Quality Deployment Function (QFD) for assessing school and teacher education program effectiveness.

Chapter 13—Characteristics of a Profession: Provides an Instructor Self-Evaluation Tool as an appendix, helping teachers engage in reflective practices to enhance their professional growth.

Chapter 14—Professionalism in Teacher Education: Highlights the critical link between teacher professionalism and student achievement. Performance indicators (PINDICS) are included to guide teacher self-assessment and professional development.

Chapter 17—Current Issues and Problems in Teacher Education: Introduces contemporary strategies to adapt teacher education to evolving educational landscapes.

This book aims to serve as a comprehensive resource for teacher trainees, educators, and researchers, equipping them to meet the challenges of modern teaching while fostering excellence in education.

We would like to thank editorial and production teams at PHI for their unstinting efforts and support. It is always a pleasure to work with such a professional and competent group of people.

We hope this edition inspires and supports your journey in teacher education.

Radha Mohan
T.V. Somashekar

Part I

REFLECTIONS ON TEACHER EDUCATION

CHAPTER 1 Stakeholders

The school has always been the most important means of transferring the wealth of tradition from one generation to the next. This applies today in an even higher degree than in former times, for through modern development of the economic life, the family as bearer of tradition and education has been weakened. The continuance and health of human society is therefore in a still higher degree dependent on the school than formerly.

—Albert Einstein

INTRODUCTION

Teacher education is, of course, at the base of all educational systems. The quality and nature of teacher training determines the nature and success of educational systems. This is what the Delors Report had to say about the crucial role of teachers:

> Our vision of the coming century is one in which the pursuit of learning is valued by individuals and by authorities all over the world, not only as a means to an end, but also as an end in itself. Each person will be encouraged and enabled to take up learning opportunities throughout life. Hence much will be expected, and much demanded, of teachers, for it largely depends on them whether this vision can come true. Teachers have crucial roles to play in preparing young people not only to face the future with confidence but to build it with purpose and responsibility (Delors et al. 1996).

GOALS OF EDUCATION

Education serves a social function when it seeks to respond to the demands of individuals or communities for education suited to their particular needs, aspirations and cultural traditions. It serves as a manpower function when it seeks to provide the economy with trained personnel, to ensure that there are sufficient teachers, nurses or engineers to meet the needs of society as a whole. Education thus seeks to discharge both social and manpower functions. So, it is necessary to understand how educational planning reconciles these functions, and to what extent manpower planning has contributed to educational planning.

PLANNING FOR BALANCE IN TEACHER EDUCATION

Teacher education is a sub-system of education. The equilibrium of this sub-system depends on the following three factors:

1. Number of seats demanded for teacher education by admission seekers and supply of seats by teacher education institutions.
2. Demand for and supply of teachers coming out of the institutions of teacher education in the job market for school teachers.
3. Number of teacher educators in the job market, seeking employment and job opportunities available in institutions of teacher education.

Maintaining equilibrium in these three areas is a complicated process. There was a period of shortage of teachers, followed by a season of excess supply of manpower in all fields, including teaching. Therefore, it is essential to work out a balanced growth of teacher education in future. For this, we have to consider the use of regulation and free market forces together in order to guide factors that affect demand and supply of teachers and teacher educators.

The demand of teacher educators depends upon the number of institutions of teacher education and enrolments of future teachers in these institutions. The number of institutions, in turn, depends on the funds available on the one hand and the demand for teachers in schools on the other.

PATTERN OF TEACHER TRAINING IN INDIA

The pattern of education in India is shown in Figure 1.1. Students can opt to become teachers with a B.Ed. after a graduate degree which they can acquire through regular courses or through distance learning programmes. For admission, it is mandatory that they fulfil the 5 + 3 + 3 + 4 grade requirements.

<table>
<tr><td>School Curricular Structure format (in years)</td><td>5</td><td>3</td><td>3</td><td>4</td><td>10+2</td><td rowspan="2">Need for multiple levels of pre-service and in-service teacher training</td></tr>
<tr><td>Break-up of age: in years</td><td>3–8, years</td><td>8–11, years</td><td>11–14, years</td><td>14–18 years</td><td>16–18</td></tr>
</table>

Standard	I	II	III	IV	V	VI	VII	VIII	IX	X	XI	XII
Age	7	8	9	10	11	12	13	14	15	16	17	18
Stages	FLN		Preparatory stage			Middle stage			Secondary stage			
	Compulsory Education											

FIGURE 1.1 Teacher education pattern in India.

However, they can after 10 + 2 years of schooling opt to do integrated teacher education programmes, B.Sc B.Ed/BA B.Ed/M.Sc.Ed or a primary teacher training programme which will give them a diploma in teaching/Nursury Teacher Training diploma which makes them eligible to teach at pre-primary level. These courses are of two-year duration. This is conducted by DIET and self-financing institutes of education. The diploma is awarded by the respective state governments. NEP-2020 prescribes four-year integrated teacher training programmes for all stages of schooling-foundation, preparatory, middle and secondary. The new Integrated Teacher Education programme (ITEP) is being implemented through NCTE in the country.

Figure 1.1 shows the different ways of getting a B.Ed. degree. One can follow the regular stream and after graduation,

- enrol for a B.Ed. in a training college, or
- do a distance education/correspondence/open university course.

Figure 1.2 gives a mind map of teacher education.

In Figure 1.2, a hub and spoke model, where the teacher trainee is the hub, the stakeholders are:

1. **Teacher trainees**—who aspire to be teachers
2. **Teacher educators**—who are motivated, interested in student development and are thorough professionals
3. **Provider**—colleges of education, institutes or universities
4. **Society**—community at large—local, national and global
5. **Funders**—students, universities, other philanthropists, industries, schools and colleges
6. **Employers**—schools, colleges, industries, district and local governments
7. **Awarding bodies**—universities, NCTE which grants recognition, and NAAC which accredits and assesses the output

The expectations of each of the stakeholder are mapped in Figure 1.2.

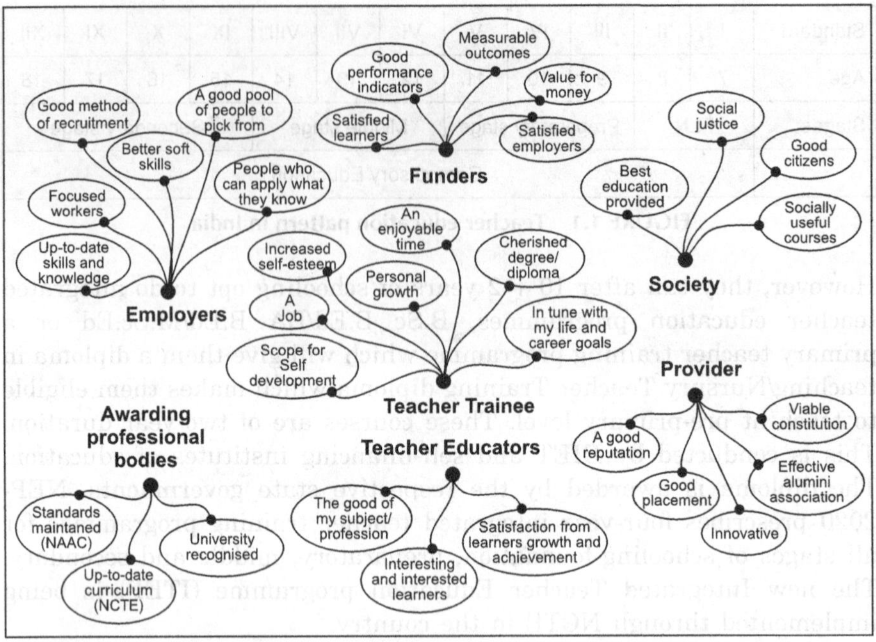

FIGURE 1.2 Mind map of teacher education.

STAKEHOLDERS IN TEACHER EDUCATION

The challenges faced by the mushrooming teacher education institutions pose questions for both the school systems and the state governments. On the one hand, the school system has to deal with poor teacher quality and increasing student and societal expectations, on the other, state and national governments have to make arrangements to provide the teacher education system with an environment encouraging innovation and meeting the needs of the school. Figure 1.3 indicates the various stakeholders in teacher education.

Stakeholders are "individuals or entities who stand to gain or lose from the success or failure of a system or an organisation". Gross and Godwin (2005) identify education's stakeholders as parents, students, alumni, administrators, employers and communities. In our Indian set-up, we could include religious groups, youth services such as NSS and NCC community organisations such as Rotaract club, senior citizens as we have a culture of respect for elders, government agencies, NGOs, and so on.

The stakeholders in education have great impact on the outcome of schooling and the purposes of learning, thus affecting how they structure educational institutions, define learning, and understand the nature of the student. These can appear to be mutually exclusive.

Teacher education is a complex system. Many contributors are involved, including state legislatures, state certification boards, national

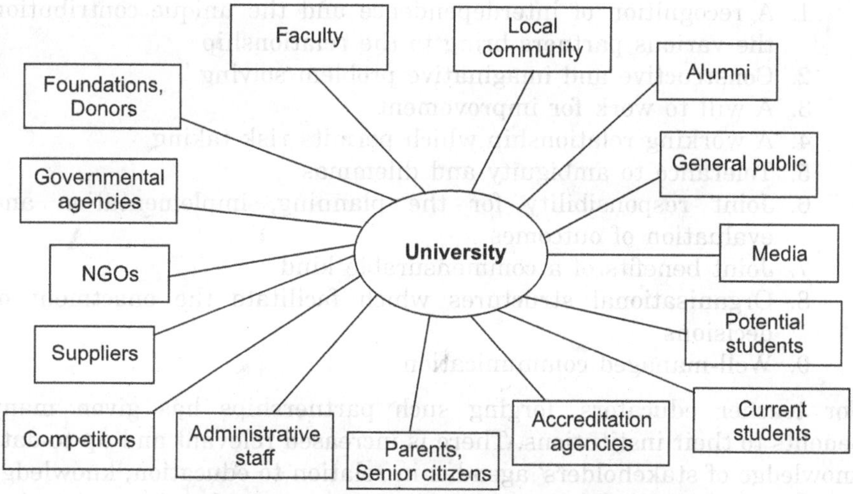

FIGURE 1.3 Stakeholders in teacher education.

and regional accreditation associations, educational professional associations, teacher unions, teacher education institutions, schools, and the federal government.

Most of the stakeholders agree that teacher education needs to change to meet the needs of digital age learners and the challenges of a rapidly changing knowledge and technology-based global society. But diverse policy contexts and a lack of shared vision pose barriers to collaborative action among the stakeholders to effect change. Although there are isolated islands of innovation and excellence in educator professional development, concerted and coordinated action by all stakeholder groups is needed to take them to scale.

Productive partnerships have drawn together previously disparate groups which recognize that

> Collaboration is necessary where parties have a shared interest in solving a problem that none of them can resolve alone. Collaboration makes sense where stakeholders recognise the potential advantages of working together—they need each other to execute a vision they all share, and they need the others to advance their educational interests. (Fullan and Watson, 2000)

The 'shared interest' is in the name of the learners in the schools—the key stakeholders—whose lives will change if exposed to a well-structured and meaningful curriculum in a humane and socially balanced environment.

The partnerships evolving between schools, teacher educators, employers and society are ones that are moving beyond consultation and advice towards genuine reciprocity. According to Groundwater-Smith et al. (2001), reciprocity between the partners is obtained in the following cases:

1. A recognition of interdependence and the unique contribution the various partners bring to the relationship
2. Constructive and imaginative problem solving
3. A will to work for improvement
4. A working relationship which permits risk taking
5. Tolerance to ambiguity and dilemmas
6. Joint responsibility for the planning, implementation and evaluation of outcomes
7. Joint benefits of a commensurable kind
8. Organisational structures which facilitate the enactment of decisions
9. Well-managed communication

For teacher educators, forging such partnerships has given many benefits to their institutions. There is increased relevant and up-to-date knowledge of stakeholders' agendas in relation to education, knowledge that can be translated into appropriate responses and actions in teacher education programmes.

Stakeholders and Responsibilities

The stakeholders who need to be involved in decisions about the profession of teacher educator include: government/educational authorities, perspectives of teacher trainees, employers of teacher educators, teacher educators themselves, employers of teachers, teachers, professional associations of teacher educators, external quality agencies, unions, university administrators, school boards, legislators, district administrators and several others.

Expectations of Key Stakeholders

The expectations of key stakeholders are listed below.

1. Society wants to educate children in order to ensure that its various economical and cultural institutions are perpetuated and expanded. Its aim is to mould students into the next generations of producers and consumers.
2. Government wants to educate children to ensure a stable, productive and powerful nation in keeping with national goals.
3. Religious groups want to educate children in order to bring them in line with their cultural norms.
4. Parents want their children to have education so that they are equipped with skills that will allow them to leave home and flourish and do them credit.
5. Students expect to be educated, so that they have plenty of choices in ways in which to comfortably realize the autonomy they so envied in their parents.

While the mechanisms for undertaking these responsibilities, and the stakeholders involved may, of course, vary according to different national contexts, it would appear that in many countries some of these key conditions are not being met, often because it is unclear who is responsible for them, with the negative consequences for the profession that have been highlighted.

The variety of purposes, definitions and understandings poses potential problems for educators in adjusting their efforts with the input from stakeholders. Gross and Godwin (2005) suggest performing a stakeholder, analysis by which once the relevant stakeholders are identified, it is determined which of these have both interest and influence on a given educational institution. It will make all the stakeholders work together to attain the common goal of teacher education.

SOME ESSENTIAL FEATURES OF TEACHER EDUCATION IN THE 21st CENTURY

Many assert that the existing system of educator preparation is not equipping teachers with the skills needed to enable their students to be successful in the 21st century. Teacher candidates continue to be immersed in antiquated preparation programmes that equip them to deliver primarily traditional stand-alone, text-based instruction in traditional classrooms. If schools of education and alternative education systems continue to prepare teachers for only traditional teaching, the future is already over. By focusing only on teacher preparation, the nation risks losing sight of the fact that schools also must change to keep pace with globalisation. Figure 1.4 shows the necessary skills a 21st century teacher trainee should have on leaving the portals of the teacher education institution. These are dependent on the following systems:

1. Learning environment
2. Professional development
3. Curriculum and instruction
4. Standards and assessments

The essential features of teacher education in the 21st century are listed below:

1. In many ways, teacher educators are working with one foot in the future and the other in the past. Their graduates will serve the most digitally savvy, socially networked generation in history.
2. Today's youth have a clear vision of what the 21st century education should provide. They participate in online communities with a wealth of learning resources that extend far beyond the bounds of their schools and well beyond the limits of a single teacher's knowledge and skill.

3. Teachers of the future will pursue careers in a globally integrated knowledge economy that rewards teamwork, continuous learning, and constant innovation.
4. Higher benchmarks for traditional teaching have to be set to meet the needs of digital age learners.
5. Schools of education must go beyond the present paradigm of teacher preparation. They must take on the exciting challenge of developing 21st century educators for 21st century schools. The time is right to reinvent teacher education.

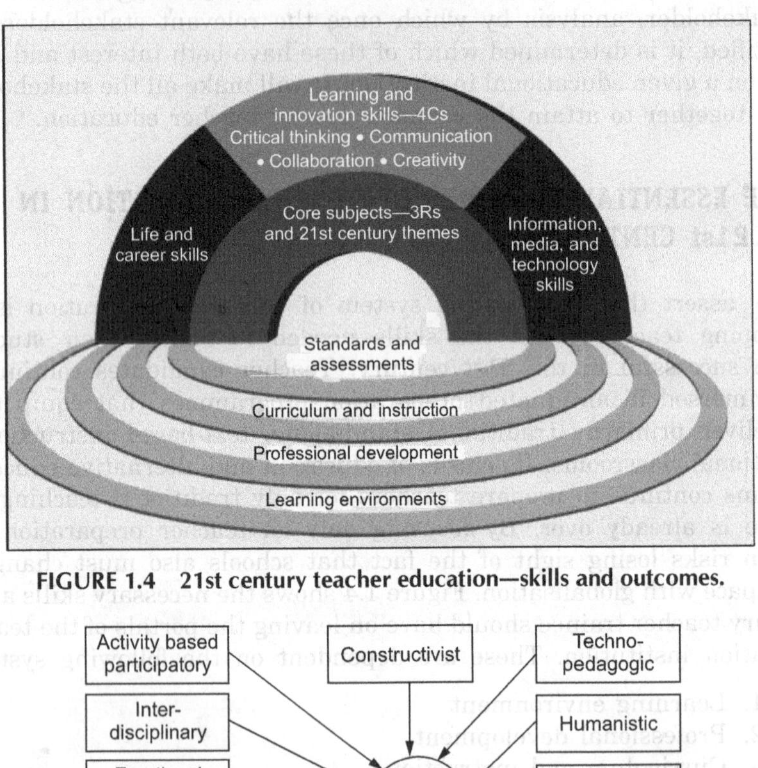

FIGURE 1.4 21st century teacher education—skills and outcomes.

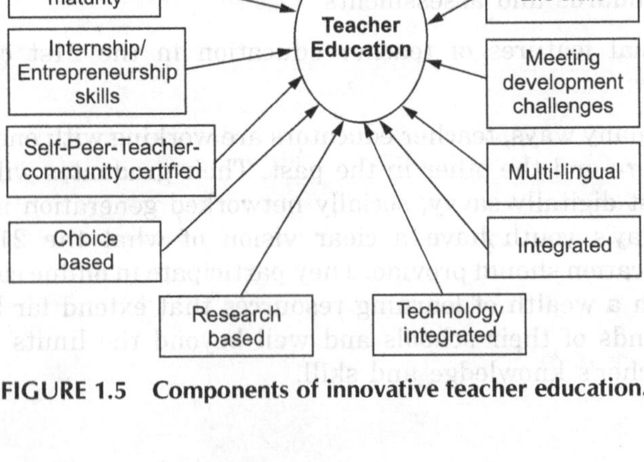

FIGURE 1.5 Components of innovative teacher education.

COMPONENTS OF INNOVATIVE TEACHER EDUCATION

Teachers who are knowledgeable can equip students with high levels of skills. This, in turn, can help the nation have a quality workforce and become more economically competitive.

Figure 1.5 shows the different components which a teacher education programme should have.

NATIONAL COUNCIL FOR TEACHER EDUCATION

The National Council for Teacher Education is a statutory body which came into existence in pursuance of the National Council for Teacher Education Act, 1993 (No. 73 of 1993) on 17th August,1995.

The main objective of the NCTE is to achieve planned and coordinated development of the teacher education system throughout the country, the regulation and proper maintenance of Norms and Standards in the teacher education system and for matters connected therewith.

The NCTE Two Year programme consists of three broad inter-related curricular areas:

(a) Perspectives in Education
(b) Curriculum and Pedagogic Studies
(c) Engagement with the field

"All the courses include in-built field-based units of study and projects along with theoretical inputs from an interdisciplinary perspective. Engagement with the Field is the curricular component that is meant to holistically link all the courses across the programme, while it also includes special courses for Enhancing Professional Capacities (EPC) of the student teachers." NCTE-Page 2

The NCTE specifies the ***hows*** of the transaction of the courses *"using a variety of approaches, such as case studies, group presentations, projects, discussions on reflective journals, observations of children, and interactions with the community in multiple socio-cultural environments."* (NCTE-Page 2)

The NCTE also promotes innovative teacher education programmes. One such innovative programmes is run by NCERT through its constituent unit, Regional Institute of Education (RIEs) in five regions of the country by offering four year integrated B.Sc B.Ed/B.A B.Ed programmes, 2 year B.Ed programmes and 2 year M.Ed programmes.

CONCLUSION

The goal of the teacher education programme is to develop highly qualified teachers who as knowledgeable, effective leaders, will be innovative, action-oriented role models in classrooms, schools, districts, and communities throughout the world. The teacher education programme should be at the forefront in preparing competent, self-confident leaders who are committed to educating children in rural and urban multicultural and international communities. Teacher trainees should be inspired to be motivated change agents, advocates for all children, creative, energetic and risk takers to touch the future through teaching.

REFERENCES

Delors, Jacques et al. (1996), Learning: The Treasure Within, Paris and Canberra: UNESCO and the Australian National Commission for UNESCO, p. 141.

Fullan, M. and Watson, N. (2000), "School-based Management: Reconceptualizing to Improve Learning Outcomes," *School Effectiveness and School Improvement*, 11(4), Taylor and Francis, London, pp. 453–473.

Groundwater-Smith S. et al. (2001), Secondary Schooling in a Changing World, Harcourt, Sydney, pp. 207–228.

Kotler, P., and Fox, K. F. A. (1995), Strategic Marketing for Educational Institutions, (2nd ed.) Prentice Hall, New Jersey.

Tran, Henry, Ed.; Smith, Douglas A., Ed.; and Buckman, David G., Ed. (2019), Stakeholder Engagement: Improving Education through Multi-Level Community Relations, Rowman and Littlefield Publishing Group Inc, Lanham.

Web References

Curriculum Framework: Two-Year B.Ed. Programme.(2015). National Council of Teacher Education. New Delhi. http://ncte-india.org/Curriculum%20 Framework/B.Ed%20Curriculum.pdf.

Gross, K. and Godwin, P. (September 2005), "Education's Many Stake-holders," *University Business*. http://www.universitybusiness.com/viewarticle.aspx articlid=174.

Natonal Education Policy 2020. Ministry of Education. Government of India. https://www.education.gov.in/sites/upload_files/mhrd/files/NEP_Final_English_0.pdf.

CHAPTER 2 Distance Education

A one-size-fits-all approach doesn't fit with our aspirations anymore. We like the idea of being able to learn when we want, how we want, in different spaces–reflecting the changing nature of work.

—PROFESSOR KIRAN TREHAN, PRO-VICE-CHANCELLOR FOR PARTNERSHIPS AND ENGAGEMENT, UNIVERSITY OF YORK

INTRODUCTION

Distance education, or distance learning, is a field of education that focuses on the pedagogy, technology, and instructional systems design that are effectively incorporated in delivering education to students who are not physically present to receive their education. Teachers and students may communicate *asynchronously* (at their own choice) through print or electronic media, or through technology that allows them to communicate in real time (synchronously). Distance education has developed as technology has advanced—from sending printed materials through the mail for students to study individually, to internet-based courses that allow students to interact with each other and the teacher in real time. It has the potential to provide quality education for all people, regardless of their location. As such, it is an important aspect of the establishment for a true human society.

Keegan (1980) identified six key elements of distance education:

1. Separation of teacher and learner
2. Influence of an educational organisation
3. Use of media to link teacher and learner
4. Two-way exchange of communication
5. Learners as individuals rather than group, and
6. Educators as an industrialized form.

Distance education has traditionally been defined as instruction through print or electronic communications media to persons engaged in planned learning in a place or time different from that of the instructor or instructors. The traditional definition of distance education is slowly being eroded as new technological developments challenge educators to reconceptualise the idea of schooling and lifelong learning. At the same time, interest in the unlimited possibilities of individualised distance learning is growing with the development of each new communication technology.

A distance education course may use the internet; one-way and two-way transmissions through open broadcast, closed circuit, cable, microwave, broadband lines, fibre optics, satellite, or wireless communications devices; audio conferencing; or video cassettes, DVDs, and CD-ROMs if used as part of the distance learning course or programme.

Correspondence education is a formal educational process under which the institution provides instructional materials, by mail or electronic transmission, including examinations on the materials, to students who are separated from the instructor. The interaction between the instructor and the student is limited, is not regular and substantive, and is primarily initiated by the student; and courses are typically self-paced.

HISTORY OF CORRESPONDENCE AND DISTANCE EDUCATION

Correspondence education began in the mid-19th century in Great Britain, France, Germany and the United States of America (California Distance Learning Project, 2005) (Clark, 2004). In Bath, England, Sir Isaac Pitman taught shorthand by correspondence in 1840, and the use of correspondence by universities grew from off-campus lectures that were given by the Scottish educator James Stuart from the University of Cambridge, England (Clark, 2004). In 1874, the Illinois Wesleyan University began offering bachelor and graduate degrees through correspondence and in 1883, the first correspondence programme began through the Chautauq Institute, America, where on Sunday school teachers were taught (California Distance Learning Project, 2005) (Clark, 2004). There was great expansion and adoption of correspondence education by institutions after World War II through political encouragement around the world (Heerema & Rodgers, 2001). In the early years, correspondence education was carried out through the use of the postal system to send written material to students and teachers. The people who benefitted most from this were the ones with physical disabilities, women who were not allowed to enrol in institutions that were only open for men, people who had jobs during normal school hours or those who lived in remote areas where there were no schools available (California Distance Learning Project, 2005).

The first Australian correspondence school was established in 1909 by the Victorian Government. However, correspondence teaching began much earlier through itinerant teachers. In 1922, a national correspondence programme was adopted. In Australia, after World War II, the 'Schools of the Air' was developed. Teaching was carried out via radio to students in distant and rural areas (Heerema & Rodgers, 2001). Correspondence education became widely available throughout developed nations, such as Britain, Germany, Scandinavia, countries of the former USSR, Australia, New Zealand, South Africa, Japan and America in the late seventies. The United Nations Educational, Scientific and Cultural Organisation (UNESCO), among other organisations, is attempting to modernise education in developing countries through correspondence education (Evans, 1995).

The development of the radio in the 1920s and of the television in the 1940s led to extended learning opportunities through broadcast programmes and educational material. Other technological advances, such as the long distance telephone systems in the early 1990s, teleconferencing in the 1980s and 1990s and the development of the Internet, World Wide Web and the new found ability of computer-network communications (California Distance Learning Project, 2005) led to new media communication developments and the use of these in education. This has led to the adoption of distance education as the more modern means for correspondence education.

In the late 1800s, at the University of Chicago, the first major correspondence programme in the United States was established in which the teacher and the learner were at different locations. Before that time, particularly in pre-industrial Europe, education had been available primarily to males in higher levels of society. The most effective form of instruction in those days was to bring students together in one place and one time to learn from one of the masters. That form of traditional education remains the model today. The early efforts of educators like William Rainey Harper in 1890 to establish alternatives were laughed at. Correspondence study, which was designed to provide educational opportunities to those who were not among the elite and who could not afford full time residence at an educational institution, was looked down on as inferior education. Many educators regarded correspondence courses as simply business operations. As the radio developed during the First World War and television in the 1950s, instruction outside the traditional classroom had suddenly found new delivery systems. There are many examples of how early radio and television were used in schools to deliver instruction at a distance. Wisconsin's School of the Air was an early effort, in the 1920s, to affirm that the boundaries of the school were the boundaries of the state. More recently, audio and computer teleconferencing have influenced the delivery of instruction in public schools, higher education, military, business and industry.

Open Learning in UK

The establishment of the British Open University in the United Kingdom in 1969 marked the beginning of the use of technology to supplement print based instruction through well designed courses. Learning materials were delivered on a large scale to students in three programmes, viz. undergraduates, postgraduates and associate students. Although course materials were primarily print based, they were supported by a variety of technologies. *No formal educational qualifications have been required to be admitted to the British Open University*. Courses are closely monitored and have been successfully delivered to over 100,000 students. As a direct result of its success, the Open University model has been adopted by many countries in both the developed and developing world (Keegan, 1980). Researchers in the United Kingdom continue to be leaders in identifying problems and proposing solutions for practitioners in the field (Harry, Keegan and Magnus, 1993). The International Centre for Distance Learning, at the British Open University, maintains the most complete holdings of literature in both research and practice of international distance learning. Research studies, evaluation reports, course modules, books, journal articles and ephemeral material concerning distance education around the world are all available through quarterly accessions lists or online.

The Indira Gandhi National Open University is modeled on the British Open University.

Correspondence Education

Correspondence education is a formal education process and system where learners and instructors are separated by distance and/or time. It is similar to distance education as it was the preceding process and term for this form of education. Class material and communication between the learner and the instructor are carried out mainly through the regular postal service. Other aids such as computer, videocassettes, videos and telecommunication methods are also used (Evans, 1995). Correspondence courses are offered by many education institutes, whether primary, secondary or tertiary, businesses, industry departments and even the defence forces, around the world.

Correspondence Study to Distance Education

The time line showing the growth of distance education in the world is shown in Fig. 2.1. In 1982, the International Council for Correspondence Education changed its name to the International Council for Distance Education to reflect the developments in the field. With the rapid growth of new technologies and the evolution of systems for delivering information,

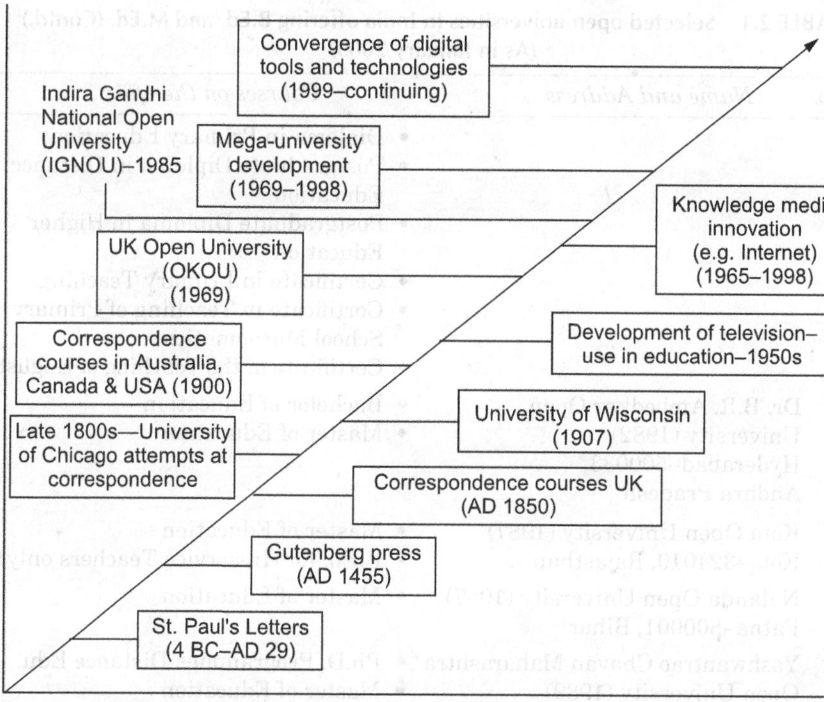

FIGURE 2.1 Timeline of growth of distance education in the world.

distance education, with its ideals of providing equality of access to education, became a reality. Today, there are distance education courses offered by dozens of public and private organisations and institutions to school districts, universities, the military and large corporations.

There are a number of open universities in the country offering various degrees/diplomas through the mode of non-formal education. The open universities have been established in the country by an Act of Parliament or State Legislature in accordance with the provisions contained in Section 2(F) of the UGC Act, 1956. These universities are, therefore, empowered to award degrees in terms of Section 22(1) of the UGC Act, 1956.

Table 2.1 lists some selected open universities in India which offer B.Ed. and M.Ed. courses.

TABLE 2.1 Selected open universities in India offering B.Ed. and M.Ed. (As in January 2005)

S.No.	*Name and Address*	*Courses on the offer*
1.	Indira Gandhi National Open University (1985)	• Ph.D. in Education • Master of Arts in Distance Education • Bachelor of Education • Diploma in Early Childhood Care and Education

(*Contd.*)

TABLE 2.1 Selected open universities in India offering B.Ed. and M.Ed. (Contd.) (As in January 2005)

S.No.	*Name and Address*	*Courses on the offer*
		• Diploma in Primary Education • Postgraduate Diploma in Distance Education • Postgraduate Diploma in Higher Education • Certificate in Primary Teaching • Certificate in Teaching of Primary School Mathematics • Certificate in the Teaching of English
2.	Dr. B.R. Ambedkar Open University (1982) Hyderabad–500033, Andhra Pradesh	• Bachelor of Education • Master of Education
3.	Kota Open University (1987) Kota–324010, Rajasthan	• Master of Education • B.Ed. for (In-service Teachers only)
4.	Nalanda Open University (1987) Patna–800001, Bihar	• Master of Education
5.	Yashwantrao Chavan Maharashtra Open University (1989) Nashik–422005, Maharashtra	• Ph.D. Programmes Distance Edu. • Master of Education • B.Ed (for In-service Teachers) Bachelor of Education • Certificate course in B.Ed/B.P.Ed.
6.	Madhya Pradesh Bhoj (Open) University (1991) Bhopal–462016 Madhya Pradesh	• B.Ed. (GE-DE) • B.Ed. (SEDE) • In Special Education (PGPC SEDE) • In Education Technology
7.	Dr. Babasaheb Ambedkar Open University (1994) Ahmedabad–380003, Gujarat	• B.Ed. • B.Ed. Special Education Distance Programme
8.	Karnataka State Open University (1996) Mysore–570006, Karnataka	• Ph.D. • M.Phil. • Master of Education (M.Ed.) • Bachelor of Education
9.	Netaji Subhas Open University (1997) Kolkata–700020, West Bengal	• Ph.D. Distance Education • Master of English Language Teaching • Certificate Course in Pre-primary teacher's training
10.	Tamil Nadu Open University (2002), Tamil Nadu	• B.Ed. Programme • B.Ed. Special Education
11.	U.P. Rajarshi Tandon Open University (1999) Allahabad–21100, Uttar Pradesh	• B.Ed. Special Education (B.Ed.S.E.) • Postgraduate Diploma in Educational Management • Diploma in Early Childhood Care and Education

Table 2.2 lists Indian universities offering B.Ed. through correspondence.

TABLE 2.2 Indian universities offering B.Ed. course correspondence courses

S.No.	*Name of the institution*	*Year of establishment*
1.	Directorate of Distance Education, Annamalai University	1979
2.	SNDT Women's University (B.Ed. and M.Ed).	1951
3.	International Centre for Distance Education & Open Learning, HP University, Shimla	1971
4.	Directorate of Distance Education, Madurai Kamraj University, Madurai	1966
5.	School of Distance Education, University of Calicut	1981
6.	Department of Correspondence Studies, Punjab University, Chandigarh	1971
7.	Directorate of Correspondence Courses, Kurukshetra University, Kurukshetra (B.Ed. and M.Ed.)	1976
8.	Bharathidasan University, Tiruchirapalli	1992
9.	Directorate of Distance Education, Maulana Azad National Urdu University, Hyderabad	1998
10.	Director of Correspondence courses and Distance Education, Bangalore	1962
11.	School of Distance Education, Mahatma Gandhi University, Kottayam, Kerala (B.Ed.)	1983
12.	Department of Distance Education, University of Kashmir (B.Ed. and M.Ed.)	1976
13.	Institute of Distance Education, Dr. Harishing Gour Vishwavidyalay, Sagar, M.P.	1997–98
14.	Central Institute of English & Foreign Language, Hyderabad (certificate courses)	1972
15.	Mahatma Gandhi Chitrakoot Gramodaya Viswavidyalaya, Satna, M.P.	1991
16.	Directorate of Distance Education, Tripura University, Tripura	1987
17.	Institute of Distance Education, University of Kerala (PGDEPMA—Post Graduate Diploma in Educational Planning, Management and Administration)	1976
18.	School of Distance Learning & Continuing Education, Kakatiya University (B.Ed. and M.Ed.)	1988
19.	Mukta Vidya Kendra, Tilak Maharashtra Vidyapeeth	2005
20.	Directorate of Distance Education, Sri Venkateswara University	1972
21.	Directorate of Distance Education, University of Jammu	B.Ed. 1977 M.Ed. 1997

(Contd.)

TABLE 2.2 Indian universities offering B.Ed. course correspondence courses (Contd.)

S.No.	Name of the institution	Year of establishment
22.	School of Distance Education, Andhra University Additional Methodology (B.Ed. & MA Education)	1972
23.	NEHU Shillong (B.Ed. Special Education)	
24.	Jamia Millia Islamia, New Delhi	1988
25.	Alagappa University—Directorate of Distance Education	1992
26.	Manonmaniam Sundaranar University—Directorate of Distance and Continuing Education	2006

NEED FOR B.Ed. THROUGH DISTANCE LEARNING

Teachers play a vital role in shaping up the future of the students. So, it is necessary for the aspiring teachers to go through formal training to acquire the skills that would assist them in becoming role models. The main objective of the bachelor of education course is to prepare individuals for this noble profession and help them learn the various aspects of it.

Candidates who are already working or those looking for flexible mode of education can opt for the distance learning programmes offered by various institutions. The comprehensive courses offered enable them to widen their understanding ability and help them judge the needs of the students. Teachers also guide the students choose the right path and achieve their goals in future.

ELIGIBILITY FOR BACHELOR OF EDUCATION THROUGH DISTANCE LEARNING DEGREE PROGRAMMES

Candidates who have completed their graduation in any discipline from a recognized university are eligible to apply for the course. In some of the institutes, it is compulsory for the students to have at least 45% marks in their graduation for taking admission to this course. At least two years of work experience is also essential for one to join a reputed distance learning institute. The course offered is a perfect blend of theoretical and practical form of education.

Students, after completing the course may look for the job opportunities available both in the government and private sectors. Most of the schools prefer candidates with a B.Ed. degree.

PROFESSIONAL ASPECT OF DISTANCE EDUCATION PROGRAMMES

The distance education programmes focus on diversified target groups with the objective to train them and upgrade the skill of those who could effectively participate in the socio-economic development of the country. Keeping in view the growth of the economy through its vision and mission, of late, attempts have been made to launch more professional and vocational programmes to meet the growing demand of the market force. In developing countries, specifically in the context of India, the need for professional education has been gaining importance. Over the last decade, due to rapid technological growth, there has been constant demand of quality professionals in various sectors of professions, both in India and overseas. This has directly contributed to the quality of life, positive use of human potential, empowerment of individual, and growth with excellence.

Ozar and Sokol (2002), while defining profession have stated certain characteristics of a profession which are as follows:

1. Its practitioners have education beyond the ordinary, both theoretical and practical.
2. Its particular expertise is a source of benefit for those who seek its assistance.
3. The profession's expertise allows its practitioners extensive autonomy in matter pertaining to it.
4. Professionals accept that they have special obligations.

Paul Rowbottom (2000) enumerated six characteristics for the recognition of a profession. These are:

1. A body of knowledge.
2. It has practical application (technology).
3. "Exclusive competence", that is, the knowledge and technology are too complicated to be employed by the laity.
4. The profession must develop and transmit its own knowledge.
5. Practitioners accept a service ethic.
6. The profession controls the entry of its members.

The most appropriate definition given to a profession in the present socio-cultural context is of Alvin Rosenblum (2001).

1. Education beyond the usual level, to continue for life
2. Self-regulation
3. Technical competence for which one is held morally responsible
4. Self improvement and
5. Service to humanity.

Hence, for a professional, there has been a growing need to update knowledge and learn such professional skills to discharge both organisational and social responsibilities effectively. This is true of teaching which has all the attributes of a profession.

INDIRA GANDHI NATIONAL OPEN UNIVERSITY (IGNOU)

Mission and Vision

The Indira Gandhi National Open University (IGNOU), one of the mega universities in the world, was established by an Act of Indian Parliament in 1985. At present, the university is offering more than 125 academic programmes and having around 1000 courses. It serves the educational aspirations of about 1.5 million learners not only in India but also in 30 countries across the world. Besides providing education globally through Open and Distance Learning (ODL) with extensive use of Information and Communication Technology (ICT), IGNOU has the additional responsibility to promote, determine and maintain standards in ODL system across the country. The vision and mission of the university gets reformulated from time to time to achieve the objectives of the university. It primarily focuses on widening access with equality of opportunity, providing for continuing professional development and training in all sectors of economy, and catering educational needs of all sections of society.

The priority of the university is to act as the National Resource Centre for Open and Distance Learning with wider international recognition. It shall provide seamless access to sustainable and learner-centric quality education, skill upgradation and training to all by using innovative technologies and methodologies and ensuring convergence of existing systems for massive human resources required for promoting integrated national development and global understanding (IGNOU Profile 2006). Hence, over the period of time, the emphasis has been laid on launching of more professional, vocational, awareness generating and non-credited extension and skill-oriented programmes, with a focus on socio-economic development and serving the disadvantaged section of the society. To have a sustainable curricular transaction system, the university provides multi-channel multiple media teaching-learning packages for instruction.

Teacher Education

Bachelor of Education (B.Ed.) Programme of IGNOU aims at developing the understanding and competencies required by practising teachers for effective teaching-learning process at the secondary stage.

The programme also provides opportunities for sharing experiences gained by practising teachers. It enables in-service teachers to select and organise learning experiences according to the requirement of learners. In addition, it provides knowledge and develops in them an understanding of areas such as educational evaluation, and school management.

IGNOU's B.Ed. programme is recognized by National Council of Teacher Education (NCTE). NCTE recognition is an important criterion for the validity of the B.Ed. Degree being awarded by a university or an institution. NCTE recognized B.Ed. degree is necessary for admission to M.Ed/MA(Education) courses offered by some universities in the country. Further, for the appointment of teachers n government schools, it is required that the candidates have an NCTE recognized degree.

Objectives of IGNOU's B.Ed. Programme

IGNOU's B.Ed. programme aims to enable practising teachers to achieve the following objectives:

1. To systematize experiences and strengthen the professional competencies of in-service teachers.
2. To imbibe knowledge and develop an understanding of the various methods and approaches of organising learning experiences of secondary school students.
3. To develop skills required in selecting and organising learning experiences.
4. To understand the nature of the learning process.
5. To develop skills involved in dealing with the academic and personal problems of learners.
6. To acquire knowledge and develop an understanding of the various procedures and techniques of evaluation and their classroom applications.
7. To develop skills involved in selecting, developing and using evaluation tools.
8. To acquire knowledge and develop an understanding of various aspects of school management.
9. To develop competencies for organising various instructional and student support activities.
10. To develop an appreciation of the role of the teacher in the prevailing socio-cultural and political system in general and the educational system in particular.

Table 2.3 gives a brief outline on the B.Ed. programme components.

In the distance education context, the transaction mode plays a very important role in acquiring new knowledge and demonstrating the same in a given situation. For acquiring professional skills using distance methodology, the channels of delivery of curricular inputs and application of new knowledge have greater importance. For the professional programmes, IGNOU, follows multi-channel multi-media teaching learning packages for instruction.

TABLE 2.3 The B.Ed. course components

Sl. No.	*Programme components* (1)	*B.Ed.* (6)
1.	Target Groups	Graduates and having two years' teaching experience
2.	Age	No bar
3.	Duration of the Programme	Minimum: 2 years Maximum: 4 years
4.	Admission	Entrance test, qualification and experience.
5.	Objectives of the Programme	• Strengthen professional competencies of teachers • Develop better understanding on organising learning experiences • Develop such skills needed to solve learners' problems • Develop skills involved in selecting, developing and using evaluation tools • Develop competencies for organising various instructional and student support activities
6.	Delivery Channel	Multi-media approaches to learning + School based practical + Workshop based practical + Practice teaching
7.	Evaluation Mechanism	• Terminal examination (theory) • Continuous evaluation • Evaluation on practical activities

Inputs for Professional Competencies

The development of professional competencies has been the main focus of all these professional programmes. These competencies not only relate to attitudinal changes for the professions in which a person is associated/ought to be associated, but also enable him/her to understand the profession deeply and adapt to the working environment. For the purpose of analysis, the following broad areas of competencies have been considered.

1. **Contextual competencies:** To provide a wider view of the development of professional education in society and professionals' role in it.
2. **Conceptual competencies:** Understanding the basic tenets of one's own profession.
3. **Curricular related competencies:** Knowledge inputs through curricular base and its transaction.

4. **Competencies on learning outcome:** Feedback mechanism in relation to assessing the competencies acquired.
5. **Competencies on management of profession:** Abilities to organise activities in professional set-up.
6. **Competencies in understanding own environment:** Internal acceptance of roles and responsibilities.

Table 2.4 gives the details of competencies along with the processes involved in the B.Ed. programme.

TABLE 2.4 Analysis on competency areas across the B.Ed. programme of IGNOU

Sl. No.	*Competencies*	*B.Ed.*
1.	Contextual	• Developing understanding on teaching-learning process at secondary stage • Updating such competencies to deal with teaching-learning process in schools
2.	Conceptual	Courses broadly offered in the areas of: • Understanding children • Curriculum and their transaction • Evaluation techniques • Understanding society
3.	Curricular related	The curricular input comprises five core courses, two courses from the content-based methodology courses and one special course. All these courses are targeted to enhance specific competencies related to teaching-learning process. This apart, the students are exposed to three areas of practical activities related to school based and workshop based activities, and practice teaching in school subjects.
4.	Learning outcome	• Assessment through practical oriented assignments • Assessment records submitted by the supervisor, mentors and headmasters of the schools • Verification of records related to school based and workshop based activities • Scrutiny of practice teaching records
5.	Management of profession	• Understanding school children and their problems • Identifying relevant instructional system and its planning • Undertaking evaluation in teaching-learning process • Understanding various issues related to school structure and its relation to the society • Demonstrating the teaching of subject-specific content in the classroom
6.	Understanding environment	• Understanding school environment • Promoting effective classroom learning

The learner-centric method in IGNOU is illustrated in Figure 2.2.

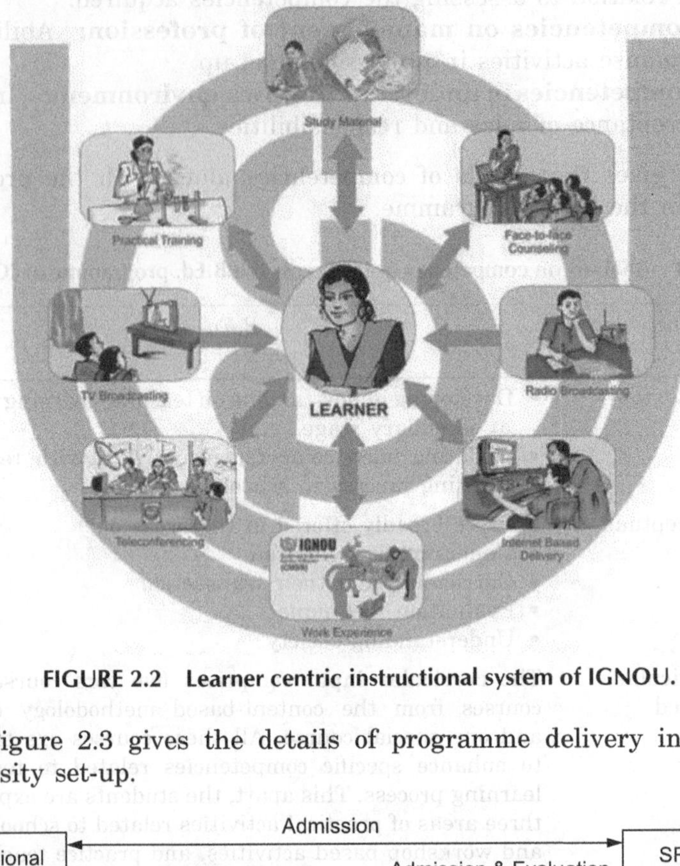

FIGURE 2.2 Learner centric instructional system of IGNOU.

Figure 2.3 gives the details of programme delivery in an open university set-up.

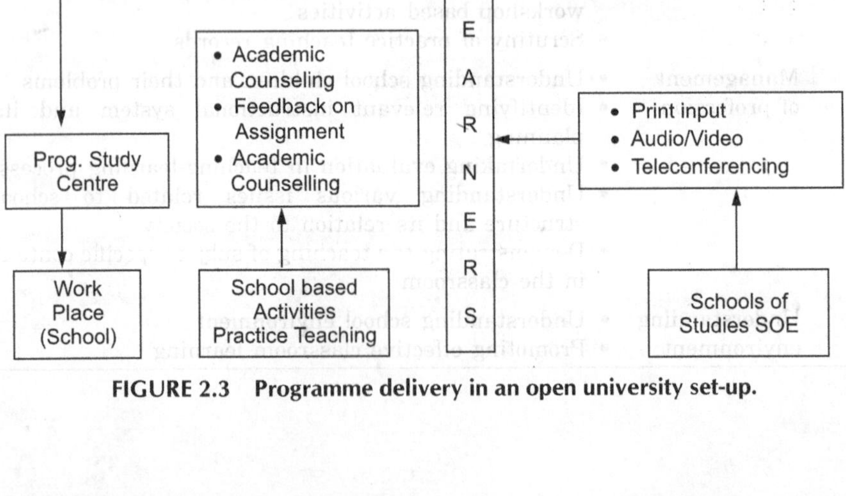

FIGURE 2.3 Programme delivery in an open university set-up.

Figure 2.4 gives the programme delivery in the B.Ed. programme of IGNOU.

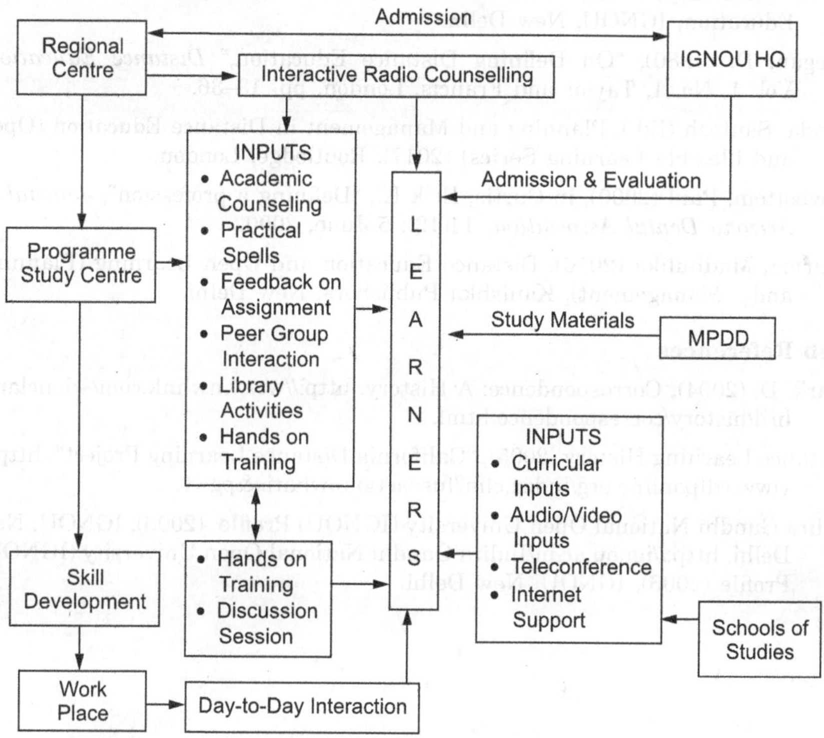

FIGURE 2.4 Programme delivery of B.Ed. programme of IGNOU.

CONCERNS OF QUALITY WITH RESPECT TO DISTANCE AND CORRESPONDENCE EDUCATION

Correspondence education offended the elitist, and extremely undemocratic educational system which characterized the early years in the United States (Pittman, 1991). Indeed, many correspondence courses were viewed as simply poor excuses for the real thing. However, the need to provide equal access to educational opportunities has always been part of our democratic ideals, so correspondence/distance education today has taken a new turn.

REFERENCES

Curtis, Erik K. (5 June 2000), "Defining a Profession", *Journal of the Arizona Dental Association*, Vol. 14, No. 12.

Distance Education, New Perspectives, Edited by Keith Harry, Magnus John, Desmond Keegan, London Routledge.

Harry, K., Keegan, D. and Magnus, J. (Eds.) (1993), *Distance Education: New Perspectives*, Routledge, London.

IGNOU (January, 2006), "Bachelor of Education Programme Guide", School of Education, IGNOU, New Delhi.

Keegan, D. (1980), "On Defining Distance Education," *Distance Education*, Vol. 1, No. 1, Taylor and Francis, London, pp. 13–36.

Panda, Santosh (Ed.), Planning and Management in Distance Education (Open and Flexible Learning Series) (2017), Routledge, London.

Rowbottom, Paul (2000), in Curtis, Erik K., "Defining a profession", *Journal of Arizona Dental Association,* 14(12): 5 June, 2000.

Sharma, Madhulika (2016), Distance Education and Open Learning (Planning and Management), Kanishka Publishers, New Delhi.

Web References

Clark, D. (2004), Correspondence: A History. http://www.nwlink.com/~donclark/hrd/history/correspondence.html.

Distance Learning History (2005), "California Distance Learning Project". http://www.cdlponline.org/index.cfm?fuseaction=whatis&pg=4.

Indira Gandhi National Open University (IGNOU) Profile (2006), IGNOU, New Delhi. http://ignou.ac.in/Indira Gandhi National Open University (IGNOU) Profile (2006), IGNOU, New Delhi.

Part II

PROCESS AND PRACTICE

CHAPTER 3 Microteaching

In learning you will teach and in teaching you will learn.

—Phil Collins

RATIONALE AND SCOPE

The teacher in the classroom uses several techniques and procedures to bring about effective learning in her students. These include introducing, demonstrating, explaining or questioning. The teacher could also make use of non-verbal behaviours such as smiling, gesturing and nodding. These group of activities are called *teaching skills*. By acquiring teaching skills, an experienced teacher can use these appropriately in her teaching, in order to achieve her lesson objectives.

The teacher trainee is introduced to a wide range of teaching skills. **Microteaching** allows the teacher trainee to practice any one skill on his own, and then combine it with others when it has been mastered.

A teaching skill has been defined in various ways. A few definitions will clarify the meaning of the term. McIntyre et al. (1977) define teaching skill as "a set of related teaching behaviours which in specified types of classroom interaction situations tend to facilitate the achievement of specified types of educational objectives".

Passi (1976) defines teaching skill as "a group of teaching acts or behaviours intended to facilitate pupil's learning directly or indirectly".

NCERT (National Council of Educational Research and Training), in its publication *Core Teaching Skills* (1982), has laid stress on the following teaching skills:

- Writing instructional objectives
- Organising the content

- Creating set for introducing the lesson
- Introducing a lesson
- Structuring classroom questions
- Question delivery and its distribution
- Response management
- Explaining
- Illustrating with examples
- Using teaching aids
- Stimulus variation
- Pacing of the lesson
- Promoting pupil participation
- Use of blackboard
- Achieving closure of the lesson
- Giving assignments
- Evaluating the pupil's progress
- Diagnosing pupil learning difficulties and taking remedial measures
- Management of the class

DEFINITIONS OF MICROTEACHING

Microteaching has been defined in several ways:

Allen and Eve (1968) defined microteaching as "a system of controlled practice that makes it possible to concentrate on specific teaching behaviour and to practice teaching under controlled conditions".

Allen (1966) defined microteaching as "a scaled down teaching encounter in class size and class time".

Buch (1974) has given a comprehensive definition of microteaching as a "teacher education technique which allows teachers to apply clearly defined teaching skills to carefully prepared lessons in planned series of 5 to 10 minutes. It encounters with a small group of real students, often with an opportunity to observe the results on videotape".

McAleese, and Unwin (1973) define microteaching as a scaled down teaching encounter in terms of time, class, size, lesson, length and teaching complexity.

Passi (1976) writes that "the most important point in microteaching is that teaching is practised in terms of definable, observable, measurable and controllable teaching skills".

Singh (1977) defines microteaching as "a scaled down teaching encounter in which a teacher teaches a small unit to a group of 5 pupils for a small period of 5 to 20 minutes. Such a situation offers a helpful setting for an experienced or inexperienced teacher to acquire new teaching skills and refine old ones."

These definitions stress the essential propositions of microteaching put forth by Allen and Ryan (1969).

1. Microteaching is real teaching, though the teaching situation is a simulated one.
2. Microteaching lessens the complexities of normal classroom teaching. Thus, class size, scope of content and time are all reduced.
3. Skills are selected and discussed in a preparatory session. Microteaching focusses on training for the accomplishment of specific tasks like practice of blackboard writing, demonstrating effectively, and so on.
4. Microteaching allows for the increased control of practice.
5. Feedback given at the end of a micro lesson helps a teacher trainee get an insight into her performance, and avoid any mannerisms.

A composite definition of microteaching technique would thus be:

Microteaching is a teacher training technique involving a specific teaching behaviour/skill of short duration—5 to 6 minutes for a small class comprising 5 or 6 fellow teacher trainees/peer group on a single concept of subject matter.

CHARACTERISTICS OF MICROTEACHING

The following are the characteristics of microteaching:

1. In microteaching, the trainee can concentrate on practising a specific, well-defined skill.
2. It is a miniaturized teaching in the sense that it scales down the complexities of real teaching with the provision for
    - Practising one skill at a time
    - Reducing the class size to 5–10 peer group
    - Reducing the duration of the lesson to 5–10 minutes
    - Limiting the content to a single concept.
3. Microteaching provides for pinpointed, immediate feedback.
4. As microteaching is scaled down teaching, there is no problem of discipline.
5. Less administrative problems arise as teaching sessions are organised with peers.
6. Microteaching provides an opportunity to undertake research studies with better control over conditions and situations.
7. Microteaching can be used as an integral part of teacher training in India as sophisticated gadgetry is not a must.

PRINCIPLES UNDERLYING MICROTEACHING TECHNIQUES

The principles underlying microteaching techniques are as follows:

1. Microteaching is based on the premise that teaching can be split into component teaching skills.

2. The teaching skills can be defined, practiced, observed, controlled, measured and evaluated.
3. Feedback is a vital part of the microteaching session. Immediate feedback critique focuses on a particular aspect of the teacher trainee's performance, and an attempt is made to replan incorporating improvements.
4. A high degree of control over time, number of students, and supervision is stressed on.
5. Skinner's theory of shaping behaviour is applied with the teach-feedback-reteach pattern of microteaching.

MICROTEACHING—THE INDIAN SITUATION (Figure 3.1)

Microteaching as a training technique involves the following steps:

***Step 1*—Orientation:** In the beginning, the teacher trainee should be given necessary theoretical background about micro-teaching on aspects such as:

- Concept of microteaching
- Rationale of using microteaching
- Procedure of microteaching
- Requirements and setting for adopting microteaching technique.

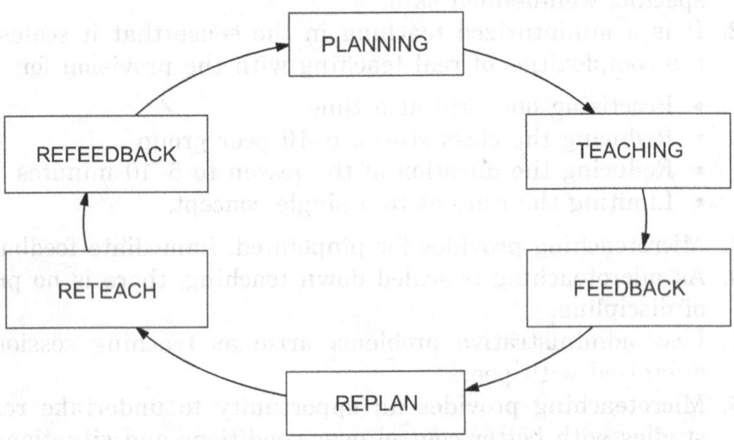

FIGURE 3.1 Microteaching cycle.

***Step 2*—Discussion of teaching skills:** This step covers the analysis of teaching into component teaching skills, rationale and role of these teaching skills in teaching.

***Step 3*—Selection of a particular teaching skill:** The teacher trainee is encouraged to select a particular skill and practice it. He is given enough orientation and background information to get through this step.

***Step 4*—Presentation of a model demonstration:** In this step, the teaching skill is presented in the form of a demonstration so that teacher trainees get an idea of what is expected of them. This demonstration can be done by the teacher educator or an expert, by showing a film or videotape, by listening to an audiotape presentation, or by providing the teacher trainees with written material such as a handbook, guide or notes.

***Step 5*—Observation of the model lesson and criticism:** Using an observation schedule, the teacher trainees critique the demonstration model micro lesson.

***Step 6*—Preparation of micro lesson plan:** The teacher trainee prepares a micro lesson based on the demonstration viewed. The duration of the microteaching cycle is as follows:

Plan	5 minutes
Teaching	5 minutes
Feedback	5 minutes
Re-plan	10 minutes
Re-teach	5 minutes
Re-feedback	5 minutes
Total	35 minutes

***Step 7*—Practice of the skill as teach session:** The teacher trainee teaches the micro lesson prepared by him/her to a class of 5–10 peer group members for 6 minutes. This is supervised by the teacher educator and peers using an observation schedule.

***Step 8*—Providing feedback on feedback session:** This is a vital aspect of microteaching. To be effective, it must be clearly related to the model of the teaching skill used. Appraisal guides add to the comments of the supervisor and fellow students. They focus on the feedback related to specific behaviour that can be used for the analysis session or be just given to the teacher trainee with a written comment or rating of his skill performance.

Feedback in microteaching is the information the teacher trainee gets about his/her attempts to practise a skill. This is generally given at the end of the teaching session from the supervisor, the peer group, pupils or the video recorder. Most of these sources of feedback are reinforced by use of appraisal guide.

The general factors for the consideration of feedback are:

1. What is being appraised?
2. Are the components of this skill discrete and measurable?
3. Can the comments be pinpointed without opinions and biases creeping in?
4. Is the feedback supportive and corrective, without destroying the confidence of the teacher trainee?

***Step 9*—Replanning/Replan session:** Keeping in mind the feedback received from the supervisor, the teacher trainee replans the micro lesson, by revising and incorporating the suggestions into the micro lesson plan or editing the existing one.

***Step 10*—Reteach:** The teacher trainee reteaches, incorporating the suggested changes, with the same students or another group of 5 students. The supervisor checks to see whether there is any improvement in skill attainment.

***Step 11*—Refeedback:** The supervisor assesses the lesson again, pointing out the improvements and lapses.

***Step 12*—Integration of teaching skills:** It means the integration of various teaching skills individually mastered by a teacher trainee. This facilitates bridging the gap between the isolated teaching episode and the real teaching situation, so that the teacher trainee can incorporate the individual skills as they are mastered into the lesson.

MERITS OF MICROTEACHING

Microteaching has proved to be an efficient and effective technique in teacher training programmes.

1. The teacher trainee is made aware of the various skills of which teaching is composed.
2. Selected skills are chosen and discussed in a briefing session.
3. Microteaching simulates the classroom scene and gives the teacher trainee an experience of real teaching.
4. Feedback enables the teacher trainee to consciously eradicate or give up undesirable habits and mannerisms.
5. Microteaching is economical in terms of time and money.
6. Microteaching is flexible and can be used in a variety of situations—business schools, nursing education, the police, etc.
7. The teacher trainee can focus his/her attention on clearly defined aspects of his/her behaviour. This reduces problems of discipline, control and other organisational activities.
8. Patterns of classroom interaction and communication between the teacher and the students can be objectively and easily studied. Time management of teach/reteach cycle can be organised.
9. Microteaching caters to the need of individual differences in the training of teachers. Here, an individual teacher trainee may work for the development of teaching skills at his/her own rate, depending on his/her teaching abilities.
10. Microteaching focuses attention on the modification of teacher behaviour and improvement of interaction process involved in the teaching learning process.

In many training colleges, the teaching session lasts between five to ten minutes. The length of the micro lesson is thus related to the skill practised, the needs of the student, the number of students, the total time available and the accessibility of pupils.

Maximum feedback about the teacher trainee's performance could be provided by video tape, supervisor comments and peer group comments. Five to ten minutes is the usually accepted length of feedback. If a video recorder is used, the teacher trainees may prefer to view the whole micro lesson. This encourages self-analysis.

In many cases, due to time constraints, the reteaching function may have to be left out. If it is included, the time between replanning and reteaching should not be too short.

MICROTEACHING SKILLS

The major premise underlying the concept of microteaching is that the complex teaching act can be split into component skills—each simple, well-defined and limited. These skills can be identified, practised, evaluated, controlled and acquired through training.

A large number of skills have been identified. The first effort made by Allen and Ryan resulted in identifying fourteen skills. Singh et al. (1987) makes reference to twenty two general teaching skills.

These skills have been chosen as they foster teacher–pupil interaction, particularly as they belong to the four areas of motivation, presentation, recapitulation and questioning. These are the skills of:

1. Set induction/introduction
2. Explaining
3. Stimulus variation
4. Reinforcement
5. Questioning
6. Blackboard writing
7. Demonstration
8. Closure

These skills are discussed giving the major components, the objectives and a simple appraisal guide.

Skill of Set Induction/Introduction

Set induction is a pre-instructional technique. Training in set helps the teacher prepare students for the lesson in order to induce the maximum pay-off in learning. **Set is more than a brief introduction**. Its purpose is to get the students in the mood, and clarify the goals of instruction, using students' present knowledge and skills to involve them in the lesson. Instructional set can vary in length and in elaborateness. It can take many forms: an analogy, a demonstration, posing an intriguing problem, storytelling, narration, problem-solving etc.

The major components of set skill are: gaining attention, arousing motivation, structuring and making links.

Skill of Explaining

A teacher is said to be explaining when he/she is describing 'how', 'why' and 'what' of a concept, phenomenon, event, action or condition. Explaining can be defined as an activity to bring about an understanding about a concept or a principle. It is an activity to fill up a gap in someone's understanding. The skill of explaining aims at making sure that the explanation is understood. All teachers should strive to perfect the skill of explaining accurately and effectively.

Major components

Explaining skill can be divided into structural and presentation components.

Structural components: These include factors such as beginning statement, key concepts, examples and summary.

(i) The aspects relevant are activities like gaining attention, arousing motivation, establishing rapport and putting the topic in its context.

(ii) The teacher clearly and concisely states the key concepts.

(iii) The teacher uses relevant, simple and clear examples to explain major ideas.

(iv) The teacher summarizes the main points of the explanation.

Presentation components: These comprise style, clarity, pointers, links and priority.

(i) The teacher uses emphasis variation—the voice level, pitch and tone, collectively known as *style*, can convey the relative importance of the content. Non-verbal communication can go a long way in emphasizing points, such as gestures, nods, and visual contact.

(ii) Clarity as a subskill contains many factors. The teacher states the purpose of the explanation, defines new terms and concepts, uses a suitable language, slowing down the word flow when ideas are difficult or complex, and does not stray from the point on hand, provided occasional summaries to refocus attention.

(iii) The teacher uses appropriate words to aid better understanding. For example,

"These are the six factors..." —***A pointer***
"From this it follows that..." —***Link words***
"We shall now come to the most important point..." —***Priorities***

Skill of Stimulus Variation

Training in the skills of stimulus variation is aimed at helping teacher trainees to avoid teaching styles likely to induce monotony in the classrooms. A stimulus situation that changes in different ways is one of the most powerful influences in maintaining interest of the students in the class. Some of the things the teacher can do are use of movements, avoidance of teaching standing in one spot, use of gestures, and development of verbal and non-verbal communication strategies to hold the students' attention.

The skill of stimulus variation covers the activities the teacher can introduce to vary the presentation methods used in a lesson. This skill is concerned with three main areas of teaching. They are:

1. The manner, voice and teaching style of the teacher
2. The media and materials used during teaching
3. The teacher/pupil relationship during the class.

Major skill components

1. **Movement** from one spot to another, say, from black board to last benches row in the class and back again.
2. **Gestures** call attention to a particular point, verbal, gestural or both.
3. **Interactional styles** encompass three areas, viz. teacher, teacher-student, and student-student.
4. **Pausing** aims at breaking an idea into clearer logical components.
5. **Shifting sensory channel**, according to the demand of the topic, becomes inevitable. This shift can be:
   - from verbal to visual—say, showing blue litmus turning red
   - from oral to oral-visual—using charts and models
   - from visual to oral-visual—films, chart/lecture
6. **Speech pattern** is varied according to the emphasis and importance of the topic.

Skill of Reinforcement

Reinforcement skill can increase students' involvement in their lessons in a number of positive ways. The skill is used when the teacher reinforces good behaviour with a smile, and when the teacher praises a good answer, or encourages a slow learner. Such positive reinforcement strengthens desirable behaviour, increases student participation. Negative reinforcement, like scolding, frowning, on the other hand, weakens undesirable behaviour.

Major components

The six major components of reinforcement skill are:

1. **Verbal reinforcement**—Comments like "Good", "Well done"
2. **Gestural reinforcement**—Facial expressions, e.g. a smile
3. **Proximity reinforcement**—Teacher moving nearer to the student evincing interest
4. **Contact reinforcement**—Patting the head, back ..., etc.
5. **Activity reinforcement**—Teacher gives the pupils a task they prefer as reinforcement, e.g. a project etc.
6. **Token reinforcement**—The teacher awards marks, merit cards, writes comments like "good".

Skill of Questioning

A good teaching technique employs different questioning levels, techniques and direction.

Questioning levels

1. **Low level question:** It is the lowest or preliminary knowledge level question, which requires the student to recall information that he has stored. Therefore, a low level response requires memorization on the part of the student and requires no processing of information.

   The simplest way to follow is that a question whereby a student has to just recall information, such as terms, facts, names and events, is a low level question.
2. **High level question:** This requires a degree of intellectual processing on the part of the student—comprehension, application, analogy, synthesis and evaluation.
3. **Description question:** Such questions are easy to ask, quite easy to answer and excellent for promoting student involvement.
4. **Comparison question:** Such questions require the learner to look at two or more objects, statements, illustrations or demonstrations and identify similarities or differences between them.

Question direction

Convergent questions refer to questions which have one correct answer. These are generally questions of fact or recall. Divergent questions have multiple answers.

Questioning techniques

1. **Redirection** involves a large number of students. It is a useful technique to help establish positive patterns and high levels of interaction in a classroom. This technique involves the framing of a single question for which there are many possible responses from the students. **Redirection is possible only in the case of high order, divergent questions.**
2. **Prompting** is required when a student is asked a question and he fails to reply or responds incorrectly.
   This technique involves the use of hints or clues which are used to aid the student in responding correctly. It requires on-the-spot practice—thinking on your feet.
3. **Probing** is used when the student's reply is correct but insufficient because it lacks depth. This helps to process information, to deal with the why, the how and is based on what.

Components of questioning skill

As there are many components and subcomponents of the skill of questioning, it is generally split into two major components: **Basic questioning** and **advanced questioning**.

Basic questioning has the following subskills:

- Phrasing
- Focusing
- Direction
- Distribution
- Pausing
- Prompting

Advanced questioning involves the following subskills:

- Varying the level
- Recalling
- Comprehension
- Application
- Analysis
- Synthesis
- Evaluation
- Probing

Skill of Blackboard Writing

The importance of effective blackboard writing cannot be stressed enough, especially in a country like India. "Operation Blackboard" aspires to equip every single school in the country with blackboards, which implies that every potential teacher should be proficient in the use of the blackboard. Good blackboard writing leads to the following:

- Clarity in understanding concepts
- Reinforcement of the matter which is being conveyed verbally by the teacher
- Presentation of a holistic picture of content
- Variety and draws attention of the pupils to the relevant points.

The major components of this skill are:

1. *Legibility in handwriting*
   (i) Distinct difference between letters spacing
   (ii) Size of the capital letters
   (iii) Size of capital and small letters
   (iv) Thickness of the lines
2. *Neatness in blackboard work*
   (i) Straightness of the lines
   (ii) Spacing between the lines
   (iii) Avoidance of overwriting
   (iv) Focusing the relevant matter
3. *Appropriateness*
   (i) Continuity in the points
   (ii) Brevity and simplicity
   (iii) Drawing attention and focusing

Skill of Demonstration

Demonstration skill is highly needed in the subjects of practical relevance in science, as the teacher has to demonstrate the working of an apparatus, functioning of an instrument, preparation of a gas, etc. This helps the students in acquiring the essential knowledge, understanding, skills and applications regarding the facts, principles, concepts and activities involved. The teacher has to take care of several component behaviours for acquisition of this skill. The components include handling of equipment and materials, relevant subject matter, pupil's participation, visibility of the demonstration work, drawing relevant inferences, emphasising cause and effect relationship, etc.

The skill of demonstration helps the students to understand the processes of scientific investigations and use inquiry and scientific ways of observing, experimenting, predicting, and validating to think critically.

Skill of Closure

Closure skill is complementary to set induction. It involves training in different methods of concluding a lesson with the student, taking steps to ensure that the pupils have understood and are able to see the connections with other phenomena. It is more than a quick summary of the portions taught and the pupils are able to relate new knowledge with the previous one.

The skill of closure assists students to establish links between new and past knowledge by reviewing and applying material to familiar and new examples, cases, and situations.

Generally, **closure** can be achieved by the following steps:

- Making a review. Both making a spoken summary and making a written summary have to be done in this section.
- Giving psychological/social encouragement to the class
- Examining how well the objectives of the lesson have been achieved
- Giving feedback
- Reflection

The major components of closure skill are:

- Summarising of major points by the teacher or the students
- Application of the present knowledge in a new situation
- Linking the past knowledge with the present knowledge
- Linking the present knowledge with the future learning

LINK PRACTICE (INTEGRATION OF TEACHING SKILLS)

No amount of expertise in any one skill can promise a good lesson. It is the integration of two or more selected microteaching skills which forms a macro lesson that is of a full 40 or 45 minutes period. The transition from a microteaching session to a macroteaching session is done by taking a few selected skills, with more content than in a microlesson through link practice. A link lesson gives a student trainee a taste of a real class without the panic and uncertainty associated with a macro-lesson. Thus, a full unit can be chosen for link practice. The unit is then divided into several smaller portions and with a few selected micro-skills, a link lesson can be framed. This gives an opportunity to use even those skills which may not have been practised before. This lesson can be demonstrated to a group of teacher trainees who can then practise continuously, with no break in subject matter.

When mastery has been attained in various skills, the teacher trainee is allowed to teach the skills together. This separate training programme to integrate various isolated skills is known as *link practice*.

1. Link practice helps the trainee to transfer effectively all the skills learnt in the microteaching sessions.
2. It helps to bridge the gap between training in isolated teaching skills and the real teaching situation faced by a student teacher.

3. The desirable number of pupils is between 15 and 20.
4. Preferable duration is 20 minutes.
5. The desirable number of skills is 3–4 skills.

Integration of teaching skills is characterised by:

1. The appropriateness of the use of skills integrated.
2. Adaptability to other situations.
3. Proper sequencing of the skills.
4. Optimum proportion of each skill in teaching.
5. Coordination of different elements involved in teaching.

Link practice or integration of skills can be done in two ways:

1. **Integration in parts:** Three or four teaching skills are integrated and then incorporated into a lesson of 15–20 minutes duration. Again, 3 or 4 skills are integrated and all are transferred within one lesson.
2. **Integration as a whole:** The student teacher integrates all the individual teaching skills by taking them as a whole and transfer them into a real teaching situation.

In most of the teacher training colleges, microteaching is used in one or all the following ways:

1. As preparation for teaching practice
2. As a remedy for teacher trainees whose classroom techniques have been found to be lacking in some way
3. As an aid to translating educational theory to practical classroom methods
4. As a way of prompting experienced teachers to reevaluate their classroom skills.

CONCLUSION

Lack of adequate and in-depth awareness of the purpose of microteaching has led to criticisms that microteaching produces homogenised standard robots with set smiles and procedures. However, proper use of microteaching leads to self-reliant, confident teachers.

REFERENCES

Allen, D.W. (1966), *Microteaching: A Description*, School of Education, Stanford University, Palo Alto.

Allen, D.W. and Eve, A.W. (1968), *Microteaching: Theory into Practice*, Vol. VII, No. 5, December 1868, “Change Agent”: The administrator in the ‘New Education’ (with Lloyd Kline), Today’s catholic teacher, March 1969, pp. 30–38.

Allen, D.W. and Ryan, K.A. (1969), *Microteaching*, Addison-Wesley, Reading, Massachusetts.

Buch, M.B. (1974), A Survey of Research in Education, Centre of Advanced Study in Education, Baroda.

Fernandez, L. Maria (2010), Investigating how and what prospective teachers learn through microteaching lesson study, *Teaching and Teacher Education, Elsevier, Amsterdam*, 26(2):351–362.

Funmi, A. Amobi, Irwin, L (2009), Implementing on-campus microteaching to elicit preservice teachers' reflection on teaching actions, Fresh perspective on an established practice, *Journal of the Scholarship of Teaching and Learning*, Indiana University Publishing, Bloomington, Indiana, 9:27–34

Koross, R. (2016), Microteaching an efficient technique for learning effective teaching skills: Preservice teachers' perspective, *IRA International Journal of Education and Multidisciplinary Studies,* IRA Academico Research, Haryana, India, 4(2):289-299.

McAleese, W.R. and Unwin, D. (January 1973), A Bibliography of Microteaching, *PLET*, Taylor and Francis, London Vol. 10, No. 1.

McIntyre, D., MacLeod, G. and Griffiths, R. (Eds.) (1977), *Investigations of Microteaching*, Croom Helm, London.

Passi, B.K. (1976), *Becoming Better Teachers—Microteaching Approach*, Sahitya Muranalaya, Ahmedabad.

Peker M. (2009), The use of expanded microteaching for reducing preservice teachers' teaching anxiety about mathematics, *Scientific Research and Essay, Academic Journals*, Nigeria, 4;9:872–880.

Singh, L.C. et al. (1987), *Microteaching—Theory and Practice*, Psychological Corporation, Agra.

Singh, L.C. and Joshi, A.N. (1990), *Microteaching in India*, NCERT, New Delhi.

CHAPTER 4

Interactional Analysis

All human interactions are opportunities either to learn or to teach.

—M. SCOTT PECK

INTRODUCTION

Recent research on teaching effectiveness based on large-scale meta-analysis conducted by Walberg (1984) indicates that there are seven factors contributing to effective teaching, like engaged academic learning time and positive classroom environment. Flanders' system of interaction reinforced these findings. Jackson (1968) reported that teachers have a minimum of 1000 verbal exchanges a day with their students.

To help students and teachers to be more self-analytical and more precise in stating their instructional objectives, many teacher training programmes and inservice efforts are using techniques such as interaction analysis. Such a system allows the individual teacher to understand more clearly the degree and kind of influence he exercises in the classroom through the activity in which he is most often engaged–talking.

Interaction analysis is a system for describing and analysing teacher-pupil verbal interactions. It has found its way into many different kinds of educational programmes—both research and development. Basically, interaction analysis has been used to help quantify teachers' verbal behaviours. It can also be used to study the relationship between teaching style and pupil achievement.

Investigators studied the following factors in their research on interaction analyses.

- Teacher–pupil interaction
- Pupil–pupil interaction

- Interaction with various materials, and the focus mainly on:
  - Affective elements
  - Cognitive elements
  - Psychomotor elements
  - Activity
  - Content
  - Physical environment
  - Sociological structure

MEANING OF CLASSROOM INTERACTION ANALYSIS

Classroom interaction analysis refers to a technique consisting of objective and systematic observation of the classroom events for the study of the teacher's classroom behaviour and the process of interaction going inside the classroom.

Satya Pal Ruhela, in his book *Educational Technology,* writes that class interaction analysis may be conveniently divided into two parts:

- Verbal interaction
- Non-verbal interaction

Class interaction analysis has been applied in teacher education. It has proven useful in educational psychology and education courses as a tool for analysing teacher behaviour. Research on teacher–pupil interaction patterns has also provided the basis for education or educational psychology courses concerned with the teacher's role and behaviour in the classroom. Interaction analysis is also a valuable tool in courses concerned with observation skills. The greatest use of interaction analysis has been in student teaching. In such activities, the tool is used for

- Developing skill in observation of teaching
- Providing a tool for analysis of teaching
- Providing a tool for feedback about one's teaching
- Setting a framework for practicing and learning specific teaching skills.

DEFINITIONS OF INTERACTION ANALYSIS

Interaction analysis is defined as:

- A research procedure used to investigate classroom communication. It involves the use of a system of categories to record and analyse the different ways in which teachers and students use language.

- A quantitative research method, which codes the content of ongoing communication between two or more individuals; identifies the verbal or nonverbal features or functions of the stream of conversational elements.

BASIC THEORETICAL ASSUMPTIONS OF INTERACTION ANALYSIS

The basic theoretical assumptions of interaction analysis are as follows:

1. Predominance of verbal communication
2. Higher reliability of verbal behaviour
3. Consistency of verbal statements
4. Teacher's influence
5. Relation between students and teachers
6. Relation between social climate and productivity
7. Relation between classroom climate and learning
8. Use of observational technique
9. Role of feedback
10. Expression through verbal statement

FLANDERS' SYSTEM OF INTERACTION ANALYSIS

Flanders et al. (1970) originally developed a research tool, Flanders' interaction analysis, using a coding system to analyse and improve teaching skills. The teaching-learning situations in the classroom involve interaction between the teacher and the student. The success of a teacher may be judged through the degree of effectiveness of his/her teaching, which may be objectively assessed through his classroom behaviour or interaction. Thus, a systematic or objective analysis of the teacher's classroom interaction may provide a reliable assessment of what goes on inside the classroom in terms of teaching and learning.

Categorization of Flanders' System

Of all the techniques of interaction analysis mentioned before in connection with their respective studies, Ned A. Flanders' system (Amidon and Flanders, 1963) is considered easy to handle and can be used as a feedback technique in teacher training. Flanders' system is an observational tool used to classify the verbal behaviour of teachers and pupils as they interact in the classroom. Flanders' instrument was designed for observing only the verbal communication in the classroom and non-verbal gestures are not taken into account. The basic assumption of the system is that in the classroom, the verbal statements of a teacher are consistent with his/her non-verbal gestures, or rather his/her total behaviour.

Flanders has categorised the interaction of teachers and pupils in classrooms (Table 4.1). There are ten categories in the system. Out of the ten categories in the system evolved by Flanders, seven categories are assigned to teacher talk and two to student talk and the remaining one category classifies pauses, short periods of silence, and talk that is confusing or noisy. The seven categories assigned to teacher talk are again divided into indirect and direct influence. Categories 1–4 represent indirect influence and categories 5–7 represent direct influence. Indirect influence encourages student participation and freedom of action. Direct

TABLE 4.1 Categories in Flanders' interaction analysis

	Influence	*Categories*	*Behaviours observed*
Teacher talk	Indirect influence	Accept feeling	• Accepting and clarifying the feeling of the students in a non-threatening manner • Feelings may be positive or negative • Predicting or recalling feeling
		Praises or encourages	• Praising or encouraging student's action or behaviour • Jokes that release tension but not at the expense of another individual • Nodding head • Saying "go on", "good", etc.
		Accept ideas	Clarifying, building or developing ideas suggested by a student
		Asks questions	Asking a question about content or procedure with the intent that a student answer
	Direct influence	Lectures	• Giving facts or opinions about content or procedures • Expressing the teacher's own ideas • Asking rhetorical questions
		Gives directions	Giving directions, commands, or orders with which a student is expected to comply
		Criticises	Making statements intended to change student behaviour from unacceptable to acceptable pattern • Scolding someone • Stating why the teacher is doing what he/she is doing • Extreme self-reference

(*Contd.*)

TABLE 4.1 Categories in Flanders' interaction analysis (Contd.)

	Influence	*Categories*	*Behaviours observed*
Student talk		Pupil's response	• Talk by students in response to teacher • Teacher initiates the contact or elicits student statement
		Student talk initiation	• Talk by students, which they initiate • If calling on students is only to indicate who may talk next, observer must decide whether student wanted to talk
		Silence or confusion	• Pauses • Short periods of silence • Periods of confusion in which communication cannot be understood by the observer

influence increases the active control of the teacher and often aims at conformity and compliance. Direct influence tends to increase the teacher's activity and restrains student behaviour. The net effect is less freedom of action for the students.

The division of student talk into categories 8 and 9 provides a clue to the nature of freedom given to the students. Usually, but not necessarily, an excessive or above average pattern of direct teacher influence is associated with less student talk. An above average indirect pattern is associated with more student talk and this will be of self-initiated type. The use of only two categories to record all kinds of student talk neglects a great deal of information, but the major purpose of this system is the analysis of teacher influence.

The purpose of category 10 is to record pauses, silence and periods of confusion. This is not intended to record longer periods of silence or confusion that exists for more than two minutes.

The major feature of this category system lies in the analysis of initiative and response which is a characteristic of interaction between individuals.

Procedure of Flanders' Interaction Analysis

1. *Encoding process*
    - Code number
    - Place of sitting
    - Recording the category number
    - Instant recording
    - Recording in uncertainty

- Not to shift into opposite classification
- No biases
- Recording categories after three seconds

2. *Decoding process*
   - Construction of an interaction matrix

Key points in the use of Flanders' interaction analysis

1. Only trained observers
2. Avoiding value judgements
3. A minimum of two observers
4. Inspecting the matrix table
5. Comparison between matrices
6. Classroom recording
7. Number of observations
8. Indicating sequence of events
9. Underlining code number

The use of Flanders' interaction analysis system involves three major steps:

- Observation or recording of classroom event
- Construction of interaction matrix
- Interpretation of interaction matrix.

Observation or recording of classroom event

The observer sits in the classroom in the best position to hear and see the participants. At the end of each 3 second period, the observer decides the category that best represents the communication of events just completed. The observer writes down this category number while simultaneously assessing communication in the next period. He continues at the rate of 20–25 observations per minute, keeping the tempo as steady as possible. The observer's notes are merely a sequence of numbers written in a column, top to bottom, so that the original sequence of events is preserved. Occasionally, marginal notes are used to explain the class formation or any unusual circumstances. When there is a major change in class formation, the communication pattern or the subject under discussion, a double line is drawn and the time is indicated. As soon as the total observation is completed, he/she retires to a room and completes a general description on each separate activity period indicated by the double lines.

Before proceeding to observe the class and mark the observations in a coding chart, it is necessary to establish certain ground rules which become conventions for coding. Since classroom interaction is so complex, category definitions, ground rules and their explanations can never completely cover all the classification problems that will arise. However, the following ground rules are helpful to decide the proper categorisation of the interactive behaviours when the observer is faced with some difficulty.

The task of observation, recording or encoding is quite complex and needs sufficient training, practice and care on the part of the observer. For maintaining objectivity and reliability of the process, there are certain ground rules which have to be kept in mind by an observer.

Rule 1 When not certain to which two or more categories a statement belongs, choose the category that is numerically farthest from category 5. For example, for choosing between 3 and 4, choose 3 and for 8 and 9, choose 9.

Rule 2 If the primary tone of the teacher's behaviour has been consistently direct or consistently indirect, do not shift into the opposite classification unless a clear indication of shift is given by the teacher.

Rule 3 The observer must not be concerned with his/her own biases or teacher's intent.

Rule 4 If more than one category occurs during the three seconds interval, then all categories used in that interval are recorded; therefore, record each change in category. If no change occurs within three seconds, repeat that category number.

Rule 5 For silence longer than three seconds, record 10 for every three seconds.

Rule 6 A teacher's joke, which is made at the expense of children, is recorded as 7, but if the joke is not made at the expense of the children, it is recorded as 2.

Rule 7 If a student gives a specific predictable answer to a narrow question, it is recorded as 8 and in the case when a number of students respond collectively, it is also recorded as 8.

Rule 8 When the teacher calls a child by name, the observer ordinarily records 4.

Rule 9 When the teacher repeats a student's answer and if the answer is correct one, this is recorded as 2.

Rule 10 When the teacher repeats a student's idea and communicates that the idea will be considered or accepted as something to be discussed, a 3 is used.

Rule 11 If a student begins to talk after another student, a 10 is inserted between 9's and 8's to indicate the change of student.

Rule 12 Reactions such as 'All right', 'Okay' are recorded as 2.

Construction of interaction matrix

After recording or encoding the classroom events into ten categories, the next task is concerned with the construction of an interaction matrix table. The matrix table consists of 10 rows and 10 columns. The category number of the record sheet is tabulated in the matrix table. Each number is entered in the form of sequence pairs, being used twice, firstly as the first number and secondly as the second number. The rows of the matrix represent the first number in the pair and the columns, the second.

Suppose the observer has written down 6, 10, 7, 5, 1, 4, 8 and 4. As the interaction proceeds, the observer will continue to write down numbers. To tabulate these observations in a 10 × 10 matrix, the first step is to make sure that the entire series begins and ends with the same number. The convention is to add a 10 to the beginning and end of the series unless it is already present. The series becomes as shown in Table 4.2.

TABLE 4.2 Convention of observation

	2nd		4th		6th		8th	
10,6 1st		10,7 3rd		5,1 5th		4,8 7th		4,10 9th
Pair		Pair		Pair		Pair		Pair

These numbers are tabulated in a matrix, one pair at a time (Table 4.3). The column is indicated by the second number, and the row is indicated by the first number. The first pair is 10–6; the tally is placed in row ten and column six cell. The second pair is 6–10; this tally is placed in row six, column ten cell. The third pair is 10–7, the fourth is 7–5, and so on. Each pair overlaps with the next, and the total number of observations, 'n', always will be tabulated by 'n–1' tallies in the matrix.

TABLE 4.3 Sample interaction matrix

	1	2	3	4	5	6	7	8	9	10	*Total*
1				1							1
2											0
3											0
4								1		1	2
5	1										1
6										1	1
7					1						1
8				1							1
9											0
10						1	1				2
Total	1	0	0	2	1	1	1	1	0	2	9

If it is a correctly tabulated matrix, the sums of the corresponding rows and columns will be equal.

Interpretation of interaction matrix

The process of interpretation of interaction or observation data is called *decoding*. There are several ways of decoding a matrix. The first and simplest way is to convert the reporting into percentages in each cell. This is done by dividing each of the column totals, 1 through 10, by the total number of tallies in the matrix. This computation gives the proportion of the total interaction in the observed classroom situation in each category. A similar procedure is used to determine the percentage of total teacher talk that falls in each category, 1 through 7, by the sum of these seven categories.

The purpose of interaction analysis is to preserve selected aspects of interaction through observation, encoding, tabulation and then decoding.

1. **The proportion of teacher talk, pupil talk, and silence or confusion:** The proportion of tallies in columns 1, 2, 3, 4, 5, 6, 7, 8, 9 and column 10 to the total tallies indicates how much the teacher talks, the student talks and the time spent in silence or confusion. In general, an average of 68 per cent teacher talk, 20 per cent pupil talk and 11 or 12 per cent silence or confusion is expected.

2. **The ratio between indirect influence and direct influence (i/d ratio):** The sum of columns 1, 2, 3 and 4 if divided by the sum of columns 5, 6 and 7 gives this ratio. If the ratio is 1 or more than 1, the teacher is said to be indirect in his behaviour. This ratio, therefore, shows whether a teacher is more direct or indirect in his teaching.

3. **The ratio between positive reinforcement and negative reinforcement (i/d ratio):** The sum of columns 1, 2 and 3 is to be divided by the sum of the columns 6 and 7. If the ratio is more than 1, then the teacher is said to be good.

4. **Student's participation ratio:** The sum of columns 8 and 9 is to be divided by the total sum. The answer will reveal how much the students have participated in the teaching learning process.

5. **Steady state cells:** Table 4.4 shows the steady state cells along the diagonal from the upper left to the lower right. If these cells are heavily loaded, it shows that the teacher remains in a particular category for more than three seconds.

The cell with the highest frequency of the entire matrix is typically the 5–5 cell, which lies on this diagonal indicating that the teacher frequently stays longer than 3 seconds when he/she provides information through lecture.

6. **Content cross cells:** The cells corresponding to the numbers 4 and 5 in the column and the row are known as *content cross cells*. If these cells are overloaded they reflect the teacher's emphasis on the subject matter.

7. **Constructive integration cells and vicious cells:** Two areas that are most sensitive to the positive and negative aspects of social skill and the teacher–student relationship. This is shown in the matrix in Table 4.5.

TABLE 4.4 Interpretation of matrix

	1	2	3	4	5	6	7	8	9	10	*Total*
1	1–1										
2		2–2									
3			3–3								
4				4–4							
5					5–5						
6						6–6					
7							7–7				
8								8–8			
9									9–9		
10										10/10	
Total											

TABLE 4.5 Content cross cells

	1	2	3	4	5	6	7	8	9	10	*Total*
1											
2		A									
3											
4											
5											
6						B					
7											
8											
9											
10											
Total											

Area A might be called *constructive integrative cells* while **Area B** might be called *vicious cells*. The cells corresponding to numbers 1, 2 and 3 are known as *constructive integrative cells*. Cells of numbers 6 and 7 are known as *vicious cells*. These cells reveal the teacher's attention to problems of classroom management and control as distinct from concern with the subject matter.

Advantages of Flanders' Interaction Analysis

The advantages of Flanders' interaction analysis are as follows:

1. The analysis of matrix is so dependable that even a person not present when observations are made can make accurate inferences about the verbal communication and get a picture of the classroom scenario.
2. Different matrices can be made and used to compare the behaviour of teachers at different age levels, sex, subject matter, etc.
3. This analysis serves as a vital feedback to the teacher or teacher trainee about their intentions and actual behaviour in the classroom.
4. It is an effective diagnostic tool to measure the social-emotional climate in the classroom.
5. It can be used for carrying out research in the areas of teaching, teacher behaviour and pre-service and in-service education of teachers.
6. It adds and supplements teacher training techniques like microteaching and team teaching.

Limitations of Flanders' Interaction Analysis

The limitations of Flanders' interaction analysis are as follows:

1. The system concentrates on verbal behaviour. Some types of behaviour may be overlooked.
2. It focuses too much on direct/indirect teacher influence or teacher talk.
3. Classroom interaction focusing on student-student interaction is not discussed at all.
4. The process of tallying, constructing and interpreting the matrix is time-consuming.
5. It requires highly trained, reliable and competent observers/interpreters.
6. This system is not economical in terms of time.
7. There is paucity of trained observers.

CONCLUSION

The heart of the educational process is in the interaction between the teacher and the student. It is through this interaction that the school system makes its major impact upon the child. The way the teacher interacts with the student is a major determinant of the quality of education the child receives.

Information on what actually happens in the classroom is, thus, very important in assessing the quality of educational opportunity. Some of the most significant aspects of the teaching learning process can be identified only by observing the actual classroom interaction. The teacher's skills in instructing, guiding, and encouraging students are demonstrated by what the teacher does and says in the classroom. The extent to which students are actively involved in the learning process is shown by their participation in the classroom activities. The way teachers and students feel about each other is evident in the way teachers and students react to one another.

REFERENCES

Amidon, Edmund, J. and Flanders, Ned A. (1963), *The Role of the Teacher in the Classroom: A Manual for Understanding and Improving Teachers' Classroom Behaviour*, Paul S. Amidon Associates, Minneapolis.

Flanders, Ned A. (1970), *Analysing Teaching Behaviour*, Addison Wesley Publishing Company, Menlo Park, California.

Hafix, M.M; Naseerud din, M and Ishitiaq, H. (2008). Teacher-student verbal interaction patterns at the tertiary level of education, *Contemporary Issues in Education Research*, The Clute Institute, USA, 1, 1: pp. 45–50.

Newman, M. (2001), PEPBL Methodology, Working Paper 6: Flanders Interaction Analysis.

Niki, F.R. (2011), Flanders Interaction Analysis, Retrieved (April 23, 2015), from http://www.slideshare.net/selvabarady/flanders-interaction-analysis.

Tisher, R.P. (2007), Classroom Interaction Analysis: the new religion, *Journal Research in Science Education*, 2: 35.

University of Queensland, Department of Education, Brisbane, Q 4067, Australia.

VanLear, C. A., and Canary, D. J. (Eds.). (2017), Researching interactive communication behavior: A sourcebook of methods and measures, SAGE Publications, Inc., Los Angeles, CA.

Veronica Odiri Amatari, (2015), The Instructional Process: A Review of Flanders' Interaction Analysis in a Classroom Setting, *International Journal of Secondary Education,* Science Publishing Group, USA, Vol. 3, No. 5, pp. 43–49.

CHAPTER 5

Practice Teaching

Providing internship opportunities......changes the whole equation.

—NCFTE, 2010

INTRODUCTION

The practice of teaching constitutes the hub of the multiple and varied activities comprising the total programme of teacher education. It is interconnected with theoretical study, field work and practicum and a wide range of institutional experiences involving school students, teachers, student teachers, and mentor teacher educators. In a way, it acts both as the evaluation tool for effective teacher education and its critical quality indicator.

In order for teachers to be sufficiently prepared for the challenges of the teaching profession, it is vital that student teachers receive comprehensive pre-service training. Vonk (1993) has pointed out that the teaching profession starts with pre-service teaching induction and continued inservice training. Practice teaching is considered the pivotal component of the B.Ed. programme. The practicum or student teaching is where theory meets practice. The performance in student teaching is the single most important criterion for predicting success in inservice teachers (Day and Brightwell, 1978).

DEFINITION OF TEACHING PRACTICE

Teaching Practice is a course or programme in which the students or trainees are posted to schools, normally lower than their institutions of learning, to teach the student subject areas of their specialization for a specified period. During the period, student teachers, as they are called, assume the position of normal subject teachers and, at the same time engage in all lawful assignments given by the cooperating school authorities. Figure 5.1 shows the teacher-career pathway.

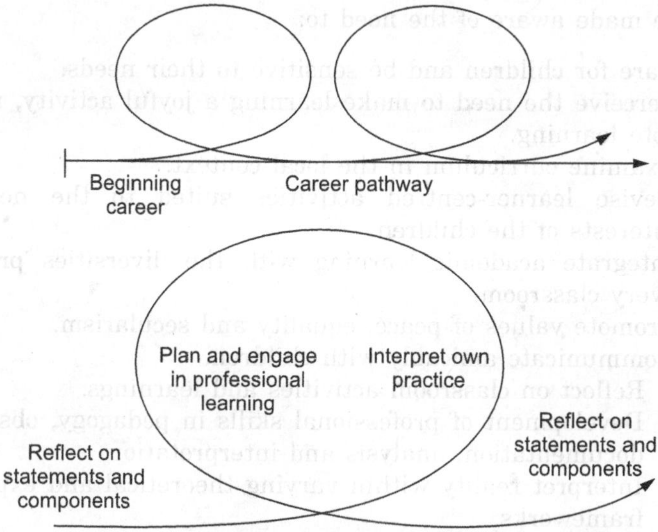

FIGURE 5.1 Teaching–career pathway.

Practice teaching is defined as **teaching by a student under the supervision of an experienced teacher.** The aim is to provide hands-on experience with children of diverse ages and contexts, and to enable a back-and-forth movement between theory and practice. Student teachers need to be given opportunities to be with children of diverse contexts such as first generation learners and street children, interact with them, organise creative activities for them with the aim to learn to communicate and relate with them.

Internship is defined as extended school based professional learning negotiated by the different stakeholders in the preservice teaching preparation phase.... The intern is mentored by the classroom teacher, with increased opportunities to involve in a broad range of teacher's work activities. There is a subtle shift in the classroom teacher and intern's relationship from evaluative to collegial.

Internship experiences need to be organised in a way that is useful in evaluating the teacher's ability, supports socialization within the profession, stimulates development of teaching-learning concepts, provides a protected field of experimentation, allows insight into new perspectives and enhances motivation to continue learning and reflecting.

OBJECTIVES OF PRACTICE TEACHING

Teacher education, when viewed as a holistic enterprise involving actions of different kinds and from multiple fronts aimed at the development of the total teacher—knowledge and understanding, repertoire of skills, positive attitudes, habits, values and the capacity to reflect, will require an intensive internship for student teachers. Thus, student teachers should be made aware of the need to:

1. Care for children and be sensitive to their needs.
2. Perceive the need to make learning a joyful activity, not mere rote learning.
3. Examine curriculum in the local context.
4. Devise learner-centred activities suited to the needs and interests of the children.
5. Integrate academic learning with the diversities present in every classroom.
6. Promote values of peace, equality and secularism.
7. Communicate amicably with children.
    - Reflect on classroom activities and learnings.
    - Development of professional skills in pedagogy, observation, documentation, analysis and interpretation.
    - Interpret reality within varying theoretical and experiential frameworks.

SCHOOL INTERNSHIP

The NCFTE 2010 has stressed the importance of *imparting professional rigour to the preparation of a teacher, the practice of teaching and associated rigorous theoretical study* which play a crucial part. Practice teaching constitutes the most functional part of the teacher preparation programme. It is the effectiveness with which the multiple components of teaching/learning—getting to know the school, observing children, observing teaching and learning in real classroom contexts, preparing lesson plans and instructional aids suitable to the needs of the students, preparing and using technology-based teaching materials based on their teaching lessons, practising teaching, developing capacities to think with educational theories and applying concepts in concrete teaching-learning situations, managing classroom learning, evaluating learners and providing feedback, learning to work with colleagues, reflecting on one's own professional practice—are drawn upon to provide appropriate learning experiences for the student teacher that is critical to the education of teachers.

In most universities in India, practice teaching comprises 20 lessons in each optional subject for a one year B.Ed. programme. However, with the proposed introduction of the integrated programme in June 2011, the hours will vary.

Components of School Internship Programme

The school internship programme comprises the following:

1. Visits to innovative centres of pedagogy and learning, for example, special schools, inclusive schools, international schools.
2. Action research projects, to help students develop the habit of reflective thinking.
3. A minimum of 40 days internship in cooperating schools for a one year B.Ed. programme.
4. Development of unit and lesson plans—not more than 4 unit plans per subject. Planning of the units would include a critical engagement with content from multiple sources including the school textbook, organisation and presentation of subject matter.
5. Creating and maintaining charts, models, etc. as well as maintenance of registers.
6. Preparation of achievement tests with scoring key; administering the tests and analysing them. This includes formulating questions, specifically to: (a) assess knowledge base and understanding of students; (b) further the process of knowledge construction and meaning-making in the classroom; and (c) assess students' learning to improve pedagogic practice and further enhance learning.
7. Conducting a case study of any particular student in the class which the student teacher is handling.
8. Getting a grip over existing systemic issues in education and developing capacity to rise to the uncertainties of a learning environment and changing learner needs and a capacity to feel empowered to make a difference.
9. Developing the ability to understand learners in context; design and choose appropriate learning experiences, activities; learn to observe and document, analyse, synthesise, interpret and reflect.

While functioning as a regular teacher for a sustained period of time, the intern would get an opportunity to learn to set realistic goals in terms of learning, curricular content and pedagogic practice.

Major drawbacks of the current model of practice teaching:

- Current practices in teacher education take the school curriculum and textbooks as 'given' and train teachers to adjust to the needs of the existing school system through fastidious planning of lessons in standardized formats, fulfilling the ritual of delivering the required number of lessons.
- Repeated 'practice' in the teaching of a specified number of isolated lessons is considered a sufficient condition for professional development.

- There is no opportunity for teachers to examine their own biases and beliefs and reflect on their own experiences as part of classroom discourse and enquiry.
- Theory courses have no clear articulation with practical work and ground realities.
- The evaluation protocol is too theoretical, excessively quantitative and lacks comprehensiveness.

—NCFTE, 2010

BLOCK TEACHING

Block teaching, which refers to an arrangement of class time into fewer, longer periods that make up a school day, has been adopted by many high schools abroad. Taking fewer classes per day reduces the instructional time lost to transitions. Students like having an extra day to complete homework assignments, and teachers gain time for planning every day. With the extended periods of class time available, teachers can build higher-order thinking skills and explore connections between disciplines. Collaborative learning and other forms of group learning are ideal for block teaching.

Example

When studying kinetic theory and phase changes, students are divided into groups and each group becomes an expert on a state of matter. The extended class period allows students within the group to cover the necessary material during two class meetings. With the block schedule, it is possible to accomplish prelab questioning, the activity, and postlab analysis in the same day.

Definition of Block Scheduling

Block scheduling was defined as the organisation into larger blocks of time (more than 60 minutes) to allow flexibility for varied instructional activities.

Cawelti (1994) identified five major components for restructuring high school level teaching, viz. curriculum and teaching, school organisation, community outreach, technology and monetary incentives. Within each of these categories, 36 specific indicators of restructuring activities were identified. One of these activities is "block teaching".

Block teaching is the reorganisation of the school year into approximately 12 'blocks' of 4 weeks each, instead of two semesters of 15 weeks each. There is no loss of curriculum time during block teaching. Changes to the curriculum are kept at a minimum.

Block teaching mimics the project management timeline in industry where designers work with short deadlines. The flow of work in block teaching allows students to ease themselves into the pace of work usually required in the professional arena, training them to think faster on their feet and conceptualise ideas more efficiently in a realistic time frame.

Workload

Subjects are taught in blocks of 4 weeks instead of over a 15-week semester. Students who used to take 6–7 subjects per semester will now take at most 2 subjects per block. It gives the students an opportunity to focus on the 1 or 2 subjects at hand and give their best in the projects assigned. Compared to the semester system, the student no longer needs to handle 6–7 projects at a time.

Advantages of Block Teaching

It has been noticed that taking 6–7 subjects at a go and having to submit 6–7 projects within a tight time frame does take its toll on the quality of the work submitted.

With only 1 to 2 projects to manage in block teaching, students would be able to concentrate on these projects. They would be able to give more dedicated time to these 2 assignments and their energies would not be as diffused as it otherwise would be. With good time management and planning skills, students are more likely to produce better quality work and do better in the long run. As block teaching is intensively taught, it would not be in the students' best interests to deliberately skip classes. Ultimately, the responsibility for learning falls on the student.

In general, the advantages of 'block scheduling' are as follows:

1. A teacher sees fewer students during the day, thereby giving them the ability to spend more time with each individual.
2. Because of the increased span of teaching time, longer cooperative learning activities can be completed in one class period. Also, there is more time for labs in science classes.
3. Students have less information to deal with over the course of a school day.
4. Because of the decreased number of classes, students have less homework on any given day during the week.
5. The teacher is able to provide more varied instruction during class. Thus, it is easier to deal with students with disabilities and differing learning styles.
6. Planning periods are longer. It seems that with a longer span of time, planning becomes easier and more gets done.

7. It facilitates the implementation of new programmes and practices.
8. It increases opportunities for students to accelerate or enroll in electives.
9. It assists students who may be slow or have missed out classes and who need time to catch up.
10. It improves teachers' class preparation, grading and record keeping.
11. Teachers get to know their students better, since the number of students seen daily and the number of classes taught daily is reduced.
12. Teachers can introduce and reinforce concepts to be learned in a single class period.
13. Teachers can utilise cooperative learning strategies.
14. It allows students to effectively utilise technology.
15. It can accommodate individual learning styles.

Disadvantages of Block Teaching

The disadvantages of block teaching are as follows:

1. Teachers see students four times a week (for example, Monday, Tuesday, Thursday, Friday) which means that students lose continuity on their off days.
2. If a student misses a day under the modular schedule, that student is actually missing two, or sometimes even more days.
3. No matter how well planned, on many days the teacher ends up with 10–15 minutes for the students to begin their homework. When all of the time is added up at the end of the semester, less information and material is covered.
4. There is no evidence to prove that block scheduling works.

Time Table for Block Teaching

The time table is reconfigured such that students focus on 1 or 2 subjects, attending class and seeing the lecturers in charge of these subjects, on a daily basis. Classes are now conducted over 4 main time slots in the school day: 0900–1200 hr, 1200–1500 hr, 1500–1800 hr and 1800–2100 hr.

Lesson Plan Format

Williams and Dunn (2008), in their text, *Brain Compatible Learning for the Block*, liken good lesson plans to recipes, blueprints, and game plans that engage students in a successful learning process. While there are endless possibilities for lesson plan formats, block scheduling will require at least three transitions during the extended class period.

Canady and Rettig (1996) propose the following three parts and the time frames for each:

1. *Explanation:* A 25- to 30-minute block of time devoted to presenting information to students through mini-lectures, reviews, modelling, demonstrations, viewing video clips, or textual reading.
2. *Application:* A 40- to 60-minute block of time when students are engaged in active learning strategies.
3. *Synthesis:* A 15- to 30-minute block of time when students reflect on and are evaluated on what they have learned.

Williams and Dunn (2008) have suggested the following format. The format has four phases, each varying in time from 10 to 25 minutes. These phases are:

Phase 1: Entice the learner, approximately 10–15 minutes in length

Phase 2: Enlighten the learner, approximately 15–20 minutes in length

Phase 3: Engage the learner, approximately 20–30 minutes in length

Phase 4: Extend the learner, approximately 20–25 minutes in length

Furthermore, in an extended time frame or block schedule, as students engage in the strategies, they can smoothly transition through each phase of the learning process, sometimes spiralling back upon one phase or another as needed, thereby not only intensifying the learning experience for them but assuring that their learning is successful.

ORGANISATION OF STUDENT TEACHING (Figure 5.2)

While teaching practice provides the trainee an opportunity to acquire practical skills through direct experience, it also provides the trainer the opportunity of assessing and guiding the trainee for both formative and summative evaluation purposes. Teaching practice enables the teacher educators develop a degree of experience in understanding the student teachers and their techniques and procedure of teaching which they put into practice under professional guidance and supervision of the teacher educator. The cooperating schools provide all the materialistic and moral support they can offer to train the student teachers in schools. It is, therefore necessary that a conducive educational environment be established for student teachers to enable them gain confidence in them

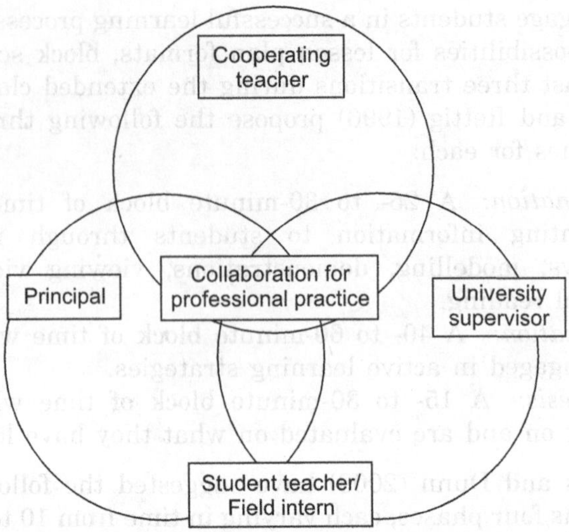

FIGURE 5.2 Teaching practice—collaborators.

and to work effectively with fellow students and the school personnel. In such environment, student teachers will have the opportunity to engage in profitable experiences in observing, sharing and in teaching with the guidance and supervision of student supervisors or tutors.

Teaching practice is a cooperative venture involving the student teachers and their supervisor on the one hand and the staff and pupils, on the other. The programme includes teaching, demonstration, participation in co-curricular activities and evaluation, which is the final assessment of the student teachers.

Being as important as it is in the curriculum of the teacher training institutions, there are certain things which the student teachers should take note of when preparing for teaching practice.

COOPERATING TEACHER SELECTION

The committee of principal and teaching staff of the training college interviews each student prior to making internship assignments. Based on the recommendations of faculty of the committee, an assessment of the student's needs for a successful experience is made. This includes attention to personality traits and special skills as well as the preferences (courses, school location, etc.) of the student teacher with respect to the selection of the cooperating teacher when possible and appropriate. Cooperating teachers are then selected on the basis of the following criteria:

1. The cooperating teacher must be certified in the specialty area for which he or she would be supervising.

2. The cooperating teacher must have a minimum of three years of successful teaching experience.
3. The cooperating teacher must be recommended strongly by the current principal or assistant principal.
4. The cooperating teacher must be willing to participate in the orientation and post-observation conferences, as well as the evaluation process.

Responsibilities of Cooperating Teacher

Cooperating teachers are to do the following during the internship:

1. Work closely with student teachers to help them meet the expectations listed in the next section.
2. Be a positive role model by showing an interest in students and in the profession.
3. Guide student teachers as they reflect upon each experience and develop their own teaching styles.
4. Guide student teachers as they develop their own philosophy of education.
5. Provide regular feedback and advice about their teaching on a daily basis.
6. Evaluate student teachers' performance during the internship. The student teacher is responsible for working with the cooperating teacher to schedule the observations and for submitting a copy of each evaluation to the college supervisor.
7. Suggest other teaching experiences that may be beneficial to the student teacher.

Tasks of Student Teachers during the Training

The student teacher must be present in his/her assigned school based on the days mentioned in the Teaching Practice Programme.

1. The student teacher must follow the school calendar and daily routine of the cooperating teacher during practice teaching. They are to arrive and leave when the cooperating teacher does and participate in all the activities that make up the day (including lunch duty, club sponsorship, etc.).
2. The student teachers are assigned progressive tasks that will eventually lead to the student teacher conducting full lessons in the classroom; the student teacher is also assigned tasks inside and outside the classroom under the supervision of the cooperating teacher, the college supervisor, and the school principal.

3. Students are assigned the responsibility of making a teaching file (every academic year has a specific colour) which contains all the assigned tasks in the schools.
4. Students must attend the seminars held in the college as well as perform the tasks in the daily journal with the college teachers.
5. The student teachers must cooperate with the supervising team (the cooperating teacher—college supervisor—school principal) during the teaching practice, and make his/her best effort to become a professional and capable teacher.
6. The student teacher must keep a lesson plan book with plans for at least three days in advance. Students do need to write complete lesson plans each day. The format may vary, but each lesson should include objectives, activities and evaluation procedures.
7. The student teacher must attend all appropriate meetings with you.
8. The student teacher must teach a portion of the day for at least four weeks and all day for at least four consecutive weeks.

Observations and Evaluations

The student teachers will be observed a minimum of 2 times formally as well as daily by the cooperating teacher on an informal basis. These observations are conducted as follows:

1. Cooperating teacher in the school, who will evaluate all activities of the student teachers allotted to her
2. Training college faculty supervisor, who will:
   (i) Provide overall advising leadership for the internship.
   (ii) Keep team members and student teachers aware and monitor the implementation of state guidelines, licensure process, and the standards of performance.
   (iii) Observe each student teacher.
   (iv) Provide feedback on progress regularly.
3. The content professor/faculty (1 observation) will:
   (i) Provide the content specific portion of EDU 400 and support the student teacher in developing the comprehensive instructional unit.
   (ii) Observe each student teacher in the specialty area a minimum of once.
   (iii) Evaluate the student's progress and performance.
   (iv) Serve as a resource throughout the internship.
4. Principal, assistant principal, or other faculty of training college (1 optional observation).

Cooperating teachers, student teachers and observers will normally participate in a conference following each observation, and specific feedback will be provided.

Student teachers, cooperating teachers, and the college faculty supervisor will participate in final evaluation conferences to determine the progress of the student teacher.

Student teachers should always have a written lesson plan available for each observer at the beginning of the class.

Evaluation Tools

Teacher education programmes tend to develop their own evaluation forms to determine student teacher effectiveness. There are three elements that should be considered when evaluating teaching effectiveness within a particular context:

1. Criteria–attributes of effective teaching.
2. Evidence–documentation of teaching considered in the review process.
3. Standards–expectations of quality and quantity.

Research indicates that student teaching grades usually are high, regardless of the evaluation instrument used. The high grades could reflect an evaluation of the student teachers' potential rather than a measure of demonstrated skills. Appendix 1 is a sample of student teaching profile used in selected training colleges. With the Covid pandemic changing the face of education, every teacher trainee will necessarily have to have a basic competency in handling technology. A good understanding of the various tools and techniques in use is definitely a must for every teacher in the 21st century.

The NCTE document provides a detailed framework and guidelines for the transaction of school internship. The NCTE envisages a comprehensive internship programme covering the curriculum of the 2-year integrated B.Ed. as well as the Diploma in Elementary Education and the 4-year B.A.B.Ed. and B.Sc.B.Ed. Prospective teachers can by practice and hands-on experience link the educational theory and pedagogical concepts in actual school settings. (NCTE document, 2016).

CONCLUSION

Practice teaching is the heart of the teacher education curriculum as it gives the teacher trainee a first hand experience of what the profession 'teaching' is like and prepares him for pursuing teaching as a profession.

REFERENCES

Canady, Robert L. and Michael, D. Rettig (1996), Block scheduling: A catalyst for change in high school, Eye on Education, Routledge, Larchmont, New York.

Cohen, Louis, Manion, Lawrence and Keith, Morrison (1996), A Guide to Teaching Practice, 4th ed., Routledge Falmer, London.

National Curriculum for Teacher Education framework 2009, GOI document.

Web References

Internship in teaching: A source book for cooperating teachers and student teachers. Regional Institute of Education, Mysore - 570 006 NCERT. http://ir.riemysore.ac.in:8080/jspui/bitstream/123456789/65/1/011-Internship%20In%20Teaching-Source%20book.pdf.

NCTE. School Internship: Framework and Guidelines (January 2016).
http://ncte-india.org/ncte_new/pdf/SCHOOL%20INTERNSHIP-%20A%20FRAMEWORK%20And%20GUIDELINES.pdf.

APPENDIX 1

Student Teaching Profile

Name of the student teacher:
Class and Section:
Date:
Period and Time:
Subject: Topic:
Supervisor from College of Co-operating School:

Criteria	*Characteristics*	*Max. Marks*	*Marks awarded by supervisor*
Content Knowledge and coverage	• Mastery • Currency • Correlation with other fields • Tolerance of divergent views • Adequacy of content	10	
Learning Objectives	• Clarity • Adequacy • Accuracy • Relevance to content • Higher Order Abilities inclusive	5	
Lesson Development	• Clear statement of learning outcomes • Appropriate to age and level of student population • Suitable methods used to assess student learning • Alignment with objectives of the course • Applications to new situations	15	

(*Contd.*)

Criteria	*Characteristics*	*Max. Marks*	*Marks awarded by supervisor*
Teaching Learning Process	• Appropriate motivation used to arouse interest • Linkage to previous knowledge • Variety of approaches • Well planned class activities • Clarification of misconceptions • Scaffolding skills • Effective communication and good rapport with students • Catering to diverse student population	25	
Teaching Aids/Use of Technology	• Appropriate use of medium, technology aligned with learning outcomes • Skilled in using technology	10	
Review and Assignment	• Recapitulation inclusive of relevant questions and activities • Attainment of learning objectives • Variety of questions used like quizzes and graded tests • Use of technology for creating an interesting recapitulation session like jam board • Nature of assignment	20	
Classroom management	• Accessibility to students • Responsiveness • Sensitive to diversity of student population while grouping students • Awareness of student resources • Rapport with students	15	
Total		100	

Name of Supervisor:
Signature:
Date:

Part III

STAGES AND PHASES

CHAPTER 6

Pre-Service Teacher Education

It isn't what you do, but how you do it.

—John Wooden

INTRODUCTION

Teacher education programmes are expected to provide some 'training' not only in pedagogy but also in behavioural attributes including attitudes, motivation, perceptions, preferences, appreciation and value orientation. The courses of study generated for the purpose have, over the years, been broadened in scope from their original emphasis on pedagogic considerations within classrooms, to include several understandings and practices useful for teachers. These have to be continually converted into appropriate curricular forms. Through these, aspiring teachers, despite differences among them, have to become capable of being effective in their tasks at least up to some comparable standards. This continues to be a challenge even today and is likely to persist in the years to come.

RECOMMENDATIONS OF DIFFERENT COMMISSIONS AND COMMITTEES FOR PRE-SERVICE PROGRAMMES OF TEACHER EDUCATION

The recommendations of different commission and committees for pre-service programmes of teacher education are given in Table 6.1.

In particular, NCFTE 2009–2010 has suggested the following with regard to pre-service teacher education:

1. A four-year integrated programme of elementary teacher education in select state universities and all central universities, in particular via IASEs and select DIETs, could be undertaken in the initial phase.

TABLE 6.1 Recommendations for pre-service programmes for teacher education

Name of Committee/ Board/Commission	*Year*	*Major recommendations regarding teacher education*
Hartog Committee	1929	• Primary teacher training • Lengthening the duration of training courses • Provision of adequate staff for training institutions
Central Advisory Board of Education	1943	• Duration of training programmes for teachers • Two years for pre-primary and junior basic • Three years for middle school • Two years for non-graduates in high schools • One year for graduates in high school
Sargent Committee	1944	• Need to strengthen practice teaching
Memorandum on the further action taken by the Provincial Governments on the Post-War Educational Development Report	1946–47	• Emergency secondary grade training course of one year to bridge the gap between supply and demand
First Five Year Plan	1950s	• Paradigm shift of teacher education as a process of total development of the individual personality
Second Conference of All India Training Colleges	1951	• Realisation that teacher education had a broader canvas than envisaged • Need for redesigning curricula
Secondary Education Commission Report	1953	• Professionalism in teacher education • Reorientation of syllabus and evaluation techniques • Need to integrate subject content and transactional strategies
University Grants Commission report of the Review Committee on Education	1960s	• Shift in stress from secondary to primary teacher education • No untrained teacher to be recruited • Setting up of correspondence courses for B.Ed. at Regional Colleges of Education. (1964–65)
Education Commission Report	1964–66	• For those who have passed the school leaving certificate or higher secondary leaving certificate, the period of training is to be two years • For graduates, the training to be one academic year

(Contd.)

TABLE 6.1 Recommendations for pre-service programmes for teacher education (Contd.)

Name of Committee/ Board/Commission	*Year*	*Major recommendations regarding teacher education*
		• Training colleges to conduct research in pedagogy • Only trained graduates with three years experience to be admitted to M.Ed. courses
NCERT	1975	• Publication of curriculum framework for school education
NCERT	1978	• Publication of curriculum framework for teacher education
Chattopadhyaya Committee	1983-85	• The minimum length of training for a secondary teacher should be five years following the completion of Class XII • Reiterated the need "... to enable general and professional education to be pursued concurrently", • Need for an integrated four-year programme ...
National Policy on Education	1986	• Reiterate that teacher education is a continuous process and pre-service and inservice components are inseparable
The Acharya Ramamurti Committee—Review of the NPE 1986	1990	• Need for an internship model as it is based on the primary value of actual field experience in a realistic situation, on the development of teaching skills by practice over a period of time
The Yashpal Committee Report Learning without Burden	1993	• The content of the programme should be restructured to ensure its relevance to the changing needs of school education. • The emphasis should be on enabling the trainees to acquire the ability for self-learning and independent thinking
NCTE	1995	• Approved norms and standards for teacher training institutions at the pre-school, elementary and secondary level
NCFTE	2009–10	• Guidelines for all aspects of teacher education with the focus on preparing humane teachers
Justice Verma Committee	2012	The recommendations include: • Pre-entry testing of candidates • Increase in duration of teacher education courses • Redesigning of prevalent teacher education programme in the light of NCFTE 2009

(*Contd.*)

TABLE 6.1 Recommendations for pre-service programmes for teacher education (Contd.)

Name of Committee/ Board/Commission	*Year*	*Major recommendations regarding teacher education*
		• Having a laboratory school with every teacher training institute • Granting of the first professional degree/ diploma in teacher education conducted in face-to-face mode • Increasing investment in research in education.
NCTE Regulations 2014 (following the recommendations of the Justice Verma Commission)	2014	Among the highlights of are: • A variety of programmes including the 4-year • B.A/B.Sc.B.Ed., 3-year B.Ed. (Part-time), and 3-year B.Ed.-M.Ed. programmes • B.Ed., B.P.Ed., M.Ed. courses have been made two years in duration in keeping with international standards. • Each programme curriculum comprises three components—theory, practicum, internship; • 25% of the programme to be focused on school-based activities and internship. • Introduction of Yoga Education, ICT, Inclusive education an important aspect of the course. • Open and Distance Learning (ODL) to be more intensive with quality assurance mechanisms in place. • Each teacher education institution to have compulsory accreditation in every 5 years from an accrediting agency recognized by NCTE. (An MoU has already been signed with NAAC in this regard).

2. XI Plan funding under the innovative education schemes should be channelised as a priority by the UGC to universities and select DIETs to institute four year Integrated Elementary Teacher Education Programmes.
3. As an interim measure, current models of Elementary Teacher Education offered by the DIETs such as the DT.Ed. are required

to redesign their courses as well as the programme structure to include the specific features and structural mechanisms proposed in the new framework in terms of curricular areas and transaction processes.

4. A review of the existing D.Ed. programmes is commissioned and the process of redesign of the curriculum in the light of the proposed process model be completed in the next one-two years.

REDESIGNING CURRENT TEACHER EDUCATION PROGRAMMES

The National Curricular Framework for Teacher Education 2009 has suggested that teacher education courses be redesigned. Thus, D.Ed. would be a two-year diploma after +2 and B.Ed. one-year degree after graduation. This would provide enough time and opportunity for self study, reflection and involvement, engagement with teachers, school, classroom and pedagogic activity and rigorous theoretical study. Any compromise on the duration of the initial education of teachers, for whatever reason, adversely affects the quality of teacher and teaching in schools. The NCFTE 2009 recommends that current models of teacher education at all levels of school education be gradually replaced by models of teacher education that integrate general education with professional development along with an intensive internship with schools. These integrated models should be designed using the specific features outlined in the curricular areas and transaction process. As an interim measure, current models of teacher education such as B.Ed. and D.Ed. are required to redesign their courses as well as the programme structure to include the specific features and structural mechanisms proposed in the new framework in terms of curricular areas and transaction processes. Transaction of teacher education programmes should follow the broad strategies presented in Flow Chart 6.1.

Three areas—Area A, Area B and Area C have been identified in this flow chart. Each area covers both theory and practice.

Area A Foundations of education

Foundations of education provides the teacher trainees with an array of opportunities to study and experience schooling over the academic year. Candidates prepare for the classroom by building a knowledge base that is deepened through observation and personal experience.

Area B Curriculum and pedagogy

The curriculum studies courses would necessarily include units of study that provide for a critical study of school curriculum materials, syllabi, textbooks in the light of theoretical frameworks and empirical research.

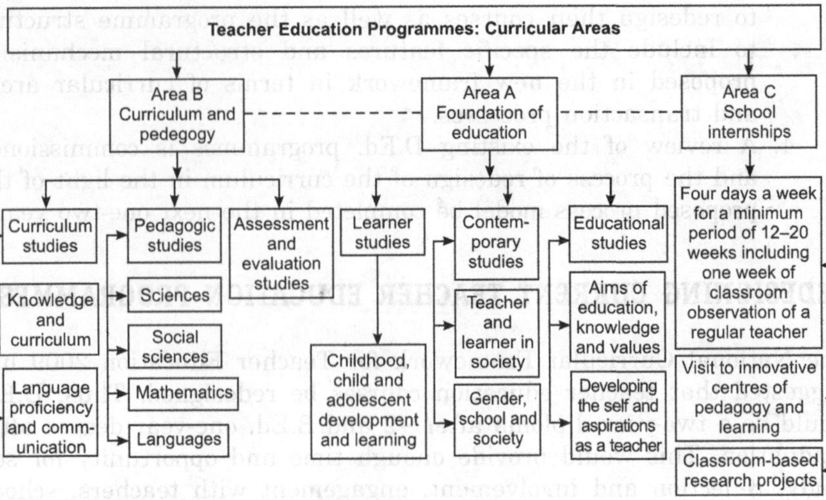

FLOW CHART 6.1 Teacher education—Curricular areas.

The pedagogic studies courses would necessarily include units of study that provide for a critical study of content, an examination of learners' thinking and learning and pedagogic processes in the light of theoretical frameworks and empirical research.

Each of the above theory courses is to be complemented with practicum courses.

Area C School internship

School internship should include the following:

1. Visits to innovative centres of pedagogy and learning, wherever feasible.
2. Classroom-based research project.
3. School internship of four days a week for a minimum period of six-ten weeks, including an initial phase of observing a regular classroom.
4. Developing and maintaining resources in the internship schools.
5. Developing unit plans and maintaining reflective journals.

The practice of teaching during school internship would include not more than four-unit plans per subject. Planning of the units would include a critical engagement with content from multiple sources including the school textbook, organisation and presentation of subject matter, formulating questions, specifically to: (a) assess knowledge base and understanding of students; (b) further the process of knowledge construction and meaning-making in the classroom; and (c) assess students' learning to improve pedagogic practice and further enhance learning.

National Education Policy 2020

The National Education Policy (NEP) 2020 replaces the National Policy on Education (NPE) 1986. The overarching goal of NEP 2020 is that of harnessing human resources (teacher and the one taught) to create value propositions (life skills, digital literacy and employment fitness), whereas the earlier NPE 1986 laid the base for training a pool of human resources for facilitating the value chain. NEP 2020 aspires to achieve multifold increase in Gross Enrolment Ratio by 2030 restructuring school education from pre-school to secondary level along with open schooling, ensuring equity and inclusion.

NEP2020 envisages not only structural changes and ambitious targets but more significantly aims to blend modern knowledge with relevant aspects of ancient knowledge. To the taught, it means life skills, value education and digital literacy, ensuring societal and employment fitness. To the in-service teacher as well as prospective teacher, it means relearning, to meet the challenge of being the guiding guru of the younger generation. Only then can India realize her demographic dividend.

TABLE 6.2 Implications of NEP2020 on teacher education

S.No.	*Aspect*	*NEP2020 Envisaged*				*NPE1986 Currently in place*	*Impact on Teacher Education*
1	Gross Enrolment ratio	50% (2035)				26.3% (2018)	More quality teachers needed
2	School Curricular Structure format (in years)	5	3	3	4	10 + 2	Need for multiple levels of pre-service and in-service teacher training
3	Break-up of age: in years	3–8, years	8–11, years	11–14, years	14–18, years	16–18	
4.	National Curriculum Framework for Teacher Education (NCTFE 2021)	Comprehensive with more practice and enhanced skill development				Theoretical with less Practice	Pre-service and in-service training to focus on imparting skills, communication and other practical aspects
5	Curriculum	Curriculum content will be reduced to its core essentials				Extensive theoretical curriculum	
6	Inclusion in schools	Development of methodologies for more successful inclusion in schools with diverse learning environment				Limited research done	Training at both pre-service and in-service level for better implementation of inclusion
7	Assessment Reforms-Exams conducted	In class 3, 5, 8, 10, 12–Objective and descriptive. Twice a year.				Each year up to class 12–Descriptive. Once a year.	Need to be familiar with latest techniques to be adopted in evaluation including online assessment

(*Contd.*)

TABLE 6.2 Implications of NEP2020 on teacher education (Contd.)

S.No.	*Aspect*	*NEP2020 Envisaged*	*NPE1986 Currently in place*	*Impact on Teacher Education*
8	Evaluation	360 degree holistic report card for students including skills	Grades instead of marks, CCE, Rating Scale	
9	Qualifications for teaching	Minimum qualification for teaching – 4 year integrated B.Ed. degree by 2030	Graduate with B.Ed.- either 1 year B.Ed. or 2 year integrated B.Ed.	Setting up of more 4-year Integrated B.Ed. courses in Colleges and Universities
10	Three language formula	3 language – Any three languages	By state, region and choice of student	Need to have trained language teachers
11	Development of National Professional Standards for Teachers (NPST) by the National Council for Teacher Education by 2022, in consultation with NCERT, SCERTs, teachers and expert organisations from across levels and regions to ensure quality teaching	Single Professional National Testing Uniform throughout the country	By state, regional with differing standards	Training pre-service teachers with professional attitudes and skills to enhance quality teaching
12	E-content	E-content in at least 8 languages	Lack of regional language e-content	More e-content materials to be developed for use in regional languages
13	Instruction Medium	Mother tongue	Mother tongue	Teachers trained to teach in mother tongue
14	Sanskrit	Emphasis on learning Sanskrit	Not given enough importance	Need for starting 4-year Integrated B.Ed.Sanskrit courses in Universities and Colleges

(*Contd.*)

TABLE 6.2 Implications of NEP2020 on teacher education (Contd.)

S.No.	*Aspect*	*NEP2020 Envisaged*	*NPE1986 Currently in place*	*Impact on Teacher Education*
15	Emphasis in promoting Cultural Ethos and Heritage	Teaching of Indian Knowledge Systems at all levels of schooling	Not given enough importance	Need to train pre-service and in-service teachers to handle IKS using appropriate methodology

(Source: Mohan, Radha. (2022) "Reshaping Teacher Education for the 21st Century-An Indian Perspective" in ***Handbook of Research on Teacher Education: Innovations and Practices in Asia*** *Springer* ***1st ed.*** *Myint Swe Khine (Editor), Yang Liu (Editor)).*

INTEGRATED TEACHER EDUCATION

Integrated teacher education programmes have been found to have a mixed scenario. The integrated teacher education programs offered by the regional institutes of education for many years have self-recognition and accreditation. There is a need to conduct research on these integrated programmes offered by the various institutions. There is also a need to mentor and monitor the innovative teacher education programmes in all the regions.

The four-year integrated programme of Elementary Teacher Education is given in Box 6.1.

BOX 6.1 Four-year Integrated Programme of Elementary Teacher Education

The B.El.Ed., Maulana Azad Centre for Elementary and Social Education (MACESE), Faculty of Education, University of Delhi (1994).

The Bachelor of Elementary Education (B.El.Ed.) is a four-year integrated professional degree programme of Elementary Teacher Education offered after the senior secondary (Class XII or equivalent) stage of school. It is currently offered in six colleges of the University of Delhi. Over seven hundred students have graduated from this programme and are widely sought in both government and private school systems. Some of them are now teacher educators after completing postgraduation in liberal arts, humanities and social sciences.

The B.El.Ed. programme is designed to integrate the study of subject knowledge, human development, pedagogic knowledge and self-knowledge. The main aim of the B.El.Ed. is to prepare reflective practitioners who are socially sensitive. It is an attempt to replace an unquestioning and meek teacher with one who can critically reflect on the 'received' curriculum and 'prescribed' knowledge. It prepares students to move beyond mere textbook knowledge. The B.El.Ed. students attempt to initiate their own inquiry, examine ideas in all gender inequities in the process of schooling and develop intervention their complexity and deal with ambiguity. The aim is to develop in students a mental flexibility needed to critically examine and synthesise knowledge from various sources and deal with the complex challenges of classroom teaching. The students learn to engage with issues of subject content, reflect on appropriate methods of assessment and attempt to evolve pedagogy in consonance with the needs of the learner.

The B.El.Ed. course attempts to develop the individuality of the student based on the assumption that it is the individual transformation that leads to social transformation. The course structure gives students the space to engage intensely with issues of understanding themselves and others. There is a special emphasis on understanding the nature of the child, the adult-child relationship and its dynamics within the classroom. The students engage with issues of politics of education within the classroom as they reflect on the best way of facilitating children's learning. This course is also designed to develop an understanding of contemporary Indian realities through a study of key historical, political, social cultural and economic issues. Students observe and analyse strategies. The B.El.Ed. curriculum is cyclic in nature whereby the same issues are dealt with at different levels of complexity and within different contexts over the four years.

The longer duration of the programme offers students critical psychological space to explore and define their own approaches to educational issues as they are in regular contact with the school setting over the four years. There is a sustained 17 weeks school internship programme in the fourth year where students attempt to translate their thoughts into action and critically reflect on this process. Students also visit institutions engaged in innovative practice in elementary education, in order to broaden their horizons. Students undertake research projects with an aim to further develop the process of reflective enquiry through classroom-based research.

Through specially designed colloquia students learn specific professional skills like using theatre, art, crafts, story telling and music in education and creating a resource centre in schools.

B.El.Ed. Programme of Delhi University mainly emphasises participative processes along with some lectures and prescriptive exercises since last 10 years. It is a four-year integrated course.

Box 6.2 gives details of the four-year integrated B.Ed. programme for secondary teachers.

BOX 6.2 Four-year Integrated Programme of Secondary Teacher Education Regional Colleges of Education, NCERT (1960)

The four-year integrated programme was introduced during the 1960s in NCERT's four Regional Colleges of Education in Ajmer, Bhubneshwar, Mysore and Bhopal. This programme was designed to prepare secondary school teachers in the Sciences and Humanities.

Over the thirty-five years of its existence, the scheme of studies of the programme has been modified several times, which is its most significant innovation. The curriculum was initially designed to develop subject-based competency of the level of graduation along with professional competencies related to methodology of teaching. To begin with, a composite degree of B/Sc. B.Ed. was awarded to the candidates on the successful completion of the course. Subsequently, a modification was introduced to award the degree of B.Sc. on the completion of three years to enable students to join postgraduate programmes of study in various science disciplines. This provision however, led to the exodus of several students at the end of three years. As a consequence, the original system of awarding one composite degree at the end of the entire four-year programme was reintroduced. Subsequently in 1996, the B.A. B.Ed. Arts programme was withdrawn on the recommendations of the Abbreviated Review of NCERT. The B.Sc. B.Ed. integrated programme in the Science is still continuing.

The minimum qualification for admission into this programme is senior secondary (i.e., 12 years of schooling). The content of this integrated programme includes courses on subject knowledge (60%), professional education (20%) and general education (20%), leading to the B.Sc. B.Ed. degree.

A number of studies were conducted to examine the effectiveness of these four-year integrated programmes. The key finding is that teachers who emerge from this programme are much better than the products of the traditional one-year B.Ed. programme. The difference in effectiveness is attributed to 'selection of meritorious students, greater length, integrated curriculum along with simultaneous teaching of content and methods of teaching.' In spite of a sound conceptual base, the availability of evidence with regard to its effectiveness and experiences of developed countries and recommendation of several expert bodies, the innovation has not been mainstreamed beyond the confines of the four NCERT regional colleges of education. The education commission, however, commented on the four-year 'integrated' teacher education programmes being offered in the RCEs of the NCERT since 1963. It felt that there was no evidence to show that the products of these integrated courses are better in anyway than teachers who have first taken their degree and then completed their professional education. Moreover, these integrated courses, even when developed to their fullest potential, can only provide very small proportion of the total number of teachers the country requires. The Commission felt that for integrated courses in teacher education the minimum length of training for a secondary teacher should be five years after 10+2. Each state may make a beginning by introducing at least one four-year integrated College of Education on the lines of RCEs of the NCERT.

The four-year programmes can be made into a five-year programme in keeping with professional courses in medicine, engineering and law.

Characteristics of a Four-year Integrated B.Ed. Programme

The vision and features of a four-year integrated B.Ed. programme designed to integrate general education with professional training are:

1. Strong foundations of education located in sociological understanding of education and philosophical thinking on education.
2. In-built courses to engage with subject content with the aim to revisit and reconstruct concepts and perspectives.
3. Core courses to engage with subject-content with the aim to revisit and reconstruct concepts and perspectives.
4. Engagement with theory of pedagogy and hands-on experience in understanding the learner, her context and processing of thinking and learning as a base to evolve relevant and appropriate pedagogic strategies.
5. Theory courses designed to enable inter-disciplinary engagement as well as visit theory in the light of personal experiences and social realities.
6. Opportunities for developing the self through drama, craft, music, self-development workshops along with a critical engagement with theoretical constructs of identity development and the individual-social interface.
7. Extensive and intensive practicum courses to equip teachers with a grip over existing systemic issues in education, a developing capacity to rise to the uncertainties of a learning environment and changing learner needs and a capacity to feel empowered to make a difference.
8. Practicum courses to develop other professional capacities such as the ability to evolve developmentally and contextually relevant pedagogies, re-arranging subject-matter to communicate effectively with learners and a repertoire of skills of relating to children, designing and choosing appropriate learning experiences, observing and documenting, analyzing, synthesizing and interpreting.
9. Sustained engagement with schools to appreciate the given constraints of a system and to learn to strategize to think out of the box. Understand and learn to negotiate formal learning spaces as sites of struggle, contestation and social transformation.
10. Pedagogic courses designed in the frame of broad disciplinary areas such as Sciences, Social Sciences, Languages and Mathematics rather than individual school subjects.
11. Theory courses to include in-built field-based units of study to enable porous boundaries between theory and practice.
12. Rigorous study of a chosen liberal course out of a pool of courses in languages, mathematics, sciences and social sciences.

Box 6.3 gives an example of Comprehensive Teacher Education Programme of Mumbai University.

BOX 6.3 Comprehensive Teacher Education Programme: Gandhi Shikshan Bhawan, College of Education, Mumbai University Mumbai (2000)

Gandhi Shikshan Bhawan, an affiliated College of Education of Bombay University, has been offering an integrated B.Ed. degree programme for secondary school teachers since 2000. It provides first hand experiences of a slum community. The aim is to make student teachers aware of the socio-economic and cultural traditions of the poor and backward and its impact on the education and development of children. Teachers are educated to develop the conviction and the professional skills to help children come out of such adverse conditions. Such an approach has now become a part of the B.Ed. degree programmes of all the colleges of education of Bombay University.

On the same line the Department of Education of Jamia Millia has proposed to incorporate the social context elements into teachers training programme.

All these innovations compel one to be convinced that drastic and revolutionary changes are possible, and the Gandhi Shikshan Bhawan of Bombay and the proposed programme of Department of Education of Jamia Millia show the readiness to change the Teacher Education programme. But only fully participative, process-oriented programmes should be adapted, which is the need of the hour. That can only change the education scenario of Indian education.

Pre-service Programmes at Secondary Stage

1. Existing B.Ed. programmes are being reviewed to facilitate the choice between a four-year integrated model after +2 or a two-year model after graduation, based on state requirements and available institutional capacity.
2. As an interim measure, current models of teacher education such as the B.Ed. are required to redesign their courses as well as the programme structure to include the specific features and structural mechanisms proposed in the new framework in terms of curricular areas and transaction processes.
3. A review of the existing B.Ed. programmes is to be done and the process of redesigning of the curriculum in the light of the suggestions of NEP2020 for teacher education is being carried out by concerned stakeholders.

Conclusion

Britzman (1991) has stated that a pre-service teacher is “marginally situated in two worlds: that of the inchoate educator who is making meaning of what a teacher is and does, and that of still being educated.” Reflecting on pre-service education can help map future teacher education programmes to best scaffold pedagogy.

REFERENCES

Agrawal, S.P. and Aggarwal, J.C. (1997), *Development of Education in India*. Vol. 4–5, Concept Publishing Company, New Delhi.

Britzman, D. (1991), Practice Makes Perfect: A Critical Study of Learning to Teach, State University Press, Albany.

Government of India NEP 1986, National Education Policy, Ministry of Human Resource Development, New Delhi.

Government of India (1948), *Report of the University Education Commission—Radhakrishnan*, Ministry of Human Resource Development, New Delhi.

Government of India (1953), *Secondary Education Commission 1952*, Ministry of Human Resource Development, New Delhi.

Government of India (1967), *Kothari Commission Report 1964–66*, Ministry of Human Resource Development, New Delhi.

Government of India (1967), *Report of the Secondary Education Commission* (1952), Ministry of Human Resource Development, New Delhi.

Government of India (1971), *Report of the Education Commission* 1964–66, Ministry of Human Resource Development, New Delhi.

Government of India (1986), *National Policy of Education 1986 Programme of Action*, Ministry of Human Resource Development, New Delhi.

Government of India (1993), *National Advisory Committee on Curriculum Load*, Ministry of Human Resource Development, New Delhi.

Government of India (1995), *National Commission on Teachers 1983–85*, Ministry of Human Resource Development, New Delhi.

Government of India (2005), *National Curriculum Framework for School Education 2005*, Ministry of Human Resource Development, New Delhi.

Government of India (2009), *National Curriculum Frameworks on Teacher Education*.

Government of India NPE 2020, *Final National Education Policy 2020 (PDF) (Report)*, Ministry of Human Resource Development, New Delhi.

Mohan, Radha Myint Swe Khine (Editor), and Yang Liu (Editor) (2022), "Reshaping Teacher Education for the 21st Century—An Indian Perspective" in Handbook of Research on Teacher Education: Innovations and Practices in Asia, Springer, Singapore, https://doi.org/10.1007/978-981-16-9785-2_25.

Right to Education Act, 2005 (2009), Ministry of Human Resource Development, New Delhi.

Web References

National Curriculum Framework for Teacher Education Towards Preparing Professional and Humane Teacher. NCTE Document 2009/10.

http://ncte-india.org/ncte_new/pdf/NCFTE_2010.pdf.

NCTE 2014.

http://ncte-india.org/ncte_new/?page_id=910.

http://dcdc.puchd.ac.in/downloads/Regulation-2014.pdf.

Vision of Teacher Education in India Quality and Regulatory Perspective Vision of Teacher Education in India Quality and Regulatory Perspective Volume 1 August, 2012 Government of India Ministry of Human Resource Development.

https://mhrd.gov.in/sites/upload_files/mhrd/files/document-reports/JVC%20 Vol%201.pdf.

CHAPTER 7 Induction

The intent of all induction programmes is to transform a student teacher graduate into a competent career teacher.

—ERIC DIGEST–4, COMPONENTS OF GOOD TEACHER INDUCTION PROGRAMMES

INTRODUCTION

Cascio (1995) defines induction as a process to inform new staff concerning:

- Standards, expectations, norms, traditions and policies.
- Social behaviour, work climate, getting to know others.
- Technical aspects of the job.

Delahaye (2000) describes induction as an introduction to the new organisation, which encompasses aspects such as procedural training and socialising the new comer to the organisational climate.

The value of induction is supported by Becker et al (2001), who examined the human resource practices in high performing organisations. Successful and highly productive organisations spent three times more hours (116.87 in the first year) inducting new staff than did low performing organisations (35.02 hours).

Induction is intended to introduce new staff to the work culture, including clarifying organisational values. Induction begins a process for new staff of identifying these values and demonstrating their importance through endorsement by the executive and hopefully demonstrated by the other members of the staff's working community.

Learning about procedures and policy related to teaching and learning is another aspect of induction. From a risk management point of view, a university has an obligation to ensure that teaching staff have all the necessary information they require to ensure that students receive the quality of education they are expecting. Where staff are not properly equipped, there is a risk of litigation.

Induction, therefore, plays a key role in clarifying expectations and values, attending to risk management issues, assisting adjustment to the new work climate and providing necessary technical and professional information in order that the new staff member can become a productive and committed part of the university community. The role of induction is summarised in Figure 7.1.

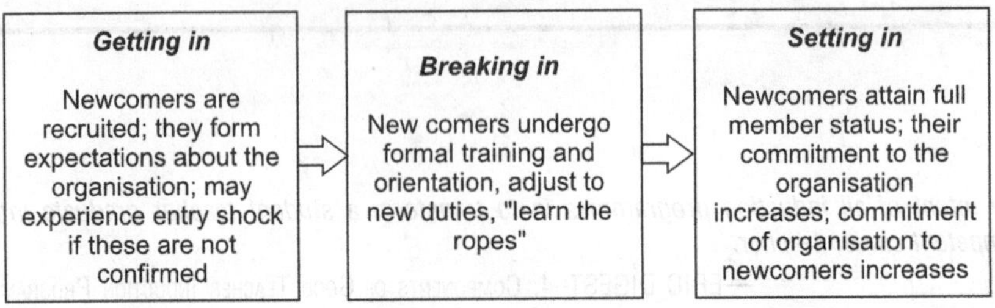

FIGURE 7.1 Organisational socialisation: its major phases. (*Source:* Baron and Greenberg, 1990, p. 306).

CURRENT INDUCTION STRATEGIES

Many schools are not getting most out of their new teachers' up-to-date skills, energy and enthusiasm. This is because when newly-qualified teachers take up their first paid teaching post, they often experience a 'praxis-shock' as they confront the daily school reality. They may feel stressed, especially in schools where they are expected to cope with this complex new situation on their own.

Not surprisingly, many new teachers leave the profession after only a few years, which is increasingly a problem in countries that face teacher shortages or where many teachers are close to retirement.

Effective induction programmes can avoid some of these problems by providing all new teachers with systematic personal, social and professional support in the early years of their career. They can, therefore, also help improve school and teacher performance.

Induction provides a vital link in the continuum of teacher education that runs from initial teacher education through induction to career-long continuing professional development.

An induction programme is that programme which provides inputs necessary for a person to start performing certain functions expected of him/her. It may have awareness inputs, attitudinal inputs and competency development inputs. The induction programme for DIET faculty, therefore, would provide inputs necessary for a person to perform functions expected of him/her in a DIET.

RATIONALE FOR INDUCTION PROGRAMMES

Figure 7.2 gives the sequence of teacher training.

The pre-service teacher training focuses on real world experience and awareness of the need to blend with school culture and climate. The teacher induction programme is designed to increase teacher retention by providing beginning teachers with support, acculturation, cross-cultural training, and skills assessment. To accommodate the different experiences of urban and rural teachers, specialized activities and supports are provided to teachers serving in urban and rural areas. The inservice training is to facilitate teachers updating themselves and keeping abreast with the changing world.

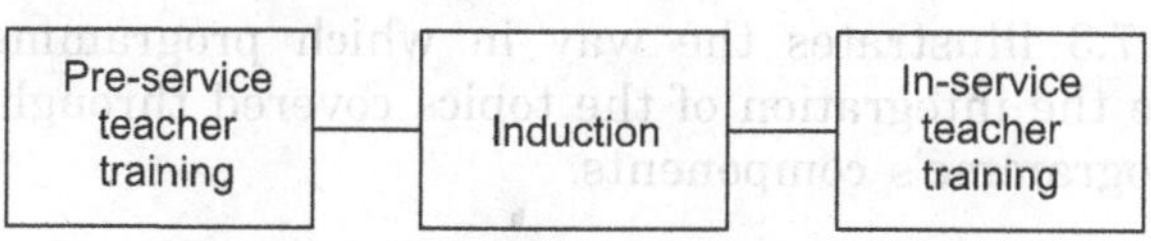

FIGURE 7.2 Sequence of training programmes.

District Institutes of Education and Training (DIET) are the district level institutions with four key functions, namely, *pre-service teacher education, in-service teacher education, research and evaluation*, and *documentation*. A newly recruited teacher educator in DIET and the faculty members who are coming by transfer and deputation need to be inducted into these functions which are not a part of the teacher education curriculum. Each of the states in India is in need of a training design with inputs/experiences to be provided to the newly recruited teacher educators. It is possible to form a project group of state level functionaries/senior DIET faculty to articulate a programme of induction and prepare content which would then be forming different modules for the programme.

WHO NEEDS INDUCTION?

An induction programme is needed for a person who is new to the nature of a work. For example, a lecturer of DIET needs induction training if he has never worked in a DIET, is newly appointed and is not having previous experience of performing those functions expected of a DIET faculty member. In a way, it is *initiation*.

Even though an induction programme is provided to a DIET faculty who is new to the DIET, a faculty member on transfer or promotion from some other level or sector may also benefit from induction training. In other words, it is not the age alone or recency of recruitment which decides who needs an induction programme.

COMPONENTS OF GOOD TEACHER INDUCTION PROGRAMMES

Any induction programme consists of the following elements:

1. Orientation for all new teachers to the school and school board
2. Mentoring for new teachers by experienced teachers
3. Professional development and training in areas such as:
   - Literacy and numeracy strategies, student success, safe schools.
   - Classroom management, effective parent communication skills, and instructional strategies that address the learning and culture of students with special needs and other diverse learners.

Figure 7.3 illustrates the way in which programme developers conceptualise the integration of the topics covered through the teacher induction programme's components.

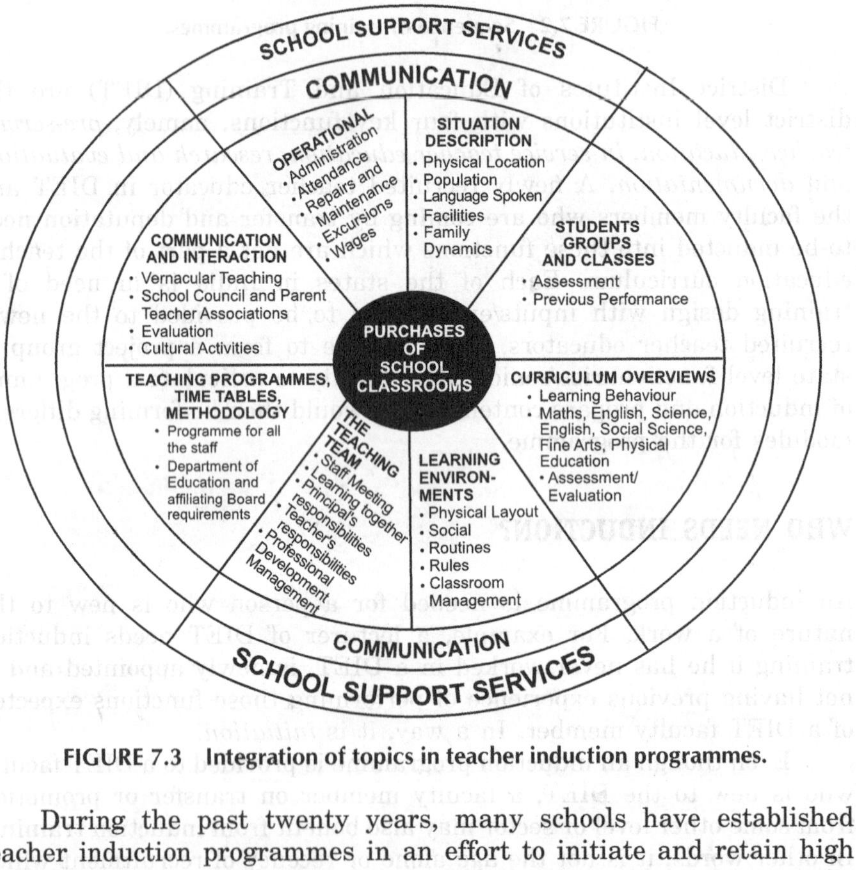

FIGURE 7.3 Integration of topics in teacher induction programmes.

During the past twenty years, many schools have established teacher induction programmes in an effort to initiate and retain high quality teachers (Galvez-Hjornevik, 1985). These programmes take many forms, the most recent borrowing from the induction techniques of nonteaching professions. Both new and old programmes are organised into segments—introduction, instruction, assessment, and adjustment. As new induction techniques are initiated, more segments are integrated into existing programmes.

WHO ARE NEW TEACHERS?

New teachers are defined as all new teachers (including teachers trained in other states) certified with a B.Ed. degree who have been hired into permanent positions—full-time or part-time—by a school board, school authority or district school to begin teaching for the first time.

WHAT MAKES A GOOD INDUCTION PROGRAMME?

The intent of all induction programmes is to transform a student teacher graduate into a competent career teacher. Schlechty (1985) suggests that signs of effective induction programmes can be observed in the faculty and administration attitude and behaviour: support of school norms and the general conformity of teacher performance to those norms. He presents a framework for evaluation of induction programmes which can be translated into a checklist of eight programme qualities. His framework is intended to apply to induction programmes of vastly differing content and delivery structures. Four programme characteristics show the influence of other professions:

1. The programme explains to the inductees that the process of their selection is based on special requirements and that induction training is crucial to their future success.
2. The induction process is divided into progressive stages of achievement.
3. The programme cultivates mutual support within peer groups
4. The training is oriented towards long-term career goals. The remaining characteristics apply directly to the needs of beginning teachers.
5. Administratively-set expectations and norms of teacher conduct are clearly articulated and disseminated.
6. Teachers must assimilate a professional vocabulary.
7. New teachers receive supervision, coaching, demonstration, and assessment.
8. The responsibility for supervision should be distributed throughout the faculty in a tightly organised, consistent, and continuous programme.

Foster (1982) and Griffin (1985) emphasise the importance of specifying programme objectives in behavioural terminology and the necessity for continuous feedback among programme participants. Griffin further cautions programme developers on the inappropriate use of research results as definitions for expected teacher behaviour.

Several references point out that induction programmes should contain three information sources: *the community*, *the school*, and *the teaching profession*. All must be introduced to the beginning teacher, with emphasis on teaching as an area of life-long learning (Hall 1982). Special needs programmes (e.g. those which introduce the new teacher into a rural or urban environment with which the teacher has had no previous experience) most often use this approach (Defino and Hoffman, 1984).

WHAT AREAS SHOULD INDUCTION PROGRAMMES COVER?

Topics of importance are usually taken from surveys of senior teachers and administrators experienced in the evaluation of shortcomings of first-year teachers. To vastly varying degrees, all programmes contain elements of faculty and facility introduction, classroom management, student discipline, professional conduct, school and school district expectations, and professional obligations. A new teacher needs to be exposed to a variety of teaching techniques and evaluation processes. Some programmes equally instruct and assess the beginning teacher; others emphasise assistance to the teacher rather than using the programme as an indicator of the beginner's competency. Crucial problems arise when evaluation is mistaken for assessment and induction programme are used as wash-out programme. Schlechty (1985) emphasises that new hires in any field are hired with the expectation that they will "survive" the induction process and start on their way to full-term careers.

HOW DO INDUCTION PROGRAMMES WORK?

Like the terms "induction" and "internship," many elements and intents of teacher induction programmes are borrowed from other professions. Business and medicine are the most common (Galvez-Hjornevik 1985; Schlechty (1985). Some are based on academic induction, such as formal seminars and informal workshops on the system and what is expected of the beginning teacher. Teacher induction started from the introductory lecture and, in some school systems, has evolved into sophisticated multipurpose programmes.

Internship status. Beginning teachers enter as teaching interns, often at reduced salary. The intern combines full teaching responsibility (albeit at reduced class loads).

Mentor. Beginning teachers are assigned to a senior teacher in their area. The senior teacher supplies information, and oversees the maturation of the beginner's teaching and classroom management skills daily.

Committee. Beginning teachers are each assigned to an induction committee. The committee is a professional development team designed to supervise, provide information to and train the beginning teacher in school-approved classroom techniques and procedures. The committee usually consists of the school principal, a consultant on curriculum and instruction, and a peer teacher, the latter often as a mentor.

Orientation seminars. The seminar is used to instruct inductees on subjects that the administration deems important, issues that peer teachers have found essential or helpful and concerns expressed by the participating inductees.

The above components are hardly a complete listing of possible induction approaches. In spite of twenty years of professional concern with the initiation of new teachers into their working environments, much more work needs to be done in developing good programmes.

CONCLUSION

It is important to note that teacher induction programmes do not operate in a vacuum. Effective teacher induction depends on a number of factors including presage variables such as quality teacher preparation programmes, real-world practice from teacher candidates, and appropriate teacher dispositions and beliefs from teacher candidates. The conceptual framework presents a linear trajectory of teacher candidates from teacher preparation programmes, which supply them with the basic knowledge, skills, and dispositions to prepare them for success in their careers, to become effective teachers. The ultimate goal of teacher induction programmes is to retain competent teachers who are reflective, adaptive, experts and effective teachers.

REFERENCES

Becker, Brian, Huselid, Mark and David Ulrich (2001), *The HR Scorecard—Linking People, Strategy and Performance*, Harvard Business School Press, UK.

Carver, C.L., and Feiman-Nemser, S. (2009), Using Policy to Improve Teacher Induction: Critical Elements and Missing Pieces, Educational Policy 23, 295–327. doi:10.1177/0895904807310036.

Cuddapah, J. L., and Clayton, C. D. (2011), Using Wenger's Communities of Practice to Explore a New Teacher Cohort, *Journal of Teacher Education*, 62(1), 62–75, https://doi.org/10.1177/0022487110377507.

Feiman-Nemser, S. (2001), From Preparation to Practice: Designing a Continuum to Strengthen and Sustain Teaching, Teachers College Record, 103(6), 1013–1055. https://doi.org/10.1111/0161-4681.00141.

Hobson, A. J., Ashby, P., Malderez, A., and Tomlinson, P. D. (2009), Mentoring beginning teachers: What we know and what we don't, *Teaching and teacher education*, Elsevier, 25(1), 207–216, UK, https://doi.org/10.1016/j.tate.2008.09.001.

Ingersoll, R. (2012), Beginning Teacher Induction: What the data tell us. Phi Delta Kappan, USA, 93(8), 47–51.

Wang, Jian (Ed.) Odell, Sandra (Ed), and Clift, Renee (ed.) (2010), Past, Present, and Future Research on Teacher Induction: An Anthology for Researchers, Policy Makers, and Practitioners, R&L Education, Lanham, USA.

Web References

Induction Training for Newly appointed Teachers SCERT, Chattisgarh, Raipur https://scert.cg.gov.in/css2013-14/CSS2023-24/INDUCTION%20TRAINING-MANUALS-%20(NEWLY%20FOR%20APPOINTED%20TEACHERS).pdf.

University Grants Commission-Faculty Induction Programme(FIP) https://www.ugc.gov.in/pdfnews/9054829_FIP-Framework.pdf.

CHAPTER 8

In-Service Teacher Education

Whoever teaches learns in the act of teaching and whoever learns teaches in the act of learning.

—PAULO FREIRE "PEDAGOGY OF FREEDOM" (1996)

INTRODUCTION

Everyone concerned with the educational system's performance agrees that the improvement of teaching qualities is a high priority in any educational effort. Teachers are assigned the role of change agents and are presented with new challenges, e.g. to make education global and permanent, flexible enough to serve in any environment (in or out of the classroom) for life, and reflective of the community. Teachers have to learn to adapt creatively to changes in science and technology and to prepare generations who are universal, critical, and creative and who have firm identities with their socio-cultural background. However, a realistic approach to in-service teacher training should consider that teachers are ordinary human beings with their virtues, defects, duties, and rights.

The expression 'in-service training' refers to training of teachers who are already in service. It is, hence, a supplementary, additional training. It must be given mostly in the teacher's spare time or in time made free by the school authorities.

DEFINITIONS OF IN-SERVICE TRAINING

For the good teacher, every facet of his knowledge, skills, personality and interests is of potential value. Hence, every experience he undergoes during his career, however irrelevant it may appear, may be described as in-service training. In-service training may, therefore be taken to include everything that happens to a teacher from the day he takes up his first appointment to the day he retires which contributes, directly or indirectly, to the way in which he executes his professional duties (Figure 8.1).

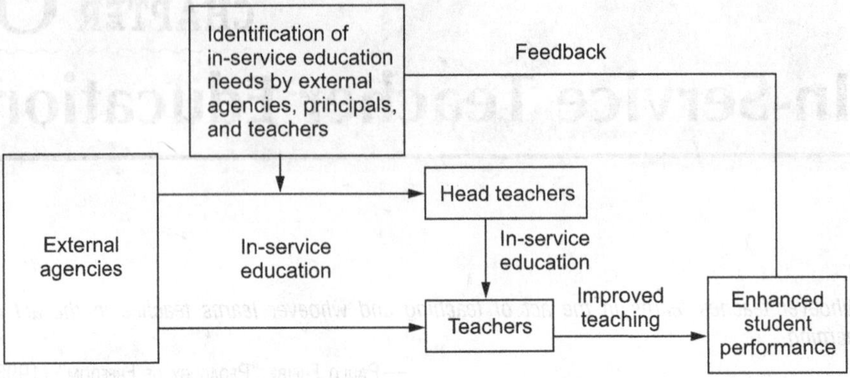

FIGURE 8.1 In-service education.

Hence, in-service training is "*any activity which a teacher undertakes, after he has begun to teach, which is concerned with his professional work.*"

—*Department of Education and Science (1970) UK.*

For administrative convenience, in-service training is defined as: "*a programme of systematised activities promoted or directed by the school system, or approved by the school system, that contributes to the professional or occupational growth and competence of staff members during the time of their service to the school system.*"

In general, in-service teacher training can be defined as "*structured activities designed exclusively or primarily to improve professional performance.*"

In-service training refers to "*designating or of training, as in special courses, workshops, etc., given to employees in connection with their work to help them develop skills, etc.*

—*Webster's New World College Dictionary (2010), John Wiley and Sons, Inc. UK*

Also, the *Dictionary of Pedagogy* (Průcha, Walterová, Mareš, 1995, p. 41) relates the notion of in-service training mainly to potential **forms and targets**, defining it as "education of teachers in course of their professional career... materialised in a wide range of organisational forms (guidance of new teachers in practice, learning for attestations, preparation of educational innovations and reforms, preparation for specialised projects, teachers' functional study, re-qualification study, specialist courses... etc)."

In-service training is defined as a *workshop for employed professionals, para-professionals and other practitioners to acquire new knowledge, better methods, etc. for improving their skills towards more effective, efficient and competent rendering of service in various fields and to diverse groups of people.* Further, such a workshop is a training designed to benefit a specific group of children at a particular school. A good in-service training should, via workshop, improve the quality of programming for heterogeneous classrooms.

RATIONALE OF IN-SERVICE TRAINING

In-service teacher training may be understood as professional development, or sometimes as part of wider professional development or growth. The **career development** is understood as growth through natural promotion, from one stage of teacher's professional career to another. The notion of the **experiential growth** is usually anchored in a succession of a few clearly delimited stages. This category is directly related to the professional and personal maturing of the teacher. **In-service teacher training** is usually defined as the provision of organised programmes for practising teachers, meant to help them as one of the possible systematic steps to support their development. These systematic steps, or planned situations, offers, possibilities, and events supporting teachers' professional development have been becoming more and more varied in the last two decades.

New information technologies, modern learning theories, a much better mobility of teachers, and many more factors, is what makes for a variety of in-service teacher training forms expanding: **study of texts and other documents in the Internet, e-learning discussion forums, international visits, student exchanges**, and mainly in-school activities, such as **action researches, project work, supervision, visits, discussion groups**, and so on.

NEED FOR IN-SERVICE TRAINING

The NCERT is the apex Central educational body with state level bodies—the State Councils of Educational Research and Training (SCERTs), District Institutes for Education and Training (DIET). With the help of Sarva Shiksha Abhiyan (now known as Samagra Shiksha) teacher-training has been conducted, covering the school education sector from preschool to higher secondary. Sarva Shiksha Abhiyan Framework 2001 (revised in 2008 and 2011) developed a 20-day teacher training under the In-service Education for Teachers (INSET) initiative. This framework has a 'split-up' model of in-service training. The teachers are first trained on specific topics for a day or two at the district or block level followed by two days of practical training through classroom observation and simulation exercises. The trained teachers then implement the recommended methods in their classrooms for the next two months. Finally, the teachers meet, reflect and share their insights.

A Cascaded model is followed for training with State-level trainers, instructing resource persons at the district level on how to conduct the training modules. This model is economic in terms of time and money and is adopted by several states like Uttar Pradesh, Madhya Pradesh, Tamil Nadu and Uttarakhand, amongst others.

> The training of teachers is a major area of concern at present as both pre-service and in-service training of school teachers are extremely inadequate and poorly managed in most states. Pre-service training needs to be improved and differently regulated both in public and private institutions, while systems for in-service training require expansion and major reform that allow for greater flexibility.
> —NCFTE 2009, p. 6

In-service training provides teachers with opportunities to learn specific skills, techniques and new instructional approaches that they can use in their own teaching.

HISTORY OF IN-SERVICE TEACHER EDUCATION IN INDIA

The in-service education of secondary school teachers at the beginning of this century consisted mainly of refresher courses, lectures, and conferences. These were generally arranged during the vacation period at a centrally located place or the teacher training institution and were seldom a regular feature of the school programme. Most of these activities were spasmodic responses to the recommendations of the various Commissions that were appointed from time to time to study the problems of the existing educational system.

Resolution on Educational Policy (1904)

An early reference to the needs of in-service education and the role of the training colleges was made in Lord Curzon's Resolution on Educational Policy.

Every possible care should be taken to maintain a connection between the training college and the school, so that the student, on leaving the college and entering upon his career as a teacher, may not neglect to practice the methods which he has been taught, and may not (as sometimes happens) be prevented from doing so and forced to fall into line with the more mechanical methods of his untrained colleagues. The trained students whom the college has sent out should be occasionally brought together again and the inspecting staff should cooperate with the training college authorities in seeing that the influence of the college makes itself felt in the schools.

Resolution on Educational Policy (1913)

The Resolution on Educational Policy of 1913 laid down the major principles for the expansion and improvement of primary education and also recommended in-service education for village teachers. The resolution stated: As teachers left to themselves in villages are liable to deteriorate, there are great advantages in periodical repetition and improvement courses for primary school teachers during the school vacations. The trend at that time was towards an increase in the quality rather than the quantity of the teachers at the primary level.

The Hartog Committee Report (1929)

The Hartog Committee of 1929 made further recommendations about the training as well as in-service education of primary teachers. The Committee observed: Even under ideal conditions, when the right type of teacher has been selected and well trained, the primary school teacher, particularly the village teacher, is much isolated and most often in need of guidance and encouragement. Journals for teachers in the regional languages, refresher courses, conferences and meetings of teachers' associations can do much to brighten the lives of teachers and improve their work. No active steps were taken, however, for the improvement of in-service education, as the report of the Committee raised controversial issues.

The report was warmly received in official circles, as it attempted to show that a policy of expansion of education in India had proved ineffective and wasteful and that a policy of consolidation alone was suited to Indian conditions. The non-official view did not accept the opinion of the Committee that quality must have priority over quantity. As a result, the report of the Committee helped little towards the progress of primary education for the next twenty years or so, and some of the valuable suggestions of the Committee such as improved salaries for teachers, improvement of curricula, progress in in-service education, and tutorial work in colleges were neglected. Advances were, however, made in secondary and university education. Departments of Education were established in some universities and refresher courses for teachers began to be organised. It is during this period that teacher training institutions developed rapidly.

University Education Commission Report (1949)

The Government of India appointed a University Education Commission in 1948, under the chairmanship of Dr. S. Radhakrishnan, to report primarily on university education in India. In order to do this, the commission had to review the position of secondary education as well and it made certain valuable suggestions. Remarking about the utilisation of the vacation period for in-service programme, the commission stated: “At present neither students nor the teachers utilise vacation; for most of them vacation is a period of want of occupation”. Stressing the need for in-service education, it recommended that in order that the scheme of refresher courses may become a real success, the authorities of schools and intermediate colleges and the government education departments should make certified attendance at a university refresher course, once in every four or five years, or qualification for promotion. Some such stimulus would be necessary until attendance at such refresher courses becomes a tradition.... Alternatively, teachers may be given leave of absence for six months after every five years of service and asked to attend advanced courses at their own or any other university and obtain a certificate of attendance and good work from the head of the Department of the University.

Secondary Education Commission Report (1953)

During 1952–53, the Secondary Education Commission, under the sponsorship of the Ministry of Education, made a national survey of secondary education, for the purpose of reorganising and improving the educational system. The study was conducted by visits to the different states and by interviews and questionnaires. As a result of this study, the commission was able to emphasise that the most important factor in the contemplated educational reconstruction is the teacher—his personal qualities, his educational qualifications, his professional training and the place that he occupies in the school as well as in the community. Regarding the in-service education, the committee was of the opinion that: However excellent the programme of teacher-training may be, it does not by itself produce an excellent teacher. It can only engender the knowledge, skills and attitudes which will enable the teacher to begin his task with a reasonable degree of confidence and with the minimum amount of experience. Increased efficiency will come through experience critically analysed and through individual and group efforts at improvement. The teacher-training institution should accept its responsibility for assisting in this in-service stage of teacher-training.

International Secondary Education Project Team Report (1954)

An International Secondary Education Project Team was appointed in 1954 by the Government of India to study the various steps and procedures needed for implementing the major recommendations of the Secondary Education Commission. One of its points of study was the in-service education of secondary school teachers. The report stated that education departments consider ways and means of helping teachers to obtain in-service training and recognising the improvement in their professional and academic qualifications by suitable salary increment.

The International Team suggested special in-service training courses immediately, "for teachers of technical, vocational and other special subjects, who are already in service but for those who have not been trained we recommend short intensive courses in the theory and practice of Education". The Team further recommended the constitution of Area Training Organisations which would take up the work of in-service education of teachers. The Team emphasised the need for the in-service programmes to be arranged in collaboration with stated department of education, schools, teacher organisations, and teacher training institutions. Thus, it is evident that from the beginning of the twentieth century, educators have felt the importance of in-service education for improving the quality of classroom instruction as well as the professional growth of the teachers. They have also realised the need for organising programmes of in-service education on a nation-wide basis.

The Education Commission (1964–66) strongly recommended that: (i) large-scale programmes of in-service education of teachers should be organised by universities and teacher organisations at all levels to enable every teacher to receive at least two or three months of in-service education in every five years of service, (ii) continuing in-service education should be based on research inputs, and (iii) training institutions should work on 12-month basis and organise in-service training programmes, such as refresher courses, seminars, workshops and summer institutes.

National Policy on Education (1968)

The Government of India was convinced that a radical reconstruction of education on the broad lines recommended by the Education Commission is essential for economic and cultural development of the country, for national integration and for realising the ideal of a socialistic pattern of society. This would involve a transformation of the system to relate it more closely to the life of the people; a continuous effort to expand educational opportunity; a sustained and intensive effort to raise the quality of education at all stages; an emphasis on the development of science and technology; and the cultivation of moral and social values. NPE 1968 stressed the need for an educational system that would produce young men and women of character and ability committed to national service and development. This would help in promoting national progress, creating a sense of common citizenship and culture, and strengthening the national integration.

The principles propounded by NPE 1968 are:

1. ***Free and compulsory education:*** According to Article 45 (Indian Constitution), education should be free and compulsory up to the age of 14. Steps should be taken to ensure that child who is enrolled in the schools should successfully complete the course.
2. ***Education of teachers:*** This involved attention to enhancements of teacher emoluments, service standard, besides academic freedom to write, study and speak on national and international issues.
3. ***Language development:*** The policy emphasised the development of Indian as well as foreign languages in the country. The three-language formula should be introduced in which a student at the secondary level should know Hindi, English and the regional language of his state. The language Sanskrit should be included as an optional subject at the secondary level.
4. ***Education opportunity for all:*** Under this policy every child of the country is to be given education irrespective of caste, religion, region or whatever the case may be. Special emphasis should be given to backward classes, minority children, girls and physically challenged children to avail the education facilities.
5. ***Uniform education structure:*** The structure of education should be uniform throughout the country. It should be a 10+2+3 pattern from higher secondary to college level.
6. Opportunities for games, sports, work experience should exist in all schools.

The Report of the National Commission on Teachers (1983–85) highlighted the absence of clear-cut policies and priorities for in-service education and lack of systematic identification of needs. It recommended 'planning ahead of time' and 'closer scrutiny of methodologies' adopted for in-service education of teachers. The report also recommended that strategies used for in-service education must be 'imaginative, bold and varied". It further stated that "the most effective among them are the services organised through the school complex. The idea of school complex...put forward by the Kothari Commission...intends to link primary and secondary schools with a view to pulling resources and including the educational process." The Commission mooted the idea of teachers' centres that could function as "...a meeting place for teachers located in a school that has resources that it would like to share with others...it is a forum where workshops of very practical nature are organised for teachers of all faculties and of all levels; it pools in the talent of all teachers of various schools who act as resource personnel for centres' workshops and it arranges book fairs." What teachers need most "... is a change in the climate of schools, an atmosphere conducive to educational research and enquiry... (select) teachers could be given study leave and sent to advanced centres of learning for furthering their professional competence...through visiting fellowships."

The landmark **National Policy on Education (1986)** linked in-service teacher education as a continuum with pre-service education. A centrally sponsored scheme of restructuring and strengthening of teacher education was evolved and implemented. The scheme visualised the establishment of DIETs in each district, upgradation of 250 colleges of education as colleges of teacher-education, establishment of 50 Institutes of Advanced Studies in Education (IASEs) and strengthening of State Councils of Educational Research and Training (SCERTs).

National Policy on Education (1986)

Teacher education is a continuous process, and its pre-service and in-service components are inseparable. As the first step, the system of teacher education will be overhauled. The new programmes of teacher education will emphasise continuing education and the need for teachers to meet the thrusts envisaged in this Policy.

District Institutes of Education and Training (DIETs) will be established with the capability to organise pre-service and in-service courses for elementary school teachers and for the personnel working in non-formal and adult education. As DIETs get established, sub-standard institutions will be phased out. Selected Secondary Teacher Training Colleges will be upgraded to complement the work of State Councils of Educational Research and Training. The National Council of Teacher Education will be provided with the necessary resources and capability to accredit institutions of teacher-education and provide guidance regarding curricula and methods. Networking arrangements will be created between institutions of teacher education and university departments of education.

The Acharya Ramamurthi Review Committee (1990) explicitly stated that "in-service and refresher courses should be related to the specific needs of the teachers. In-service education should take due care of the future needs of teacher growth; evaluation and follow-up should be part of the scheme."

NPE 1986 which was modified in 1992, states that teachers will have multiple roles to perform. Initial and in-service training will be made mandatory for faculty members and adequate training reserves will be provided. Staff development programmes will be integrated at the state, and coordinated at regional and national levels.

It may be noted that the in-service programmes have drawn their themes from the emerging needs and concerns of education as faced from time to time. As a result, these programmes have, at best, been awareness programmes in respect of specific concerns, and not teacher development programmes, as visualised. As a sequel to the National Policy on Education (1986), orientation of school teachers gained momentum on a mass scale. Efforts have been initiated over the past few years to gradually develop a network of institutions like DIETs, IASEs and CTEs with the mandate of providing in-service education to primary and secondary school teachers respectively. So far, 500 DIETs, 87 CTEs, 38 IASEs and 30 SCERTs have been set up as teacher education resource institutions in the country. In the case of IASEs and CTEs, only a handful of institutions have started in-service education programme for secondary school teachers. During the last decade, satellite interactive television-based activities have been provided for teacher upgradation as part of the SOPT and DPEP projects. The majority of them, however, continue to perform their legacy functions (NCERT, 2004).

National Knowledge Commission (2008) stresses the need to strengthen the teaching community qualitatively [Box 8.1]. It states the following:

1. Provide more incentives for qualified and committed teachers.
2. Non-teaching official duties such as electoral activities should not be allowed to interfere with the teaching process.
3. Forums that allow and encourage teachers to exchange ideas, information and experiences, including a web-based portal, should be developed.
4. Pre-service training needs to be improved and differently regulated in both public and private institutions.
5. Systems for in-service training require expansion and major reform that allows for greater flexibility.

BOX 8.1 National Knowledge Commission—Teaching Profession

Revitalise the teaching profession to attract and retain quality teachers: The working condition of teachers needs to be drastically improved. Rewards and recognition should be publicised and given at all levels. Teachers at the school and college levels should be encouraged to develop innovative teaching methods. Research should be promoted in colleges by building linkages between colleges and research institutions. Academic autonomy and flexibility should be encouraged. Further, a mentoring programme for young faculty members should be started in universities and colleges. Many reserved faculty posts remain vacant in the absence of innovative or flexible appointment modes to fill these posts, creating enormous practical difficulties in teaching. **There is a need to start a systematic affirmative campaign** 2 **to rectify this situation.** Young students who can eventually fill these posts could be selected from an early age and nurtured and trained carefully to induct them into a career in teaching.

National Knowledge Commission (2nd May 2008)
Government of India
http://www.knowledgecommission.gov.in/recommendations/math&science.asp

National Curriculum Framework for Teacher Education (NCFTE 2009–10)

The National Knowledge Commission recognized the teacher as a key figure in the school system and emphasized the need to build teachers' competence through inservice courses. The NCTE formulated the NCFTE (2009-10) to fulfill these needs to promote quality education by enhancing teachers' professional capabilities. This National Curriculum Framework for Teacher Education details the context, concerns and vision underlying teacher education and school education. There is a need for developments in both sectors for qualitative improvements of the education.

The major indicator of quality of training is its relevance to the needs of teachers. The potential for radical shifts in the school practices and programmes via effective in-service education programmes has been acknowledged by most education committees and commissions. They have articulated their concern regarding the neglect and inadequacies of current in-service education practice.

Part Played by Other Organisations

In addition to the recommendations and programmes of the various all-India committees that stressed the need for in-service education, several organisations such as educational institutions, teacher organisations, educational department of the state, and private organisations have arranged, from time to time, in-service education of one type or another. These activities have been varied in nature in the different states of India.

Professional Development

According to the thesaurus of the Educational Resources Information Centre (ERIC) database, *professional development* refers to "activities to enhance professional career growth." Such activities may include individual development, continuing education, and in-service education, as well as curriculum writing, peer collaboration, study groups, and peer coaching or mentoring.

Fullan (1991) expands the definition to include "the sum total of formal and informal learning experiences throughout one's career from pre-service teacher education to retirement".

Considering the meaning of professional development in the technological age, Grant suggests a broader definition of professional development that includes the use of technology to foster teacher growth:

"Professional development ... goes beyond the term 'training' with its implications of learning skills, and encompasses a definition that includes formal and informal means of helping teachers not only learn new skills but also develop new insights into pedagogy and their own practice, and explore new or advanced understandings of content and resources. [This] definition of professional development includes support for teachers as they encounter the challenges that come with putting into practice their evolving understandings about the use of technology to support inquiry-based learning .... Current technologies offer resources to meet these challenges and provide teachers with a cluster of supports that help them continue to grow in their professional skills, understandings, and interests."

When a teacher begins her career, the knowledge and skills acquired by her in college serve only as basic necessities or minimal requirements to launch her work. The first few years of teaching will lead the new teacher to identify, re-examine and evaluate his/her goals of subject teaching, methods, the nature of the content and one's own personal aspirations. An excellent education for subject teaching can merely provide the basic tools for the creative teacher to implement, supplement, and modify knowledge to meet the everyday challenges of young people in a school classroom.

The subject teacher, like any other professional, does not commence her career with a complete understanding of methodology of teaching her particular subject to students. It is necessary that she continues to learn not only from day-to-day teaching experience but also from the many opportunities that are available. In order to remain in touch with the latest development in the field and in the world around, the teacher can take the following measures:

1. Attend seminars, workshops, conferences.
2. Pursue higher qualifications like M.Sc., M.Ed.
3. Exchange teaching position, either in the same school or through exchange programmes.
4. Visit other schools to study different methods of teaching, the facilities, etc.
5. Write articles, for professional journals like *School Science.*

6. Active participation along with other science teachers in various science clubs and professional associations like All India Science Teacher's Association.
7. Participate in refresher courses to get acquainted with the latest developments in the field.
8. Participate in the National Integration Camps which are being introduced for primary school teachers organised in different parts of the country. Each camp is attended by primary school teachers drawn from different states and regions.

SUMMER INSTITUTES FOR SCIENCE TEACHERS

Summer institutes in India can be classified into the following categories:

1. **Unitary institutes:** In these institutes courses are held once a year in science to update teachers on the developments in different fields of science as well as in new techniques in teaching.

2. **Sequential institutes:** A follow-up of the unitary institutes, the purpose of the sequential institute is to prepare a team of resource persons for state level summer institutes. Hence, the best five teachers in the unitary institutes are trained in imparting instruction both in content and in methods by an intensive programme.

3. **Special institutes:** These institutes stress on improvement of textual material for the use of training colleges in science and on the development of improved techniques of teaching and educational technology.

4. **Project technology institutes:** These institutes provide intensive training in laboratory work and workshop skills. Teachers are encouraged to develop improvised aids using indigenous resource materials and audio-visual materials.

CURRENT STATE OF AFFAIRS IN INDIA

Need to Establish Meaningful Links between Pre-service and In-service Teacher Education

Most initiatives of the 1990s have focused on 'in-service' training of teachers at the elementary stage. In-service training of teachers in the DPEP, for example, ranged from three to a maximum of twenty days and included a range of topics, with little focus on the teaching-learning process. Information on the education of teacher training in the eleven DPEP I and II States is fragmented and imprecise. The impact of these trainings still remains to be understood in spite of a massive infrastructure and investment that went into creating them.

One of the key fallouts of the undue emphasis on sporadic, short-term training of in-service teachers has been the accentuation of the divide that already exists between pre-service and in-service teacher education. These continue to function as insular mechanisms, despite the fact that both coexist in university departments for Secondary Education (IASEs) and are also the joint responsibility of DIETs in the country. A centrally sponsored scheme to establish Institutes of Advanced Studies in Education (IASE) and upgrade university departments of Education (offering B.Ed. and M.Ed. programmes) was started post-NPE 1986 to initiate the in-service training of secondary school teachers. IASEs were mandated to work concertedly on elementary education as well. This objective, however, is yet to be realised as reiterated in the Tenth Five Year Plan for Teacher Education. One pioneering effort in this regard came into effect with the establishment of the Maulana Azad Centre for Elementary and Social Education (MACESE) in the Department of Education of the University of Delhi, as a modified IASE. MACESE is the only IASE that initiated concerted work in Elementary Education, leading to the creation of the Bachelor of Elementary Education (B.El.Ed.) Programme in 1994. Under the centrally sponsored scheme, DIETs were established as premier institutions to work in elementary education.

Linking pre-service and in-service teacher education is the real need of the day.

In 2001, India launched another prestigious programme, which is known as **Sarva Shikha Abhiyan (SSA)**. Its goals are the following:

- All children in school by 2003.
- All children complete five years of primary schooling by 2007.
- Focus on elementary education of satisfactory quality.
- Bridge all gender and social category gaps.
- Universal retention by 2010.

For the development of in-service teachers, there is a provision of 20 days in-service training for all teachers and 30 days induction training for new recruits working at the elementary level. Enormous human and material resources are being invested into elementary education with a view to achieving the said goal.

"There is widespread agreement that the achievement of successful schooling is crucially dependent on the quality of teaching workforce" (Husen et al. 2003). Teacher education—both pre-service and in-service—is responsible for developing quality teaching workforce. It is generally observed that the quality of pre-service teacher education is low. It does not equip prospective teachers with requisite knowledge, skills and attitudes to perform effectively in their work-situation. In-service education of teachers is considered to be key aspect of school improvement efforts (Sparks and Loucks—Horsley 1990). *The training, retraining and updating of practicing teachers are widely recognised as essential factors in the development of teachers' quality.* Teacher quality is a major factor, contributing to improvement in learning outcomes of students (Husen et al. 2003).

Prior to 1986, in-service education of teachers was a sporadic affair. The National Policy on Education (1986) laid a great deal of emphasis on in-service education of teachers on a continuing basis to improve school quality and thereby to achieve Universal Primary Education (UPE) and Universal Elementary Education (UEE). Enormous resources—human and material—are being invested into in-service education of teachers. Presently every teacher is being imparted in-service education for 20 days in a year under Sarva Shiksha Abhiyan—the flagship programme of the Government of India.

Though in-service education programmes for teachers are being organised on a continuing basis, very little is known about the effectiveness of these programmes. Also very little information is available whether the training experiences have improved classroom processes of teachers or not. There are studies which reveal that pupils' achievement only increases when teachers present appropriate content in effective ways in the classroom. Teachers attending in-service courses often complain that in-service courses are too theoretical, and are too far removed from their daily working experiences.

The Tamil Nadu State Council for Science and Technology organises in-service training for teachers in subjects such as physics, chemistry, biology, and mathematics so that the updated syllabus in the school curriculum can be taught effectively to students.

Mass Orientation of School Teachers (MOST)

School teachers are being given orientation on a mass programme in regard to the new perspectives under the NPE. During 1985–87, nearly a million teachers have been oriented. This programme will continue till the end of the Eleventh Plan. The objective of the scheme, known as the Programme of Mass Orientation of School Teachers (**PMOST**), is to sensitise teachers to the emerging concerns in education, UEE, use of learner-centred approach, action research, the emerging role and responsibilities of teachers, enrichment of their knowledge in curricular areas, and other thrust areas enlisted in the NPE. The duration of training is 10 days. The programme during 1986–90 covered about 1.8 million teachers. The training programme was strengthened by media support. Films relating to various modules constituting the training print package were telecast on the national network for the benefit of teachers in different parts of the country. Each viewing session was preceded and followed by discussion. A participatory, interactive approach was followed in the training. The programme is implemented by the NCERT in collaboration with the SCERTs in different states.

Special Orientation Programme for Primary School Teachers

Special Orientation Programme for Primary School Teachers (SOPT) was launched in the year 1993–94 to improve the quality of primary/elementary education as part of the strategy to achieve UEE. The main focus of this programme is implementing the MLLs identified for the primary stage, training in the use of Operation Blackboard materials provided to primary school teachers, and encouraging teachers to adopt a child-centred approach to teaching. It envisages covering 0.45 million teachers every year. During the past few years, these two schemes of mass orientation have covered more than 2 million teachers. Like PMOST, this programme, too, is strengthened by media support. Films on various themes covering the course design are shown to teachers during training programmes.

District Institutes of Education and Training (DIETs)

Teacher education programmes are being revamped by the establishment of DIETs. These institutes give training and resource support to primary school teachers. Existing institutes are upgraded by provision of appropriately qualified staff to ensure professionalism. They are also being provided infrastructure support in terms of buildings and equipment. Wherever there is need, new institutes are being set up too.

INTEL

The Intel® Teach In-service Programme offers K–12 classroom teachers a curriculum designed specifically for their needs. Teachers learn how, when, and where to incorporate technology tools and resources into their teaching. They also learn how to create assessment tools and align lesson plans with provincial learning outcomes. The goal is to prepare today's teachers and students for tomorrow's demands.

Under the programme, training has been conducted for teachers from schools of Central Board of Secondary Education (CBSE), Indian Certificate of School Examination (ICSE), State Education Boards and Projects and Support Organizations under the administrative control of Union Department of Education.

Intel Teach programme provides both face-to-face and online instruction to help teachers integrate technology into their classrooms. The Intel Teach trainings emphasise on the effective use of technology in the classroom, research, communications, productivity, strategies and working in teams to solve problems. Teachers learn how, when and where to incorporate technology into their lesson plans, with a focus on developing students' higher-order thinking skills. They experience new approaches to create assessment tools and align lessons with educational learning goals and state syllabus outcomes. Teachers are provided with all the necessary curriculum materials.

IGNOU Institute of Professional Competency—Advancement of Teachers (IIPCAT, 2009), IGNOU

The vision of IIPCAT encompasses improvement in the quality of education by continuously striving for competency advancement of teachers of different disciplines at all stages of education, that is, pre-school, primary, upper primary, secondary, senior secondary, and tertiary stages of education. It shall endeavour to develop itself as an effective vehicle to transform the modality of curriculum transaction in educational institutions so as to improve the quality of education in particular and of human life in general.

The mission of the IIPCAT shall include competency advancement of teachers of all levels and in all aspects of teachers' functions and responsibilities. To accomplish this mission, the IIPCAT shall use multiple strategies, such as, organisation of in-service education, preparation of quality reference material, making arrangements for practical training. There is hope that as a result of the interventions of the IPCAT, the teachers will relatively be more enlightened, professionally competent and socially responsive.

The Indian Institute of Teacher Education, Gujarat (Bill, 2010)

The Indian Institution of Teacher Education is a Bill to establish the Institute of Teacher Education to promote teachers' development of integral personality, wide vision of nationalism and internationalism and to fulfil their role exemplars, friends, philosophers and guides, scientists, psychologists, artists and technologists, and above all, as ideal communicators who can spread uplifting influence by the processes of awakening, inspiration, and enthusiasm, also to new trends of syntheses of the East and the West and agents of change from old to the new and to confer the status.

Limitations of In-service Programmes before pandemic

Research points to training activities not resulting in improvement in teachers' instructional behaviours (Van Tulder, 1992). Bolam (1987), too, reported that information imparted to teachers is insufficiently related to the specific needs and concerns of the participants. They tend to offer theory which is unrelated to practice. They tend to overuse lecture and discussion methods. In consequence, they are ineffective in influencing teacher performance and school improvement. It can be effective only if it is based on the entry level capabilities of teachers. A look into the effectiveness of contemporary staff development literature reveals that teachers learn little from traditional in-service training workshops (Smylie, Mark and Miretzky, Debra (Eds.) (2004).

1. Participants have to be persuaded to take part in summer institutes as motivation to attend such programmes is low.
2. There is no follow-up programme to keep alive the knowledge and skills assimilated in the in-service programmes.
3. Inadequate planning by the coordinators leads to a colossal waste of time for all concerned.
4. Shortage of books leads to teachers having nothing to take back to their schools, where they could use what they have learned.
5. The examination-ridden system leaves teachers with scarcely any time to practice what they learn at the summer institutes.
6. There is dichotomy between what is taught at the summer institutes and other programmes conducted by the NCERT.
7. Training programmes conducted by ill-equipped and in-experienced resource persons lead to waste of resources—both human and material. Therefore, only experienced and well-equipped teachers should be selected as resource persons.
8. Sometimes teachers are asked through mobile phone a day before the commencement of the training programme to participate. In such a situation, teachers come to the training programme unprepared to gain experiences from training situation. They need to be informed well in advance about their participation in the training programme.
9. Training programmes spoil many school working days and students learning hours. Therefore, there is an urgent need to review the duration of training with a view to reducing it suitably.
10. In-service education and training is important. But too much of anything does not provide the desired dividends. Like this, too much of training does not result in improvement in teachers' classroom processes.
11. Training sessions should be participatory and interactive. Resource persons should use transactional approach(es) which produce conducive environment in the training session for learning to happen. Training approaches presently being used by facilitators are not appropriate.
12. Training under SSA is not useful to highly experienced teachers as they know how to teach.

Designing Relevant Inservice Training Programmes for Teachers

The COVID-19 pandemic brought prolonged school closures globally. The impacts of school closures were wide-ranging, affecting not only children's schooling and learning, but also all stakeholders of school education. Pedagogical adaptations were pivotal as transitions from the traditional models of teaching-learning to a remote learning environment had to be made. Further, teachers needed to be creative, besides being technologically sound to keep students engaged in their homes, whether urban or rural. Teachers had to learn to use technology at a rapid rate to ensure continuity of learning in their students as well as to minimize learning gaps due to poor connectivity. The pandemic has resulted in teachers having to divide their time between teaching, engaging with students, and administrative tasks. Teachers needed to be aware of ground realities, more so when using technology, as many students may lack smart phones and other gadgets to log into classes online.

This period saw:

- Training workshops held online to facilitate teachers to teach effectively using different learning platforms and technology confidently.
- Training teachers handled multigrade students, like in tribal areas, where a single teacher must be capable of handling students of different grades, as enrolments are low in remote areas.
- Language development workshops with a wide range of supplementary materials suitable to the socio-cultural background of the diverse nature of the student population. States were developing materials and using technology to facilitate effective transaction based on their infrastructure.
    - ♦ Tamil Nadu has Kalvi TV Educational programmes for classes 1 to 12, where all subjects are taught by experts. It is also working on a mobile application called Tamil Nadu Vagupparai Nokkin to provide in-class support to teachers. States and UTs like Himachal Pradesh, Delhi, and Chandigarh have also adopted similar program.
- Inservice Programmes combined high-tech and low-tech approaches to help teachers better support student learning.

CONCLUSION

In-service teacher education helps teachers adapt to changes by providing them with the requisite knowledge, skills, and support to align with the latest educational policies and technological advances effectively.

REFERENCES

Government of India NEP1986, *National Education Policy Ministry of Human Resource Development,* New Delhi.

Government of India (1948), *Report of the University Education Commission—Radhakrishnan,* Ministry of Human Resource Development, New Delhi.

Government of India (1953), *Secondary Education Commission 1952,* Ministry of Human Resource Development, New Delhi.

Government of India (1967), *Kothari Commission Report 1964–66,* Ministry of Human Resource Development, New Delhi.

Government of India (1971), *Report of the Education Commission 1964–66,* Ministry of Human Resource Development, New Delhi.

Government of India (1985), *National Commission on Teachers 1983–85,* Ministry of Human Resource Development, New Delhi.

Government of India (1986), *National Policy of Education 1986 Programme of Action,* Ministry of Human Resource Development, New Delhi.

Government of India (1993), *National Advisory Committee on Curriculum Load,* Ministry of Human Resource Development, New Delhi.

Government of India (2001), Sarva Shiksha Abhiyan, Education Policy.

Government of India (2005), *National Curriculum Framework for School Education 2005,* Ministry of Human Resource Development, New Delhi.

Government of India (2009), *National Curriculum Frameworks on Teacher Education.*

Government of India, Acharya Ramamurti Review Committee (1990), *Towards an Enlightened and Humane Society,* Ministry of Human Resource Development, New Delhi.

Mohan, R. (2022), Reshaping Teacher Education for the Twenty-First Century: An Indian Perspective. In: Khine, M.S., Liu, Y. (eds) Handbook of Research on Teacher Education, Springer, Singapore. https://doi.org/10.1007/978-981-16-9785-2_25.

Myint Swe Khine (Editor), and Yang Liu (Editor), Handbook of Research on Teacher Education: Innovations and Practices in Asia, Springer, Singapore, 1st ed.

Right to Education Act, 2005, (2009), Ministry of Human Resource Development, New Delhi.

Smylie, Mark A. and Miretzky, Debra (2004), Rethinking Teacher Workforce Development: A Strategic Human Resource Management Perspective, *Yearbook of the National Society for the Study of Education, Sage Publications, USA* Vol. 103, No. 1, pp. 34–69, April 2004.

Sparks, D. and Loucks-Horsley, S. (1990), "Models of Staff Development", in W.R. Houston (Ed.), *Handbook of Research on Teacher Education,* Macmillan Publishing, New York.

Web References

Government of India NPE2020.Final National Education Policy 2020 (PDF) (Report). Ministry of Human Resource Development. https://niepid.nic.in/nep_2020.pdf.

National Curriculum Framework for Teacher Education Towards Preparing Professional and Humane Teacher. NCTE Document 2009/10.
http://ncte-india.org/ncte_new/pdf/NCFTE_2010.pdf.

National Knowledge Commission–Report to the Nation 2006, Government of India, New Delhi.
https://www.aicte-india.org/downloads/nkc.pdf.

Part IV

METHODS AND TECHNIQUES
General and Modern

CHAPTER 9

General Methods of Teaching

Teachers are those who use themselves as bridges, over which they invite their students to cross; then having facilitated their crossing, joyfully collapse, encouraging them to create bridges of their own.

—Nikos Kazantzakis

INTRODUCTION

A teacher can use a variety of methods and techniques for daily teaching. While choosing a method, she should assess its advantages and disadvantages in relation to other methods and also correlate the correct method with the objectives of education and the specific conditions in which learning is to take place. In general, there is an interaction between the teacher and the learner. To enhance this interaction, teachers use new instructional materials.

DEFINITION

The word 'method' means 'mode' in Latin. *The methods of teaching can hence be defined as the manner in which teachers impart knowledge and skills while teaching, and students acquire this knowledge and skill in the process of learning.* Thus, method of teaching implies the teaching-learning process involving both teaching and learning activity.

Gage defines teaching methods as:

Patterns of teacher behaviour that are recurrent, applicable to various subject matters, characteristic of more than one teacher, and relevant to learning.

Figure 9.1(a) represents teacher-centred methods whereas Figure 9.1(b) represents student-centred method.

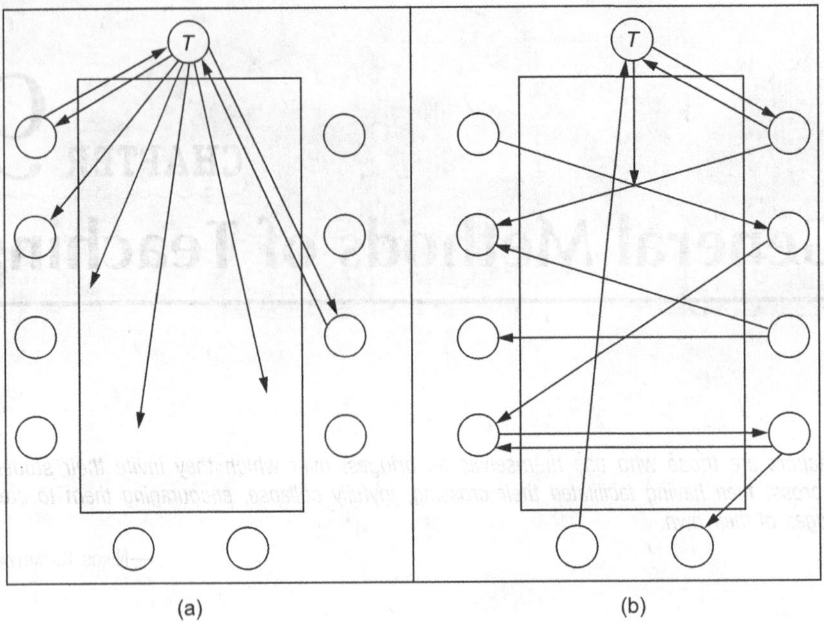

FIGURE 9.1 Participating dynamics.

LEARNING CYCLE

The learning cycle is an established planning method in science education and consistent with contemporary theories about how individuals learn. It is easy to learn and useful in creating opportunities to learn science. The learning cycle model is considered as having five parts, though these parts are not discrete or linear. The learning cycle (Figure 9.2) used in lesson plans follows Bybee's (1997) five steps of **engagement,**

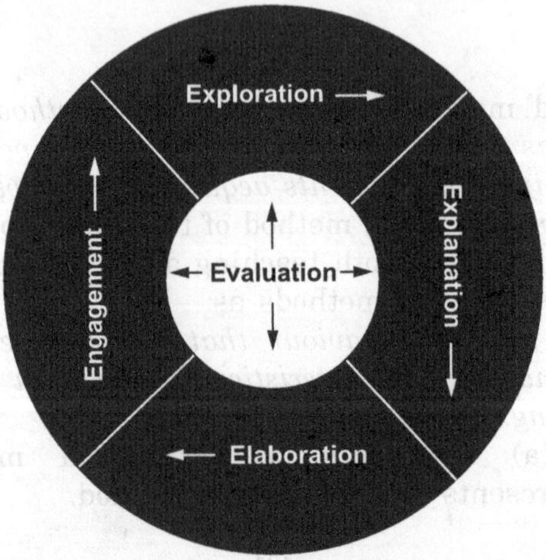

FIGURE 9.2 The learning cycle.

exploration, explanation, elaboration, and **evaluation**. As in any cycle, there is really no end to the process. After elaboration ends, the engagement of the next learning cycle begins. Evaluation is not the last step. Evaluation occurs in all four parts of the learning cycle.

Engagement

Engagement is the time when the teacher is on centerstage. The teacher poses the problem, pre-assesses the students, helps students make connections, and informs students about where they are heading.

The purpose of engagement is to:

1. Focus students' attention on the topic.
2. Pre-assess students' prior knowledge.
3. Inform the students about the lesson's objective(s).
4. Remind students of what they already know that they will need to apply to learning the topic at hand.
5. Pose a problem for the students to explore in the next phase of the learning cycle.

Evaluation of engagement: Evaluation's role in engagement revolves around pre-assessment that is funding out what the students already know about the topic at hand. The teacher could ask questions and have the students respond orally and/or in writing.

Exploration

Now the students are at the centre of the action as they collect data to solve the problem. The teacher makes sure the students collect and organise their data in order to solve the problem. The students need to be active. The purpose of exploration is to have students collect data that they can use to solve the problem that was posed.

Evaluation of exploration: In this portion of the learning cycle, evaluation should primarily focus on process, i.e., on the students' data collection, rather than the product of the students' data collection. Teachers ask themselves questions such as the following:

1. How well are the students collecting data?
2. Are they carrying out the procedures correctly?
3. How do they record the data?
4. Is it in a logical form or is it haphazard?

Explanation

In the explanation phase of the process, students use the data they have collected to solve the problem and report what they did and try to figure out the answer to the problem that was presented. The teacher also introduces new vocabulary, phrases or sentences to label what the students have already figured out.

Evaluation of explanation: Evaluation here focuses on the process the students are using—how well can students use the information they have collected, plus what they already knew to come up with new ideas? Using questions, the teacher can assess the students' comprehension of the new vocabulary and new concepts.

Elaboration

The teacher gives students new information that extends what they have been learning in the earlier parts of the learning cycle. At this stage, the teacher also poses problems that students solve by applying what they have learned. The problems include both examples and non-examples.

Evaluation of elaboration: The evaluation that occurs during elaboration is what teachers usually think of as evaluation. Sometimes, teachers equate evaluation with "the test at the end of the chapter." When teachers have the students do the application problems as part of elaboration, these application problems are "the test."

Methods ***teachers*** use to support the learning cycle should:

1. Create interest.
2. Generate inquisitiveness.
3. Raise questions and elicit responses.
4. Facilitate cooperative learning.
5. Refer to and include previous learning experiences as they relate to new learnings.
6. Incorporate alternate assessments.

Teaching methods should allow ***students*** to:

1. Show interest by asking questions.
2. Use inquiry to explore or investigate new concepts.
3. Form predictions and hypotheses.
4. Formulate experiments with alternatives.
5. Record ideas and observations.
6. Use various resources to seek explanations.
7. Make connections between prior knowledge and new concepts.
8. Self-evaluate.

CRITERIA FOR THE SELECTION OF METHODS

The criteria for the selection of teaching methods are manifold. However, the most important factors are:

1. Human factor
2. Objectives of teaching
3. Subject area
4. Time and material factor

Human Factors

The human factors influencing the selection of teaching methods are: (a) the teacher, (b) the students, and (c) the environment from which they come.

Teachers

The knowledge, teaching experience and personality of the teacher are the factors of primary importance. The teacher should have a clear and significant message to convey and a personality acceptable to the students for establishing effective communication links. If these conditions are fulfilled, a well chosen and properly used method is likely to stimulate the process of learning; otherwise, the method may be a failure and become an end in itself.

Students

The methods of teaching adopted should take into account the following factors:

1. The intellectual level of the students
2. The age and practical experience of the students
3. The social and cultural environment.

For example, while teaching the students from a rural background, concrete examples of applications in day-to-day life would be appreciated and well-received. Similarly, in schools where laboratory facilities are poor, lectures supported by visual aids would help bring alive the experiments.

Environment

In general, any participative method may be used in any environment, provided it is instilled gradually, with prior knowledge of the environment and is accordingly modified. It shows the ability of the teacher to create their own teaching-learning environment by considering the objectives of teaching the subject and creating suitable classroom climate for the same. This could be done by hanging charts relevant to the subject or posing simple and prompting questions or narrating a general real-life situation or by providing relevant examples.

Objectives of Teaching

The objectives are defined in terms of changes to be effected in knowledge, skills and attitudes. Methods will have to be selected with regard to their ability to impart new knowledge, influence attitudes and develop practical skills.

Subject Area

Each subject area (physics, chemistry, history, maths, etc.) has its own specific features. For example, in physical chemistry, extensive use of mathematics is made. It could be taught through a combination of lectures (using audio-visual aids) and numerical exercises during which the concepts could be mastered. The teacher should, therefore, know when to use which method and how. It should be noted that it is often possible to choose from several methods. Thus, a particular topic could be taught in different ways using different methods by different teachers.

Time and Material Factors

Decision on the choice of teaching methods depends on time, financial resources and availability of learning resources as factors. Preparation time varies for the different teaching methods and also depends on the abilities of teachers.

The teaching facilities may be a limiting factor in some schools in small townships. Factors such as the number of rooms available, accessibility of ICT tools, audio-visual aids, and laboratory facilities should be anticipated and the methods selected should conform to the specific needs.

PRINCIPLES OF EFFECTIVE LEARNING

Any educational process accomplishes its role only by creating situations which are favourable to learning and in which learning actually takes place. Of course, the principles of learning are not put into effect through the teaching method alone.

Some selected aspects of the relationship between the principles of learning and teaching methods are discussed below:

1. **Motivation:** The motivation to learn is enhanced if the presentation of the teaching material is interesting and emphasis is laid particularly on applied value. The main purposes of motivating the learner is to enhancing their readiness for learning, arousing their interest towards learning and sustaining it for the entire period. This can be done

using various techniques like-narration, storytelling, reciting a poem, demonstration and by posing questions. To some extent, this can be obtained through any method, including a good lecture. However, many participative methods are directly concerned with applying theoretical knowledge to real-life situations. The diverse ways in which they can be combined and sequenced can add to the joy of learning, and minimise the fatigue.

2. **Active involvement:** The principle of active involvement implies that the deeper the involvement, the higher the motivation, the more the students retain and the better they are equipped to apply it.

3. **Individual approach:** Individuals have different capabilities of learning, and have personal styles of study and application. They should be subject to individual control of performance. The overall methods of teaching have to initiate not only 'work in groups' but also provide the opportunity for individual reading, thinking and applying knowledge gained. This can be done through:

(i) Compulsory individual assignments (e.g., reading, exercises, projects).

(ii) Use of teaching aids for individual learning, like audio and video tapes, teaching machines, computer terminals accessible to individual students.

(iii) The breaking down of projects into modules of assignments for each individual.

(iv) Voluntary additional work by the more gifted students.

Some methods are better suited than others, for they have more scope of introducing new topics and ideas and correctly sequencing them, or for explaining the logical structure of a vast and complex topic. For instance, to teach optical instruments in Class X, the teacher should check if the students are familiar with lenses, mirrors, image formation, etc. That is why in certain situations, the teacher cannot do without lectures and reading assignments.

(v) Different types of feedback are needed and have to be provided in learning. They are:

(a) Feedback on the student's competence and behaviour

(b) Feedback on the effectiveness of the teaching method in achieving the stated objectives.

(vi) The principle of transfer requires that education should help the student to transfer what he has learned, to live situations.

Keeping in view the principles of learning, it is necessary to properly combine and sequence various teaching methods in order to secure the greatest impact on learning.

GROUPING OF TEACHING METHODS

Teaching methods can be classified into (a) oral, (b) observation, and (c) practical.

Oral methods include talks, narration, discussions, lectures and work at a book. Observation methods involve demonstrations of natural objects, charts, models, slides and films. Practical methods involve conducting experiments and doing relevant laboratory work. There are other known classified methods on the basis of activity. If the student is active, the method is called **student-centered,** whereas if the students are mere passive participants in the learning process and the teacher is active, the method becomes **teacher-centered**.

Pesson has classified teaching methods into three general classifications, viz. individual contact, group contact and mass contact. The first two are one to one contact and one to much contact. The third classification—mass contact—is what is used in distance education and correspondence courses.

The major areas to be considered while selecting a method are:

1. Human factors—target audience
2. Classification of subject matter—specific subject and its nature
3. Desired change—objectives to be attained, knowledge, skill and attitude
4. Learning theories—motivation, readiness, and so on.
5. Main function of the method chosen—feasibility of methods in terms of time, cost and availability.
6. Need and time factors—right techniques at right time
7. Availability of the method—in the case of power connections, laboratory facilities and the like.

Figure 9.3 illustrates the various factors involved in the selection of teaching methods.

1. HUMAN FACTORS • Teacher (trainer) • Target audience • Environment	4. PRINCIPLES OF LEARNING • Motivation • Active involvement • Individual approach • Sequencing and structuring • Feedback • Transfer
2. SUBJECT AREA • Specific subject • Inter-disciplinary problem	
3. OBJECTIVE • Knowledge • Skills • Attitudes	5., 6. and 7. TIME AND MATERIAL FACTORS • Time • Finance • Teaching facilities

FIGURE 9.3 Factors for the selection of suitable teaching methods.

GENERAL METHODS OF TEACHING

The methods suitable for teaching are:

1. Lecture and discussion
2. Demonstration
3. Seminars
4. Symposium
5. Supervised study
6. Workshops
7. Panel discussions
8. Programmed instruction
9. Computer-aided instruction
10. e-learning.

Lecture Method

Lecture method is an educational presentation usually delivered by an instructor to a group of students with the use of instructional aids and training devices. Lectures are useful for the presentation of new material, summarising ideas, and showing relationships between theory and practice. In lecture method, the teacher orally presents the material of the course in an organised way to the students, going from theory to examples and back again. Lectures may contain a varying level of student participation, and notes are generally taken.

The lecture is one of the oldest and most basic pedagogic tools. Although experience and educational research show that the lecture is less effective than activity methods at school level, many teachers find themselves spending at least 30–50 per cent of their teaching time in lecturing.

Lecture method lays emphasis on the penetration of contents. The teacher is more active and students are passive, but she also uses question-answers to keep them attentive in the class. It is used to motivate, clarify, expand and review the information.

Lecture, as a method of instruction, does place enormous weight and attention on the teacher. Unlike other methods, there is no hiding place for the teacher. The spotlight is on the teacher. She is the centre of attention, and for many students it is the lecturer, rather than the lecture content, that is of greatest interest. If the lecture method is to be one that is successful, the teacher must be aware that the lecture requires great attention, hard work, creativity, and a certain type of personality on the part of the performer.

The use of lecturing depends on the subject matter, the teaching philosophy of the teacher and the overall learning situation. Formal lecturing is used largely to build up basic theoretical knowledge, which must be gained before practice of skills. If the number of students in a class is large, teaching resources are scarce or a limited number of periods are available on the time table, lecturing may be the only alternative.

Meaning of lecture method

Carter Good's dictionary defines lecture method as:

An instructional procedure by which the lecturer seeks to create interest, to influence, stimulate, or mould opinion, to promote activity, to impart information, or to develop critical thinking, largely by the use of the verbal message, with a minimum of class participation; illustrations, maps, charts, or other visual aids may be employed to supplement the oral technique.

Wasley and Wronski (1958) suggested that the lecture method serves four basic purposes (a) to motivate, (b) to clarify, (c) to review, and (d) to expand. In general, the lecture directly conveys information to generate understanding and to stimulate interest. Also, it helps to get immediate feedback from the student, besides on spot solution to the questions raised.

The lecture is an exposition of knowledge, facts, principles or other information which a teacher wishes to present to her students. In brief, a lecture means one person addressing many students.

Planning the lecture

Before starting to prepare a lecture, the teacher must be able to answer four basic questions:

Who is your audience? —Who (Learner)
What is the purpose of your lecture? —Why (Objectives)
How much is the time available? —How long (time period)
What is the subject matter? —What (content knowledge)

1. **The audience:** What is the target audience, their background, likes and dislikes—cultural features, level of education, prior knowledge of the subject? What can you assume about their level of understanding before you start your lecture? It may be helpful to start with a general discussion or question-answer session.

2. **Purpose of the lecture:** What does a lecturer expect from students after delivering the lecture? The approach varies, depending on the objectives in her mind.

The objectives may be to:

(i) Give general information on a subject.
(ii) Gain acceptance for a new point of view.
(iii) Change basic attitude.
(iv) Give detailed information.
(v) Teach a particular skill.

With a clearly defined objective in mind, it will be easier to select appropriate material and to decide on the most effective way to present it.

3. **Time available:** The teacher should realise that after some time the students' interest may start waning. The lecture should be planned in such a manner that the interest is sustained throughout, accordingly sprinkled with interesting examples, questions, discussion and so on.

4. **Subject matter:** Lack of sufficient knowledge about the subject matter virtually leads to the 'death of a lecture'. The presentation of a few ideas at a time will give the teacher an opportunity to evolve meaningful and logical relationship within the topic, which is well understood by the students.

All notes should be reorganised in a logical order and a detailed outline worked out. A schematic illustration of organisation is given in Figure 9.4.

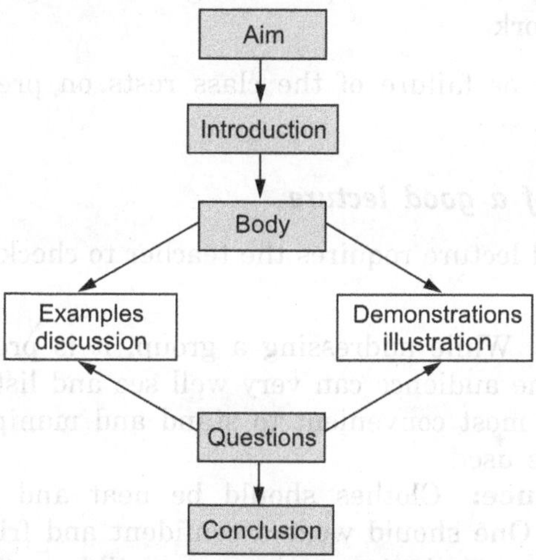

FIGURE 9.4 Format of the lecture.

The introduction should give a brief outline of the objective and theme of the lecture to students in a manner designed to keep alive the interest and arouse curiosity of the class right from the beginning. In the body of the lecture, the important points are highlighted in logical sequence, i.e. each step should naturally stem from the previous one.

Illustrative examples are added, related to the student's experience wherever possible. Demonstrations help to clarify the points discussed. Audio-visual aids will help students to further understand and retain the important points in their mind. The teacher should put these in a logical sequence as each new point is raised. Due time for questions and discussion to clarify meanings is required.

The type of conclusion will depend largely on the objectives of the lecture, but a brief recapitulation of the main points is essential. The conclusive summary determines how well the overall objective has been achieved.

Purpose of a good lecture

A teacher needs to note a few points while using the lecture method. The lecture becomes effective if the purpose is clearly understood. In general, the lecture is used for the following:

1. **Introduction of a new topic:** It not only motivates the students but gives guidelines for the students on what is to follow.
2. **Summarising a topic:** The lecture method is effective in summarising the lesson, as the points highlighted would help focus the attention of the students.
3. **Supplementary information:** This method is invaluable in supplementing textbook information, as a follow-up or prior to laboratory work and in presenting the findings of field trips and project work.

The success or failure of the class rests on presentation of the lecture.

Characteristics of a good lecture

Delivering a good lecture requires the teacher to check on the following points.

1. **Posture:** While addressing a group, it is preferable to stand so that the audience can very well see and listen you. Besides, it is also most convenient to stand and manipulate the visual aids to be used.
2. **Appearance:** Clothes should be neat and suitable for the occasion. One should wear a confident and friendly look while lecturing as students are very susceptible to first impressions.
3. **Manner:** To hold the attention of the group during the lecture, a teacher requires to be poised and courteous.
4. **Gesture:** Actions and gestures must be natural and spontaneous. Mannerisms like playing with the chalk, or any other similar object should be avoided, as they are distracting and sometimes extremely annoying.
5. **Voice:** The tone of the voice can be accordingly altered to convey confidence, emotion, emphasis and indignation. Pace and pitch of the voice-should also be varied occasionally to avoid monotony.
6. **Vocabulary:** It is best to use simple language avoiding jargons, metaphors and slangs, which could be misinterpreted. Sentences should be kept simple and short as far as possible.

7. **Use of audio-visual aids and blackboard:** A well-planned lecture, divided into parts, highlights focal points and can improve the instructional value of the lecture. The use of visual aids should be planned and well prepared.
8. **Time:** Time available must be used effectively, keeping in mind the students' listening threshold. Thus, recapitulation should form a part of the lecture, say, the last ten minutes. Questions should be encouraged, and discussions conducted to make the class more interactive.

The students may be asked to assess the performance of a lecturer, by using a lecture rating form like the one given in Table 9.1. This will help the teacher improve her/his teaching capabilities.

TABLE 9.1 Lecture rating form

Name of Teacher: . . . . Date: . . . .

Subject: . . . .

	Very Good	*Satisfactory*	*Weak*
Organisation and content			
1. Clear purpose			
2. Appropriate introduction			
3. Clear main points—principles			
4. Development of points/theme/ (use of examples)			
5. Conclusion			
6. Adaptation to group needs and interests			
7. Interest or novelty of topic or approach.			
Presentation			
8. Animation and directness			
9. Use of voice (tone, expression)			
10. Body and gesture			
11. Use of notes			
12. Total speaking ability			
Other methods (where applicable)			
13. Use of visual slide (comment, if necessary)			
14. Handling questions/directions/discussions			
15. Timing of session			
Total handling of session			

Remarks:

The lecture method is appropriate when:

- The objective is to present information.
- Information is not available in accessible sources.
- A particular organisation is required.
- The information is original or must be integrated from different sources.
- An introduction **must** be made.
- A summary or synthesis is required.
- Alternative points or clarification are required.
- Supplementary explanations are needed.

(after Good and Brophy, 1999; Gage and Berliner, 1992; Henson, 1988)

Advantages of lecture method

The advantages of the lecture method are as follows:

1. The lecture method is the most economical way of getting a large amount of information across to a large class. A teacher can convey the information in minimum time, thus enabling the syllabus to be covered within the stipulated time. It is economical in terms of both money and time.
2. The lecture is useful in imparting in an efficient manner factual information to convey facts to students who have difficulty reading their texts.
3. The lecture helps to channelise the thinking of students in a given direction.
4. Some abstract topics in science are best taught by the lecture method. The teacher, through tact, style and presentation, can get her message through.

Disadvantages of lecture method

The disadvantages of the lecture method are as follows:

1. The lecture method is apt to be misused. The 'pouring in' of information is psychologically unsound unless it can be done in a meaningful way.
2. Science is best learnt by doing. There is no provision for activities in this method as the students are passive (listeners).
3. The rate of imparting information by the teacher may seem too fast for the students who are restless by nature, preoccupied with their own immediate problems and often handicapped by limitations of vocabulary and background of experience.
4. A poorly planned, poorly delivered lecture fails to motivate the students.
5. The lecture method is not very successful in imparting attitudes and skills, as it does not touch the affective and psychomotor faculties of the learner.

6. As student interaction is minimum, social attitudes and values may not be fostered.
7. The lecture method cannot cater to individual grasping capacities of the students.

Lecture-cum-demonstration Method

The lecture demonstration method includes the merits of the lecture as well as demonstration method. It attempts to filter out the disadvantages of both. The teacher performs the experiment in the class with the active participation of the students. Thus, the students observe the experiment, help in taking down readings as well as assist in setting up the apparatus. The teacher helps the students draw inferences.

This method serves the following two purposes:

1. To provide means of making certain parts of subject matter clear by objectifying it.
2. To be as economical, both time-wise and finance-wise, as possible.

The lecture demonstration method can prove to be one of the best methods if the demonstrations are well planned by a skilful teacher.

Now, it will be easy to define what is lecture-cum-demonstration method.

This method includes the merits of lecture method and demonstration method. The teacher performs the experiment in the class and goes on explaining what she does. It takes into account the active participation of the student and is thus not a lopsided process like the lecture method. The students see the actual apparatus and operations and help the teacher in demonstrating experiments and thereby they feel interested in learning. So, this method also follows the maxim of moving from *concrete to abstract*, wherein the students observe the demonstration critically and try to draw inferences. With the help of lecture-cum-demonstration method, their power of observation and reasoning are also exercised. So, the important principle on which this method works is "*truth is that works.*"

Steps needed to conduct a lecture-cum-demonstration lesson

1. **Planning and preparation:** Great care should be taken by the teacher while planning and preparing her demonstration. She should keep the following points in mind while preparing her lesson.

(i) *Subject matter.*
(ii) *Questions to be asked.*
(iii) *Apparatus required for the experiment.*

To achieve the above stated objectives, the teacher should thoroughly go through the pages of the textbook, relevant to the lesson. After this, the teacher should prepare the lesson plan which should essentially include the principles to be explained, experiments to be demonstrated and type of questions to be asked form the students. These questions should be arranged in a systematic order to be followed in the class. Before actually demonstrating the experiment to a class, the experiment should be rehearsed under the condition prevailing in the classroom. In spite of this, some thing may go wrong at the actual lesson, so reserve apparatus is often useful. The apparatus has to be arranged in a systematic manner on the demonstration table. Thus, for the success of the demonstration method, a teacher has to prepare herself as thoroughly as possible.

2. **Introduction of the lesson:** As in every subject, the lesson in the case of science should also start with proper motivation of the students. It is always considered more useful to introduce the lesson in a problematic way which would make the students realise the importance of the topic. The usual way through which the teacher can introduce the lesson is by telling some personal experience or incident of a simple and interesting experiment. A good experiment carefully demonstrated is likely to leave an everlasting impression on the mind of the young students and would set the students talking about it in the school.

3. **Presentation:** The method of presenting the subject matter is very important. A good teacher should present her lesson in an interesting manner, and not in a boring manner. To make the lesson interesting, the teacher may not be very rigid to remain within the prescribed course, rather she should make the lesson as much as broad-based as possible. For widening the lesson, the teacher may think of various useful applications taught. The teacher has also the liberty to take examples and illustrations from the allied branches of science like history and geography. Constant questions and answer should form part of every demonstration lesson.

Questions and cross-questions are essential for properly illuminating the principles discussed. Questions should be arranged in such a way that their answers may form a complete teaching unit.

4. **Performance of experiment:** A good observer has been described as a person who has learnt the use of senses of touch, sight, and smell in an intelligent way. Through this method, teachers want students to observe what happens in an experiment and to state it carefully. They also want them (students) to make generalisation without violating the scientific spirit, i.e. teachers should allow students to learn from one experiment or observation. The following steps are generally accepted as valuable in conducting science experiment generally:

(i) Write the problem to be solved in simple words.
(ii) Make a list of activities that has to be used to solve the problem.
(iii) Gather material for conducting the experiment.
(iv) Work out a format of steps in the order of procedure so that everyone knows what is to be done.
(v) Teacher should try the experiment before conduction.
(vi) Record the findings.
(vii) Assist students to make generalisation.

5. **Blackboard summary:** A summary of important results and principles should be written in the blackboard. The blackboard should also be frequently used to draw sketches and diagrams. The entire procedure should be displayed to the students after the demonstration.

6. **Supervision:** Students are asked to take the complete notes of the blackboard summary, including the sketches and diagrams drawn. Such a record will be quite helpful to the student while learning his lessons. Such a summary will prove beneficial only if it has been copied correctly from the blackboard, and to make sure that it is done, the teacher must check it frequently during this stage.

Common errors in demonstration lesson

Apparatus may not be ready for use:

1. There may not be an apparent relation between the demonstration experiment and the topic under discussion.
2. Blackboard summary may not be up to the mark.
3. Teacher may be in a hurry to arrive at a generalisation without allowing students to arrive at a generalisation from facts.
4. Teacher may talk too much, which will mar the enthusiasm of the students.
5. Teacher may not have allowed sufficient time for recording of data.
6. Teacher may fail to ask the right type of questions.

Merits of lecture-cum-demonstration method

1. It is an economical method as compared to a purely student-centred method.
2. It is a psychological method and students take an active interest in the teaching-learning process.
3. It leads the students from concrete to abstract situations.
6. In comparison to heuristic, project method, it is time saving but purely lecture method is too lengthy.
7. It can be successfully used for all types of students.
8. It improves the observational and reasoning skills of the students.

Limitations of lecture-cum-demonstration method

1. It provides no scope for "learning by doing" for the students as students are only observing the teacher performance in the class.
2. Since the teacher performs the experiment at their own pace, many students may not be able to comprehend the concept being taught.
3. Since this method is not student-centred, it makes no provision for individual differences; all types of students including slow learners and genius have to proceed with the same speed.
4. It fails to develop laboratory skills in the students.
5. It fails to impart training in scientific inquiry and promoting development of scientific attitude among students.

Project Method

The project method of teaching is the practical outcome of the John Dewey's philosophy of pragmatism. Pragmatism has made a unique constribution in the shaping up of project method enunciated by the Kilpatrick, the follower of Dewey. In the project method, study through workshop and source methods are also studied. Concrete activity rather than academic work takes the dominant place in the project method. In the project method, the teacher, instead of following the lecture method, substitutes "the subject" with a few outstanding problems and proceeds to solve the same by the experiment method with the active cooperation of the students. The purpose of this method is to turn students into trained investigators and prepare them for learning by doing.

Definitions

Ballard: A project is a bit of real life that has been imparted into the school.

Burton: The problem is a project which results in doing. The motor element is not what makes the activity a project, but the problem-solving of practical nature accompanying the activity.

Stevenson: A project is a problematic act carried to completion in its natural setting.

Snedden: Project is a unit of educative work in which the most prominent feature is some form of positive and concrete achievements.

Charters: In topical organisation principles are learned first while in the projects, the problems are proposed which demand in the solution the development of principles by the learner as needed.

Thus, a project is:

- A problematic act.
- A purposeful activity.
- A whole-hearted activity.
- An activity in natural setting.
- An activity in a social setting.
- A bit of real life introduced in school.
- A problem solving of a practical nature.
- A positive and concrete achievement.
- An activity through which solution of various problems are found out.

Main principles of the project method

The main principles of the project method are as follows:

1. **Principle of purpose:** Knowledge of purpose is a great stimulus, which motivates the student to realise his goal. The student must have an ideal. Purpose motivates learning. Interest cannot be aroused by aimless and meaningless activities.
2. **Principle of activity:** Opportunities should be provided to students that make them active and learn things by doing. Physical as well as mental activities are to be provided to them. They are to be allowed to 'do' and to 'live through doing'.
3. **Principle of experience:** Experience is the best teacher. What is learnt must be experienced. The students learn new facts and information through experience.
4. **Principle of social experience:** The student is a social being and must be prepared for social life. In the project method, the students work in groups.
5. **Principle of reality:** Life is real and education, to be meaningful, must be real. The project method is a method of education to the student and, therefore, it must also be real. Real life situations should be presented in the life of the school.
6. **Principle of freedom:** The desire for an activity must be spontaneous and not forced by the teacher. The student should be free from imposition, restrictions or obstructions so that he may express himself fully and freely. S/He must be given the freedom to choose an activity, to do an activity according to their interests, needs and capacities.
7. **Principle of utility:** Knowledge will be worthwhile only when it is useful and practical. This method develops various attitudes

and values which are of great significance from the practical point of view.

8. **Principle of correlation:** Correlation of subject is possible in the project method, where knowledge from different subjects can be viewed holistically.

Types of projects

1. **Producer type:** In this, the emphasis is directed towards the actual construction of a material object or article.
2. **Consumer type:** In this type of project, either direct or vicarious experience is got, such as reading and learning stories and also listening to a musical selection.
3. **Problem type:** In this type, the chief purpose is to solve a problem involving the intellectual process such as determining the density of a certain liquid, etc.
4. **Drill type:** In this type, the objective is to attain a certain degree of skill in a reaction as learning vocabulary.

Various steps in conducting project

1. **Creating the situation:** The students themselves should define, state and choose their problems. Through discussions, the teacher helps in the making of a proposal by the students. The teacher should cater to the needs, interests and abilities of the students.
2. **Selection of project:** Not all projects are feasible at the school level. The teacher needs to participate and make the projects clearer to the students.
3. **Planning:** After the project is decided and accepted, the teacher may develop an outline and ask the students to study it deeply at home. A class period may be devoted for this work. The teacher should draw attention of the students to the need of planning before undertaking the activity. Different proposals should be discussed and alternatives considered. The best plan is agreed upon after a good deal of discussion, suggestions counter suggestion and rejections. The teacher needs to divide the work among the students according to their interest and ability and see that they move towards accomplishing the task.
4. **Execution of the plan:** In this, the students start collecting the facts and the teacher ensures that the students are on the right track. This is the stage at which the students perform many activities and learn various useful experiences.
5. **Evaluating the project:** The work is to be reviewed when it is completed. The students evaluate their own project against the objectives they had framed and assess how well they have

reached the objectives. This is a crucial stage and the teacher has a vital role to play here.

6. **Recording:** In this step, a complete record of all activities connected with the project must be maintained. The students write in details about all the five steps of the project with giving details of reference books, aids, details of task, etc. The procedure of providing a situation and of choosing the project, duties assigned, difficulties felt and experience gained should be recorded in detail.

Merits of the project method

1. The project strategy is based upon the following laws of learning:

> (i) **Law of readiness:** According to this law, we learn most when our minds are ready to receive. The project method prepares the mind of the students by providing them with suitable situation.
> (ii) **Law of exercise:** Learning to be effective must be practised. The project method affords many opportunities to the students to learn by doing.
> (iii) **Law of effect:** This law states that if learning is to be effective and fruitful, it must be accompanied by satisfaction, pleasure when they manipulate their own activities.

2. This method makes learning practical and application oriented. When meaningful and purposeful activities are provided to the students, they get opportunities to acquaint themselves with the real-life problems.
3. The project method gives unity to the curriculum. Different subjects get intertwined in the carrying out of projects. Students are able to perceive the interdisciplinary nature of learning.
4. The method encourages adopting cooperation and collaboration strategies in learning.
5. This method helps inculcate team spirit along with qualities like tolerance, independence and open mindedness.
6. It helps in all-round development of the students.
7. Dignity of labour is encouraged through the project method. They learn skills like soldering, making charts, displaying models, communication and other such skills.
8. The students work with great enthusiasm for the competition of their self-chosen project.
9. The students get training in citizenship.

Limitations of the project method

1. This method needs gifted teachers who can guide, facilitate and keep track of several ongoing projects in the class.

2. Students can learn particular aspects of a topic. Many key concepts may be missed in the process.
3. The whole syllabus cannot be covered by this method.
4. This method is time-consuming and may require a reframing of the school timetable.
5. Preparation of books suitable for the project work is by no means an easy task.
6. Projects can lead to lazy students becoming even lazier, brilliant ones overshadowing the not so brilliant.
7. The school teaching can become disorganised and irregular because the method needs freedom and flexibility.
8. Library facilities may be insufficient to meet the demands of the students.

Essentials of a good project

- Timely
- Usefulness
- Interesting
- Challenging
- Economical
- Rich in experiences
- Cooperativeness

Role of a teacher

1. The project to be successful must be based on a definite procedure.
2. The teacher has to provide those situations to the students wherein they should feel a spontaneous urge to solve some of their practical problems.
3. The teacher must be on the lookout of discovering their interests, tastes, aptitudes and needs. As far as possible, problems or situations which are provided to the students should be social ones. These provide better social training and give more satisfaction.
4. The teacher may converse with the class on different topics of interest to them.
5. The teacher is to tap all resources to provide worthwhile situations.
6. The teacher should be well read and be aware of the sources of information to guide his/her students effectively.

Heuristic Method

The word 'heuristic' is derived from the Greek word heuriskin, meaning discovery. Heuristic method was advocated by Professor Armstrong, who felt that by placing a student in the position of a discoverer, he would learn much more than being merely told about things. It is based on the principle of learning by doing. *Heuriskin* method is basically training in scientific method. Knowledge is a secondary consideration. Students learn to collect data, interpret data and arrive at solutions by rejecting superfluous statements.

Heuristic is an adjective for experience-based techniques that help in problem solving, learning and discovery. A heuristic method is particularly used to rapidly find a solution that is hoped to be close to the best possible answer, or 'optimal solution'. Heuristics are "rules of thumb", educated guesses, intuitive judgments or simply common sense.

> The term "heuristic methods" can be used to describe any problem solving or creativity technique that involves creating a basic model as a starting point for further experimentation or refinement. Heuristic methods are trial-and-error approaches.

Ryburn (1963) says: "This method as the name implies is a method by which the student discovers things for himself. The student is put in the position of a pioneer and he finds his way along the path of knowledge as did those who first discovered the facts, principles and laws which are now known to all."

Objectives of heuristic method

The objectives are:

1. Develop in the student the habit of enquiry and research.
2. Instil in the student the habit of listening, observing, asking and discovering.
3. Make the students more reflective.
4. Lay the foundation for future learning.
5. Inculcate the spirit of scientific inquiry.

The heuristic method also gives all these opportunities to the student to acquire knowledge which is fully based on learning by self-experimenting.

> The essential conditions for heuristic learning are:
>
> - Freedom of action to the student
> - Providing a responsive environment
> - Acquire guidance of the teacher, when required
> - Encouragement to continue learning through heuristic method.

Advantages of heuristic method

1. The method lays stress on individual practical work, careful observation and independent thinking which makes a student self-reliant.

2. It imparts knowledge of scientific method of thinking and inculcates scientific attitude among students.
3. It is based on the important psychological principle of learning by doing.
4. Individual differences can be catered to, as each student can work at his own pace.
5. Students develop research skills, including setting up and fitting apparatus conducting experiments; habits of neatness and patiently attending to details are acquired.

Disadvantages of heuristic method

1. This method is feasible only with a gifted teacher and a small class. Both these basic requisites are difficult to attain practically.
2. Suitable textbooks are not available.
3. It is very uneconomical in terms of time. The pressurised teacher will not be able to complete the syllabus in the given time.
4. The stress is more on skills than on knowledge. Hence, the heuristic method could lead to an imbalance in learning, as knowledge is of secondary consideration.
5. As a lot of experimentation is done, it implies that suitable infrastructure is needed to follow this method. Hence, it can prove costly.
6. It demands too much of our students. Not all students can cope with this kind of learning.
7. This method cannot be used for all classes.
8. Practical problems like time-tabling can creep in, making this method not quite suitable for the school.

Role of the teacher

The success of the heuristic method depends on the teacher.

1. Finding a suitable problem is the key to the success of the method. The teacher should keep in mind the age, ability and level of the student, along with the facilities available.
2. The teacher should act as a guide and instructor to the students, providing them with sufficient background information and help to get students going.
3. Detailed instruction sheets should be given to the students.
4. The teacher should help in developing values and attitudes consistent with science, by allowing freedom of thought and action.
5. Arrangement for supplementing the students' knowledge should be made by the teacher—be it library facilities or field trips.
6. A gifted teacher should help the students draw inferences from their experiments and observations.

CONCLUSION

The appropriate combination of teaching methods will lead to enhancement of learning in the school environment.

According to Dewey:

> The mind is not a piece of blotting paper that absorbs and retains automatically. It is rather a living organism that has to search for its food, that selects and rejects according to its present conditions and transmutes into parts of energy of its own being.

REFERENCES

Armstrong, Henry E. (2010), The Heuristic Method of Teaching, Wiley, New Jersey.

Bloom B. S., Engelhart M. D., Furst E. J., Hill W. H., and Krathwohl D. R. (1956), Taxonomy of educational objectives: The classification of educational goals, New York, NY: David McKay.

Brown, A.H., and Green, T.D., (2015), The essentials of instructional design: Connecting fundamental principles with process and practice, Routledge, UK.

Gage, N. and Berliner, D. (1992), *Educational Psychology,* 5th ed., Houghton Mifflin, Boston.

Gage, N.L. (1972), *Teacher Effectiveness and Teacher Education: The Search for a Scientific Basis*, Pacific Books, Palo Alto, CA.

Good, T.L. and Brophy, J.E. (2000), *Looking in Classrooms*, 8th ed., Longman, New York.

Henson, K.T. (1996), *Teachers as Researchers*, in Sikula, J. (Ed.) (1996), *Handbook of Research on Teacher Education,* 2nd ed., Macmillan, New York pp. 53–64.

Kilpatrick, W.H. (1918), *The Project Method*, Teachers College Record, Sage Publishing, California 19, 319–335.

McIver, D., Fitzsimmons, S., and Flanagan, D. (2016), A Knowledge-in-practice approach to choosing instructional methods, *Journal of Management Education,* Sage Publishing,California, Vol 40 Issue 1.

Myint Swe Khine (Editor), and Yang Liu (Editor), Handbook of Research on Teacher Education: Innovations and Practices in Asia, Springer, Singapore, 1st ed.

Nilson, L. (2016), Teaching at its best: A research-based resource for college instructors, John Wiley & Sons, Hoboken.

Snedden, David (1920), *Vocational Education,* Macmillan, New York.

Stevenson, J.A. (1921), *The Project Method of Teaching*, Macmillan, New York.

Web References

Britannica Online: http://www.britannica.com/EBchecked/topic/ 198415/Experience-and-Education.

Dewey, John (2010), Experience and Education, in Encyclopaedia Britannica, Retrieved November 10, 2010 from Encyclopaedia.

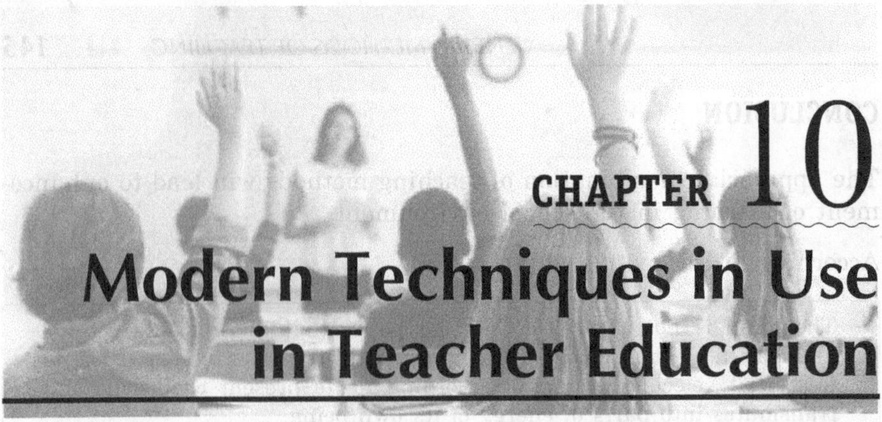

CHAPTER 10

Modern Techniques in Use in Teacher Education

More important than the curriculum is the question of the methods of teaching and the spirit in which the teaching is given.

—Bertrand Russell

INTRODUCTION

Teaching methods can be defined as ways of organising the learner's cognitive activity to ensure the acquisition of knowledge, skills and attitude necessary for allround growth in students. The proper use of modern techniques in education can make the process of instruction more effective. It helps the student acquire a better understanding of the phenomena he learns, by rousing a high degree of interest in him; It also relieves the teacher of purely mechanically lecturing all the time. The problem of improving teaching methods through the use of modern techniques is closely connected with curriculum development and teacher training. There are several techniques and strategies today which a teacher can use effectively to get the message through, besides facilitating development of other aspects of a student's growth.

DISCUSSION

Discussion method is defined as a learning experience in which students participate in a teacher-controlled, interactive process of sharing information and experiences related to achieving an instructional objective. —*Babylon online dictionary*

In the discussion method, as is true with any group learning effort, the teacher typically relies on the students to provide ideas, experiences, opinions, and information. A teacher may use this method during classroom periods, and after the students have gained some knowledge and experience. Fundamentally, the discussion method is almost the opposite of the lecture method. The teacher's goal is to draw out what the students know, rather than to spend the class period telling them. The teacher should remember that the more intense the discussion and the greater the participation, the more effective the learning. All members of the group should follow the discussion. The teacher should treat everyone impartially; encourage questions, exercise patience and tact, and comment on all responses. Sarcasm or ridicule should never be used, since it inhibits the spontaneity of the participants. In a guided discussion, the teacher acts as a facilitator to encourage discussion between students.

Planning a Guided Discussion

Planning a discussion is basically the same as planning a lecture. The teacher will find the following suggestions helpful in planning a discussion lesson.

1. **Select a topic the students can profitably discuss:** Unless the students have some knowledge to exchange with each other, they cannot reach the desired learning outcomes by the discussion method. If necessary, make assignments that will give the students an adequate background for discussing the lesson topic.
2. **Establish a specific lesson objective with desired learning outcomes:** Through discussion, the students develop an understanding of the subject by sharing knowledge, experiences, and backgrounds. Consequently, the objective normally is stated at the understanding level of learning.
3. **Conduct adequate research to become familiar with the topic:** While researching, the teacher should always be alert for ideas on the best way to tailor a lesson for a particular group of students. The teacher should also earmark reading material that appears to be especially appropriate as background material for students. Such material should be well organised and based on fundamentals.
4. **Organise the main and subordinate points of the lesson in a logical sequence:** The guided discussion has three main parts—introduction, discussion and conclusion. The introduction consists of three elements: **attention, motivation** and **overview**. In the discussion, the teacher should be certain that the main points discussed build logically with the objective. The conclusion consists of the summary, reactivation, and closure. By organising in this manner, the teacher phrases the questions to help the students obtain a firm grasp of the subject matter and to minimise the possibility of a rambling discussion.

5. **Plan at least one lead-off question for each desired learning outcome:** In preparing questions, the teacher should remember that the purpose is to stimulate discussion, not merely to get answers. The teacher should avoid questions that require only short categorical answers, such as yes or no. Lead-off questions should usually begin with how or why.

Use of Questions in a Guided Discussion

In the guided discussion, learning is achieved through the skillful use of questions. Questions can be categorised by **function** and by **characteristics.** Understanding these distinctions helps the teacher become a more skilled user of questions.

The teacher often uses a question to open up an area for discussion. This is the **lead-off question** and its function is indicated by its name. The purpose is to get the discussion started. After the discussion develops, the teacher may ask a **follow-up** question to guide the discussion. The reasons for using a follow-up question may vary. The teacher may want a student to explain something more thoroughly, or may need to bring the discussion back to a point from which it has strayed.

In terms of **characteristics,** questions can be identified as **overhead, rhetorical, direct, reverse,** and **relay**. The overhead question is directed to the entire group to stimulate the thought and response from each group member. The teacher may use an overhead question to pose the lead-off question. The rhetorical question is similar in nature, because it also spurs group thought. However, the teacher provides the answer to the rhetorical question. Consequently, it is more commonly used in lecturing than in a guided discussion.

Types

- **Overhead**—How/Why–Directed to the entire group
- **Rhetorical**—Spurs group thought
- **Direct**—Asked of a specific student
- **Reverse**—In response to a question, ask another question
- **Relay**—Relay the question to the group if asked by a student

Effective Questions

- Select a suitable subject.
- Establish the objective.
- Research the subject.
- Organise the main and subordinate points logically.
- Plan a lead-off question for each desired outcome.
- Guide students in their preparation.

Structure of Guided Discussion

The teacher must have a set of goals and/or ideas that she wants to convey to the student.

1. **Introduction:** This should be something that poses a question or narrates a current event to help get the discussion off the ground.
2. **Discussion:** The teacher should keep the discussion confined to the topic. She should listen attentively and try to continually evaluate the knowledge of the student
3. **Summary:** The teacher should summarise each section before moving on.
4. **Conclusion:** The teacher should take a couple of minutes to review and recap what was covered in the discussion. This will help the student grasp the "larger picture". The teacher should also clarify any questions.

Objectives of Discussion Method

The objectives of using discussion as a method of teaching science are to:

1. Share information.
2. Clarify ideas.
3. Inspire interest.
4. Evaluate progress.
5. Develop self-confidence in expressing views.
6. Develop tolerance to views different from one's own.

Student Preparation for a Guided Discussion

It is the teacher's responsibility to help students prepare themselves for the discussion. Each student should be encouraged to accept responsibility for contributing to the discussion and benefiting from it. Throughout the time the teacher prepares the students for their discussion, they should be made aware of the lesson objective. In certain instances, the teacher has no opportunity to assign preliminary work and must face the students straight away for the first time. In such cases, it is practical and advisable to give the students a brief general survey of the topic during the introduction. Normally, students should not be asked to discuss a subject without some background in that subject.

Guiding a Discussion—Teacher Technique

The techniques used to guide a discussion require practice and experience. The teacher needs to keep up with the discussion and know where to intervene with questions or redirect the group's focus. The following information provides a framework for successfully conducting the guided discussion.

Introduction

A guided discussion lesson is introduced in the same manner as the lecture. The introduction should include an attention element, a motivation element, and an overview of the key points. To encourage enthusiasm and stimulate discussion, the teacher should create a relaxed, informal atmosphere. Each student should be given the opportunity to discuss the various aspects of the subject, and feel free to do so. Moreover, the student should feel a personal responsibility to contribute. The teacher should try to make the students feel that their ideas and active participation are wanted and needed.

Discussion

The teacher opens the discussion by asking one of the prepared lead-off questions. After asking a question, the teacher should be patient. The students should be given a chance to react. The teacher should have the answer in mind before asking the question, but the students have to think about the question before answering.

The more difficult the question, the more time the students will need to produce an answer. Sometimes, students do not understand the question. Whenever the teacher sees puzzled expressions, the question should be rephrased in a slightly different form. The nature of the questions should be determined by the lesson objective and desired learning outcomes.

Once the discussion is underway, the teacher should listen attentively to the ideas, experiences, and examples contributed by the students during the discussion. As the discussion proceeds, the teacher may find it necessary to guide the direction, to stimulate the students to explore the subject in greater depth, or to encourage them to discuss the topic in more detail. By using how and why follow-up questions, the teacher should be able to guide the discussion towards the objective of helping students understand the subject.

When it appears the students have discussed the ideas that support this particular part of the lesson, the teacher should summarise what the students have accomplished. This will summarise the ideas developed by the group and show how they relate to, and support, the idea discussed. An interim summary reinforces learning in relation to a specific learning outcome. In addition to its uses as a summary and transitional device, the interim summary may also be used to keep the group on the subject or to divert the discussion to another member.

Advantages of Discussion Method

Guided discussion is a non-hierarchical verbal interaction among a group of persons on a specified topic with a purpose. There are several benefits to the discussion method as a technique in this course.

1. Provides an active learning role. Research shows that students learn more and retain learned information longer when their role in the learning process is active.
2. Encourages students to listen to and learn from each other. Discussion encourages *cooperative learning* rather than *competitive learning*.
3. Involves high level thinking, critical thinking skills
4. Exposes students to viewpoints other than their own.
5. Helps develop oral advocacy and other skills.
6. Provides an opportunity for students to bring their opinions and feelings to the study of the topic in science.

A guided discussion is closed by summarising the material covered. In the conclusion, the teacher should tie together the various points or topics discussed, and show the relationships between the facts brought forth and the practical application of these facts.

PANEL DISCUSSION

The panel discussion technique was introduced by Harry A. Overstreet in 1927. It is a discussion in which a few persons (the panel) carry on a conversation in front of the audience. At the end of the discussion, the audience puts important questions to the experts who answer them.

A panel discussion is designed to provide an opportunity for a group to hear several people knowledgeable about a specific issue or topic present information and discuss personal views. A panel discussion may help the audience further clarify and evaluate their positions regarding specific issues or topics being discussed and increase their understanding of the positions of others.

Definitions of panel discussion on the Web

- Discussion of a subject of public interest by a group of persons forming a panel usually before an audience.
  wordnetweb.princeton.edu/perl/webwn
- Instructional technique using a group of people chosen to discuss a topic in the presence of an audience.
- A structured conversation on a given topic among several people in front of an audience.

Objectives of Panel Discussion

The objectives of the panel discussion are to:

1. Provide information and new facts.
2. Analyse a problem from different angles.
3. Identify the values involved.
4. Give an opportunity to interact with experts in the field.

Guidelines for Conducting a Panel Discussion

The guidelines for conducting a panel discussion are as follows:

1. **Identify**, or help participants identify, **an issue or topic** that involves an important conflict in values and/or interests. The issue or topic may be set forth as a topical question, a hypothetical incident, a student experience or an actual case.
2. **Select panelists** who are well informed about and have specific points of view regarding the issue or topic. A panel discussion that includes three to five panelists is usually most workable. Select a **leader** or **moderator**.
3. **Specify the objectives** to panelists of the panel. The discussion is designed to promote and allow time for panel members to prepare for the discussion. In some situations, ten or fifteen minutes may be sufficient time for preparation while in other situations, panel members may need to prepare several weeks in advance of the scheduled discussion.
4. **Decide upon the format** the panel discussion will follow:
   (i) The leader or moderator introduces the topic and the panelists present their views and opinions regarding the issue or topic for a set amount of time.
   (ii) The panelists discuss the issue or topic with each other by asking questions or reacting to the views and opinions of other panel members. A specific amount of time should be established.
   (iii) The leader or moderator closes the discussion and provides a summary of panel presentations and discussion.
   (iv) The leader or moderator calls for a forum period during which the members of the class may participate by addressing questions to various panel members or by voicing their views and opinions. The forum period should be conducted by the panel leader or moderator.

Principal Responsibilities of the Teacher

1. Identify, or help participants identify, issues or topics upon which to base a panel discussion.

2. Ensure that all panelists and the moderator are familiar with the procedures for panel discussion in advance of the discussion itself so that they will be able to fulfil the responsibilities of their roles.
3. Assist panelists and participants (when necessary) in preparation for the discussion by directing them to various source materials, authorities in the field, etc.
4. Help participants understand the need for fair procedures in discussing an issue or topic.

Advantages of Panel Discussion

The advantages of the panel discussion are as follows:

1. Encourages social learning.
2. Develops higher cognitive and affective objectives.
3. Develops the ability of problem solving and logical thinking.
4. Develops tolerance of views other than one's own.
5. Provides opportunities of assimilation of theme and content of discussion.
6. Helps understand the nature, problem or theme of discussion.
7. Develops the ability of presentation of theme and giving logical explanations.
8. Develops creative thinking.
9. Helps acquire manners in posing questions and answering them.

Limitations of Panel Discussion

The limitations of the panel discussion are as follows:

1. There are chances of deviation from the topic under discussion.
2. Some members may dominate.
3. The panelists may split the audience for and against unless the moderator calls the shots.

SEMINAR

Seminar is generally a form of academic instruction, either at a university or offered by a commercial or professional organisation.

Seminar has the function of bringing together small groups for recurring meetings, focusing each time on some particular subject, in which everyone present is requested to actively participate. This is often accomplished through an ongoing Socratic dialogue with a teacher, or through a more formal presentation of research. The idea behind the seminar system is to familiarise students more extensively with the methodology of their chosen subject and also to allow them to interact with examples of the practical aspects of the problems. It is essentially a place where assigned readings are discussed, questions can be raised and debates conducted.

Seminars dealing with "special topics" have actually been around for decades, and are an older form of information exchanges that have seen quite a resurgence of interest in the past ten years.

Seminars are simply a group of people coming together for the discussion and learning of specific techniques and topics. Usually, there are several keynote speakers within each seminar, and these speakers are usually experts in their own fields, or topics.

Advantages of Seminar

The advantages of the seminar are as follows:

1. A wealth of knowledge, usually presented by many speakers at one time in one place. It is a time saver for teachers. The syllabus can be covered on time.
2. A sense of camaraderie, where students can meet others with the same interests/problems/concerns that they may have in their chosen field. It encourages social learning. A great way for students who do not like to read, or attend classes, to improve their knowledge of a specific subject.
3. A seminar helps develop tolerance of views other than one's own.
4. It helps develop higher cognitive and affective objectives.
5. A seminar develops ability of problem solving and logical thinking.

Disadvantages of Seminar

The disadvantages of the seminar are as follows:

1. There is a chance that the speakers may be sharing incorrect knowledge, or not at all knowledgeable themselves. Careful thought is needed here.
2. There is a chance that the topics may not actively help understanding of the topic and that the seminar will be a waste of time, where nothing learnt is of any use to the students.
3. There is a chance that students will expect too much from a seminar and thus be disappointed.

Overall, seminars, if chosen carefully, can be a good experience.

SYMPOSIUM

The word **"Symposium"** originally referred to a drinking party (the Greek verb *sympotein* means "to drink together"), but has since come to refer to any academic conference, or a style of university class.

A symposium is a meeting or conference for discussion of a topic, especially one in which the participants form an audience and make presentations. —*The Free online dictionary*

"We think of a symposium as a group of comments, either spoken or written, which portrays contrasting or at least different points of view."

—*Struck*

The **symposium**, among the newer techniques in high school teaching, deserves a place in science teaching. In the past, it has been closely associated with the adult education field and with meetings and conferences of various kinds. The symposium method, however, possesses many interesting possibilities also for the high-school classroom, the school assembly, school clubs and organisations, and other extra classroom activities.

In many classrooms, however, the majority of students in the regular learning procedures are passive. Students are generally content to let the responsibility of the mental work rest on the teacher.

Advantages of Symposium Method

The advantages of the symposium method are as follows:

1. A symposium provides students greater opportunity for self-expression.
2. It develops creative thinking.
3. It helps develop greater self-confidence and good communication skills.
4. It shifts the focus from "passive" learning to "active" learning.

In a symposium, the participants present to the audience through speeches or paper reading their views about various aspects of a selected problem or topic.

Disadvantages of the Symposium Method

1. The students may be so used to "passive" learning that this method may prove beyond their capabilities. The symposium method may, in that case, be a waste of time.
2. The chosen topics may not actively help understanding of the topic.

3. There is a chance that students will expect too much from a symposium and thus be disappointed.

TEAM TEACHING

Team teaching is an arrangement whereby two or more teachers cooperatively plan, teach and evaluate one or more class groups in appropriate and agreed upon teaching plan and in given length of time so as to take advantage of specific competencies of the team members.

—*Singer, Ira J.* (1964)

Definition of team teaching on the Web:

- A method of coordinated classroom teaching involving a team of teachers working together with a single group of students.
wordnetweb.princeton.edu/perl/webwn
- A teaching method in which two or more teachers teach the same subjects or theme. The teachers may alternate teaching the entire group or divide ...

Team teaching is traditionally thought of as when more than one teacher is involved in instruction within a classroom. There are a few different models of team teaching, and more than one model may be carried out within one class period.

Significance of Team Teaching

Higher expectations are placed on students and teachers of the 21st century than ever before. Different studies have been conducted that address different teaching methods for helping students meet these expectations. Team teaching is just one of the methods that has been explored.

Types of Team Teaching

Traditional team teaching is a model in which two teachers within a classroom take equal responsibility for teaching the students and are actively involved at all times. One may be teaching while the other may be writing notes on the board.

Supportive instruction is a second model of team teaching in which one teacher teaches the material and the other provides follow-up activities.

Parallel instruction is a form of team teaching in which students are split into two groups and each teacher is responsible for teaching her group.

Differentiated split class team teaching involves splitting students into two groups based on achievement. One teacher provides remedial instruction to students who are struggling on a skill while the other provides enrichment to those who have grasped the skill.

The monitoring teacher is another form of team teaching. In this model, one teacher assumes the role of instruction while the other walks around the class and monitors students' behaviour and progress. Different types of team teaching may be used within one class period.

Effects of Team Teaching

When team teaching is organised and carried out effectively, positive effects are felt by students, parents and school faculty. Research shows that students taught using a team teaching approach have higher levels of achievement. There is also more contact with parents by teachers in a team teaching situation. Additionally, schools that employ team teaching have teachers who are more satisfied with their job, resulting in an improved work climate.

Points to Consider When Implementing Team Teaching

The following points should be considered while implementing team teaching:

1. Are the teachers involved open to trying new methods of instruction?
2. Are the teachers involved open-minded, optimistic people?
3. Are the teachers involved resourceful, flexible, and able and willing to communicate effectively?
4. Are the team members honest, trustworthy, respectful people who will not be offended by constructive criticism?

Teachers involved in team teaching need to:

1. Define what team teaching will look like in their classroom before implementing this model of instruction.
2. Include everything from goals and responsibilities to planning time.

Disadvantages of Team Teaching

The disadvantages of team teaching are as follows:

1. Lack of a unified definition or vision for team teaching could result in confusion by all involved, including the students.
2. An inconsistent classroom environment in which students play one teacher against the other.

Benefits for teachers

- Improved teaching and learning
- Less correction
- Less stress as the portions are divided
- More support from team members
- Greater sense of achievement
- Opportunity to learn new methodologies
- Less time spent on maintaining discipline

Benefits for students

- Better teaching and learning
- Improved participation, self-esteem, group dynamics, written work
- Fewer distractions due to improved discipline
- Improved attendance
- Better teacher/student relationships

Criteria for Successful Use of Team Teaching

1. Students should communicate regularly and faithfully with the team teacher.
2. Students and team teachers should follow all rules on the syllabus concerning attendance, deadlines, make-ups, etc.
3. Students should attend all meetings called by the team teachers.
4. Students should participate actively and contribute to course meeting discussions.
5. Students should submit all requested material for exams and quizzes on time.
6. All corrections should be done on time and returned to students on time.
7. Good rapport should be developed between team teachers.

INDIVIDUALISED INSTRUCTION

Schools exist not to cram facts into the students heads, but rather to help them acquire learning for themselves ...

—Niles

For instruction to be considered individualised, the instruction is usually designed to account for specific learner characteristics. This could include alternative instructional methods for students with different backgrounds and learning styles. The instructional method used can be considered in terms of extremes. In the first extreme, one instructional method is used for everyone. There are two basic extremes when the pace of instruction, content and method is considered. The first is when someone other than student, usually a teacher or instructor, controls the pace, content and the method. In this case, specific due dates are defined before instruction begins. This is currently the predominant model in most educational systems. The opposite extreme would be if the learner had exclusive control over the pace of instruction, without a time limit. Between these two extremes are situations where control of the pace of instruction is shared or negotiated, not necessarily equally, by the teacher and the learner.

Definitions of Individualised Instruction

The following definitions of individualised instruction are available on the Web:

"Instruction of a student based on his or her unique learning style."

"One of the key tenets of special education. The specific instruction and types of services provided to the student is tailored to fit the student and wholly depends on the educational needs of the student."

"Curriculum content and instructional materials, media, and activities designed for individual learning. The pace, interests, and abilities of the learner determine the curriculum."

All of these are accurate. But none of them is an adequate definition of individualised instruction.

Individualised instruction is a method of instruction in which content, instructional materials, instructional media, and pace of learning are based upon the abilities and interests of each individual learner.

> Individualised instruction is that tailored to the needs of individual students and situations characterised by such features as clear objectives or outcome specification; detailed repertoire assessment of the student; active responding or frequent monitoring of student responses; ... immediate and frequent feedback; use of successive approximations; self paced learning; mastery learning ...
>
> — *International Dictionary of Education*

> Individualized learning, or individualized instruction, is a method of teaching in which content, instructional technology, and pace of learning are based upon the abilities and interest of each learner.
>
> http://www.dreambox.com/individualized-learning

This definition clearly indicates that individualised instruction is more than a method of teaching; it is a philosophy of education. It is an arrangement which makes it possible at all times to provide the most appropriate education for the learner, since it adjusts the education of the individual to cater to his or her specific needs or special circumstances. Individualised instruction is the accommodation of instruction to the abilities, goals, pace of learning of each student. This method of teaching places the responsibility of learning on the students, which results in improved motivation for learning.

Each approach to individualised instruction is different, but they all seek to manipulate the following three fundamental variables:

1. **Pace:** The amount of time given to a student to learn the content
2. **Method:** The way the instruction is structured and managed
3. **Content:** The material to be learned

Need for Individualised Instruction

Individualised instruction is a method which has an enormous potential in a country like India, where mass educational techniques have not been overly successful.

1. This method allows a student to proceed at his own pace, depending on his aptitude and past history of achievement.
2. Individualised instruction caters to the individual differences. Thus, slow, medium and gifted students can be placed on different but suitable programmes based on their unique needs and abilities.
3. Individualised instruction helps an individual to develop his potential to the full.
4. The feedback provided at regular intervals helps the students gain mastery over the unit under study.
5. This method is ideal for remedial purposes as it can, by drill and practice or by tutorial, identify the weak areas of the student and provide appropriate learning experiences to suit him.

Characteristics of Individualised Instruction

The general characteristics of individualised instruction have been listed below:

1. It allows the system/teacher to manoeuvre teaching methodology according to the particular level and understanding, learning style and ability of each individual student.
2. It is self-paced.

3. The material to be taught must be broken down into smaller chunks. Extensive design effort is needed to create each chunk, i.e. module.
4. The skills required to use this method are different from traditional teaching skills.
5. It can be used as a reinforcement tool, for remedial purposes as well as for distance learning.

PROGRAMMED INSTRUCTION (PI)

Programmed instruction has a long past but only a short history. The contributors in developing this method are as follows:

1. **Socrates:** Socrates was one of the earliest programmers who developed a programme in Geometry. This was recorded by Plato.
2. **S.L. Pressey:** In Ohio University, S.L. Pressey (1926–27) was first to devise a machine which could teach as well as test.
3. **B.F. Skinner:** Programmed learning got historical momentum only after the publication of Skinner's paper "The Silence of Learning and the Art of Teaching" in 1954.
4. **Co-workers of Skinner:** The associates and co-workers of Prof. Skinner gave a movement for programmed instruction by publishing a number of papers on its various aspects based mainly on laboratory experimental observations.

Definition

Programmed instruction is a method of instruction in which the information to be taught is broken down into small units which are to be presented to the student (usually in written form) in a carefully planned sequence. Each unit or 'frame' contains not only conformation but is also terminated with a question. *—Michael J. Apter (1974)*

Programmed instruction is the process of arranging the material to be learned into a series of sequential steps. Usually it moves the student from a familiar background into a complex set of concepts, principles and understanding. *—Smith and Moore*

Programmed instruction is systematic, step by step, self-instructional program aimed to ensure the learning of stated behaviour.

—Edgar Dale

Programmed instruction is instruction through information given in small steps with each requiring a correct response by the learner before going on to the next step.

—Merriam Webster's Online Dictionary

Programmed instruction is the name of the technology invented by the behaviourist B.F. Skinner to improve teaching. It was based on his theory of Verbal Behaviour as a means to accelerate and increase conventional educational learning.

—*Wikipedia, the free encyclopedia*

Programmed instruction typically consists of self-teaching with the aid of a specialised textbook or **teaching machine** that presents material structured in a logical and empirically developed sequence or sequences. Programmed instruction may be presented by a teacher as well, and it has been argued that the principles of programmed instruction can improve lectures and textbooks. It allows students to progress through a unit of study at their own rate, checking their own answers and advancing only after answering correctly. In one simplified form of PI, after each step, they are presented with a question to test their comprehension, then are immediately shown the correct answer or given additional information. However, the objective of instructional programming is to present the material in very small increments.

This idea was later adapted by Robert M. Gagné, who adapted programmed learning for use in teaching in schools. *The difference between programmed instruction (PI) and programmed learning (PL) is that PI is intended to modify behaviour, whereas PL is used for teaching facts and skills.*

Essential Characteristics of Programmed Instruction

The essential characteristics of programmed instruction are as follows:

1. **A logical sequence of small steps:** Students are led through a presentation of small amounts of information sequentially arranged to progressively approximate the final complex behaviour. Thus, a programme consists of a series of steps or frames (**pieces of information + a question = stimulus**), e.g. to learn how to find refractive index of materials, the student would first learn to compute sine functions.
2. **Active response:** The student is asked to operate on the information in an appropriate way. Typically, the student must complete a sentence with the appropriate word, or answer a question.
3. **Immediate feedback:** The student is reinforced by being given the correct answer as soon as the response is completed.
4. **Individual rate:** Each learner is allowed to progress through the sequence at his/her own rate, providing for individual differences.
5. **Objectives:** The sequence of logical steps does not exist in a vacuum. These steps are all carefully designed to lead to predefined goals or objectives.

6. **Mastery of each step:** Progress in programmed instruction depends on the success at each step, mastery of each piece of information.

   In order to make sure that the student masters the step, the programme should be made up of:

   (a) Appropriate sized steps
   (b) Branched or cues (provided wherever necessary)
   (c) Thoroughly trial tested programmes.
7. **Motivation:** The object of programmed instruction is to maximise the desire to learn. This is achieved in part, by knowledge of results, feedback, which encourages the student.
8. **Testing:** Testing of the programme is necessary at every stage. This may be in the form of revisions, summaries, subtests and postests.

Thus, while learning in a programmed learning method, a student is

- Presented with a small amount of information (stimulus).
- Encouraged to answer a question based on the information (response).
- Given the correct answer on the basis of her response (feedback).

The basic features of programmed instruction are:

1. The student works at her own pace through a series of logical steps.
2. All these steps lead to predefined objectives.
3. Each step is actively responded and mastered.
4. The student receives the feedback which motivates her to continue.
5. The programme is thoroughly tested before it is in a written form.

Fundamental Principles of Programmed Learning

The following are fundamental principles of programmed learning:

1. Principle of small steps
2. Principle of active responding
3. Principle of immediate confirmation
4. Principle of self-pacing
5. Principle of evaluation

Principles for Developing Programmed Learning Material (PLM)

The principles for developing PML are as follows:

1. Determining the objectives
2. Choosing the content
3. Choosing a suitable programming model
4. Designing the program
5. Writing the individual frames

Styles of Programming

The three conventional styles of programming are:

1. Linear programming
2. Branched programming
3. Adaptive

Linear or extrinsic programming

The linear style of programming was developed by Skinner and his associates (1954). This is also known as the *Skinnerian style of programming*. The techniques associated with this style of programming are based on the principle that the learner's original response should be gradually altered or shaped until she meets some standard of acceptable performance.

Basic assumptions of linear programming

1. Active response
2. Small units of information
3. Immediate reinforcement to response
4. Logical arrangement of contents
5. Freedom to respond
6. Hindrance by errors

Features of linear programming

1. Linear arrangement of frames
2. Small steps of information
3. Controlled responses to questions
4. Response is emphasised
5. Structural responses to stimulus
6. Active responding
7. Immediate feedback to response
8. Prompting cues to help respond
9. Self-pacing catering to individual differences
10. Minimum errors emphasised
11. Best suited for certain topics of science like radioactivity and atomic structure.

Example of Linear Programmed Instruction

Frame 1

1. Stimuli
   (a) bit of information question based on the bit of information
2. Response space for response—a completion type of question
3. Cues

Frame 2

1. Correct answer to Frame 1
2. Information

3. Stimulus
4. Response
5. Cues

Frame 3

6. Correct answer to Frame 2
7. Information
8. Stimulus
9. Response
10. Cues

Applications of linear programming: Linear programmes have effectively been used in the following situations:

1. Children in the primary sections
2. Slow learners in science
3. Homogenous classrooms
4. Hierarchical order of subject
5. Immediate feedback to response
6. Difficult study material broken into small manageable steps of information
8. Specific terminology in topic, like definitions, formulae
9. Less motivated teachers who need a helping hand to cope
10. Remedial instruction and self-study of students lagging behind
11. Complete mastery of the topic under consideration

Limitations of linear programming

1. Lack of motivation of students due to monotonous nature of programme
2. No freedom of choice, due to frames following one after the other
3. No development of discriminative power, as choice is limited
4. Serial order learning
5. Not student-centered
6. No specified role of teacher except to monitor the students moving from frame to frame

Branched programming

The branching or intrinsic style (method) of programming was originated by Norman A. Crowder. He defined branched programming as a programme which adapts to the needs of the student without the medium of an extrinsic device such as computer.

Branched programme may be produced for use on a teaching machine or in a book form. The book form is known as a *scrambled text* because the pages do not follow in a normal sequence.

Principles of branched programme

1. Principle of exposition
2. Principle of diagnosis
3. Principle of remediation

Requirements of branched programme: There are two requirements in this type of programming.

- There must be two or more choices of response for each question.
- The incorrect response should result in directing the student to information which will help remedy the error and guide him back to the main stream of the programme.

Types in branch programming

1. *Backward branching:* It is based on the principle of 'repeating the missed frames'. As shown in Figure 10.1, the learner from Frame No. 1 of the main stream goes to Frame No. 2 of the main stream only if he makes a correct choice. But if he makes a wrong choice, he is led to remedial frame wherein he is given some more help in understanding the concept and in solving the solution by a better logic. He will be then directed to the original Frame No. 1 so that he can read it again and answer it correctly in the light of the remedial material he has received. So, the learner who has committed error goes through the same frame twice (once before the remedial material and once after the remedial material).

2. *Forward branching:* In the forward branching, whether the learner makes a wrong choice, or correct choice he will always be going to new pages, thus physically progressing from page to page.

Example of branched programmed instruction: In branched programmed instruction, a single question, usually of multiple choice type, is asked. If the student answers correctly, she is taken to the next frame in the main teaching sequence. If her answer is wrong, she is taken to a remedial frame where her mistake is analysed and the topic under discussion is further explained with other examples. After this, she is led back to the original frame to check her learning. According to the alternatives selected, the student will be directed to go to a particular frame. Thus, branched programming is useful for remedial teaching.

The main frames (F1, F2 ... in Figure 10.1) is the content frame of the teaching sequence.

A **content frame** will have the following features:

1. Repeating students' response
2. Positive confirmation
3. New information
4. Question
5. Alternatives (A, B, C and D)

The **remedial frame** will have the following features:

1. Repeating the students' response
2. Negative confirmation

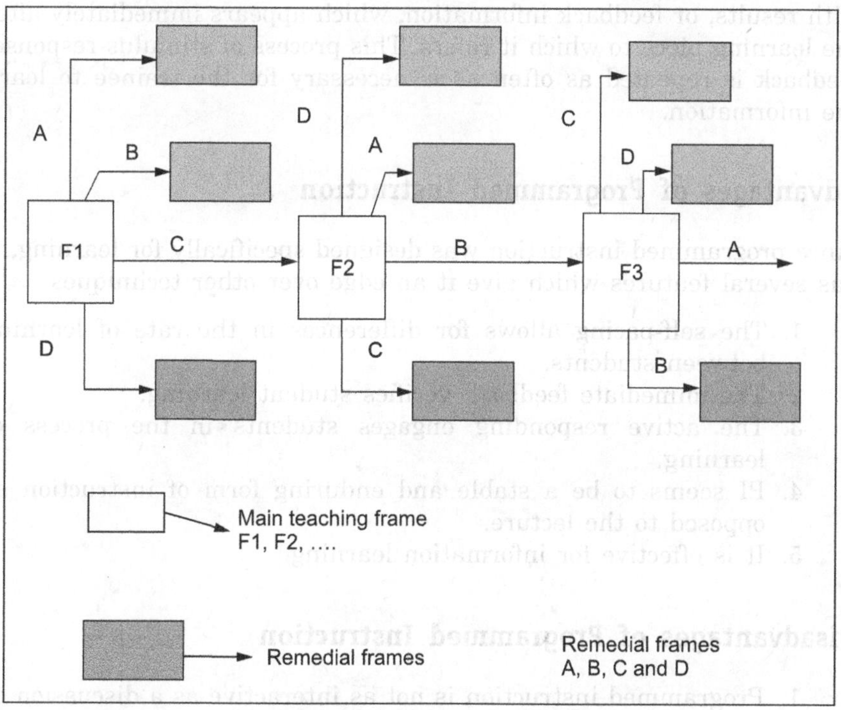

FIGURE 10.1 An example of branched programming.

3. Reasons as to why the answer is wrong
4. Simple explanations to correct misconceptions
5. Directions on how to proceed, for example go to page 3.

When the frames of a branched pragramme are presented in a book form, the book is known as a *scrambled book*. Here, the alternatives are scrambled across the book, which is why the book cannot be read sequentially.

Adaptive programming

Gordon Pask, a British Electronics Engineer, developed a form of programming known as *adaptive programming*. This form of programming makes allowances for mere variations in students' ability. These programmes can only be presented in teaching 'machines' which "adapt" to the students, hence the name.

Evidently, the three forms of programmed instruction differ, yet they are all, to some degree, based on a theory of stimulus-response-feedback.

The "stimulus" is a limited item of information plus a related question. When the student has read the information and the question, he is called on to reply or "respond". Following this, he is presented with results, or feedback information, which appears immediately after the learning piece to which it refers. This process of stimulus-response-feedback is repeated as often as is necessary for the trainee to learn the information.

Advantages of Programmed Instruction

Since programmed instruction was designed specifically for learning, it has several features which give it an edge over other techniques.

1. The self-pacing allows for differences in the rate of learning between students.
2. The immediate feedback verifies student learning.
3. The active responding engages students in the process of learning.
4. PI seems to be a stable and enduring form of instruction as opposed to the lecture.
5. It is effective for information learning.

Disadvantages of Programmed Instruction

1. Programmed instruction is not as interactive as a discussion or computer assisted instruction.
2. The student cannot alter the scope or sequence of learning.
3. Programmes, which are generally limited to requesting students to filling in missing words, can prove monotonous.
4. It can, especially branched programming, can prove extremely expensive.

COMPUTER-ASSISTED INSTRUCTION (CAI)

Computer-assisted instruction (CAI) is a narrow term and most often refers to drill-and-practice, tutorial, or simulation activities offered either by themselves or as supplements to traditional, teacher-directed instruction. This clearly indicates that computers can be useful in *individualising instruction*, as they can be geared to cater to individual needs of students. Computers, with their large memory, ability to diagnose students' level of mastery and capability of providing varied learning sequences, have considerable potential for individualisation of instruction in terms of students' different abilities and pre-existing knowledge.

Definitions of CAI

CAI is a programme of instructional material presented by means of a computer or computer systems.

—*Britannica Online Encyclopedia*

Computer Assisted Instruction (CAI) is the teaching process in which a computer is used to enhance the education of a student.

—*Glossary of Distance Education and Internet Terminology*

Use of a computer to assist in the presentation of instructional materials to a student, to monitor learning progress, or to select additional instructional material in accordance with the needs of individualised learners.

—*International Dictionary of Education (1985)*

Instruction in which a computer is used to present substantial amounts of learning material to the student; it often represents an auto, instructional technique enabling students to progress at their own individual rates.

—*The Concise Dictionary of Education (1982)*

Modes of CAI

The various ways in which CAI can be used are called **modes.** The common modes of CAI are as follows:

1. *Drill and practice mode* is a method of learning on the computer where the student becomes familiar with the use of a procedure by repetition, until it is invariably performed correctly. The control of the situation rests with the computer, for example solving problems related to Newton's laws after a class where the teacher explained the laws.
2. *Tutorial mode* is a type of CAI in which the computer interacts with the learner in a similar manner as to a tutor, engaging in a dialogue whose course depends on the responses made by the learner, for instance pre-laboratory session on titration before actual laboratory work in this mode may be useful.
3. *Simulation* deals with the representation of physical systems and phenomena by the computer. Information is entered in the computer to represent the factors in the real process and computer produces the information that represents the results of the process and the process itself, for example demonstrating the phenomenon of radioactivity on the computer screen.
4. In *Modelling mode*, computer programmes can be used to build complex mathematical models and explore them quantitatively, rapidly and in detail. Modelling is a rehearsal for reality, a way of making a trial that minimises the penalties of error.
5. *Problem-solving mode* enables a student to tackle a wide variety of problems and helps in developing problem-solving skills.
6. *Gaming mode* is resorted to when the student is pitted either against the computer or another student in an educational game. This is best suited for teaching rules and procedures.

Choice of mode is an important guide. The choice of mode of CAI lies in the objectives set out for the learning situation. The learning situation, in turn, is dependent on the content of instruction and learning activity.

Advantages of CAI

The research evidence suggests that CAI can improve student performance, particularly if used in combination with the other techniques.

1. The graphic capability of computers allows students to use the simulation mode to their advantage. Immediate feedback helps students verify their learning.
2. Self-pacing is possible if the tutorial mode is used.
3. Computers are absolutely impartial.
4. Higher cognitive abilities are achievable with the right mode.
5. Students can improve their writing skills using the computer and internet by blogging using BLOGGER and WORDPRESS.
6. The use of computers in the classroom has helped many students learn how to write well composed sentences and paragraphs using BUSUU APP.
7. CAI is instructor independent and is consistent, well structured and thorough.
8. CAI can be used effectively for remedial instruction, as computers are infinitely patient.
9. CAI is beneficial for distance-learning and continuing education programmes.

Disadvantages of CAI

1. There is a lack of the personal touch if the entire course is taught using CAI.
2. It is not always possible for a programmer to respond sensibly to unexpected inputs.
3. Computer-phobic students may not take easily to this mode of teaching.
4. It is difficult to get suitable software for the requirements of Indian schools.
5. Teachers competent in computer usage are not easily available.
6. It can result in teachers resorting to CAI instead of using the traditional methods as an easy way out.
7. Cost may be an important factor of consideration for the school as using the computer for all classes can be prohibitively high.
8. It does not promote communication skills as effectively as a traditional classroom would.

Selected Methods Used in the Classroom

- **Flipped Classroom**
  A flipped classroom is a type of blended learning where students first learn about the subject on their own, and practice working through it in the classroom, through collaborative projects to resolve questions. This method helps students have an active role and develop more autonomy in their learning. It also enables the teacher to teach through videoconferencing or WhatsApp group to clarify doubts. Students develop self-reliance and self-direction through this method.
- **Tactile Learning/kinesthetics learning**
  Tactile learning can take place at home or in the classroom with the teacher demonstrating an activity and learners practicing simultaneously from their locations. It is best suited for skill learning and lab activities. With immediate feedback, learners are prevented from learning a wrong technique.
- **VAK Learning (visual, auditory, and kinesthetic)**
  This enables different types of learners to maximise their learning using their strengths. Thus, visual learners take in information better when they view the content, whereas auditory learners respond to listening podcasts, videos) and Kinesthetic act out the content.
- **Game-Based Learning**
  Game-based learning is pretty much what the term describes–using games as part of the instruction process. Games have an element of active learning and are particularly engaging as they are a sort of "distraction" from typical learning. The online, group, or role-playing games can all be part of the syllabus. Games automatically make the learning environment entertaining, and learning becomes an adventure.

NEW TECHNOLOGY TO PROMOTE LEARNING

The effective use of technology in education has transformed the learning experience. Students now have access to a wide range of opportunities. Technology facilitates students learning to collaborate, share, learn new skills besides developing digital citizenship skills.

- **Amazon Kindle**
  This is a tablet which uses an electronic ink screen. Students can buy electronic books and read them on Kindle. The choice of books is amazing and the reading habit can be inculcated in both teachers and students.

- **Smart Boards**
  This interactive whiteboard is being used extensively in classrooms. Used with discretion, the Smartboard can prove to be an invaluable source of learning experiences for both the teacher and the student.
- **Wifi smart pen—LiveScribe Echo 8GB**
  This wifi smart pen records sound, wirelessly synchronizes notes and audio to an Evernote account which can be later organized and shared.
- **Smart Phones-mobile technology**
  Students and teachers can use this easy-to-use light phone to download and listen to audio lessons, educational apps and watch live streaming of Youtube and TeachersTube educational videos.
- **Virtual technology**
  Use of tools like SKYPE enables easy communication of students with their remote teachers. Online education makes access to study material easy.
- **Web 2.0 Tools**
  This provides a digital way of creating, collaborating, editing and sharing content online. Students and teachers can interact easily by mastering the different tools of Web 2.0.

SUPERVISED STUDY

The need for supervised study is much higher in the Indian context, with overcrowded classrooms and a tight, heavy curriculum. The classes generally comprise heterogeneous groups with bright, average and below average students in each class. It is, thus, impossible for a teacher to cater to individual differences. This situation can be remedied by supervised study.

Need for Supervised Study

Supervised study allows student to study in the classroom under the direction of the teacher. The classroom has some advantages for study because it is an environment relatively free from distractions, equipment and resources are available, and the teacher is on hand to answer questions and work individually with students. Many students have poor study habits and have no idea about how to extract information from a variety of sources to draw inferences or solve problems. Group supervised study sessions give the teacher an opportunity to foster good study habits, to deal with study problems, and to relate to students as individuals.

Teacher's role in providing the Study Environment

To conduct an effective group study session, then, the teacher should—

- Take responsibility for maintaining a pleasant, businesslike study environment.
- Help students formulate questions to direct their study.
- Help students set objectives for the study session.
- Locate and select resources in advance which students can use in their study.
- Recommend resources to students suitable to their level of ability and understanding.
- Direct students to resources which they might not otherwise find or might have difficulty finding.
- Help students find pertinent information in the resource materials.
- Control environmental conditions such as lighting, temperature, ventilation, and noise, so that students are free from distractions.
- Maintain an orderly, businesslike study setting.
- Move quietly and inconspicuously about the room giving individual help.
- Provide students with feedback during the study session to let them know whether they are progressing in the right direction.
- Hold a discussion to summarise what was achieved during the session.

Individual Attention

Group supervised study provides an opportunity for the teacher to get to know another aspect of student behaviour. It enables the teacher to become more knowledgeable about each student's interests, abilities, and personal characteristics. Students learn to relate to the teacher as a helper and a friend. If a student has a genuine study problem, the teacher should probe deeper into the cause of the problem and try to help the student overcome it.

Supervised Study as Supplementary Individual Instruction

Supervised study should promote self-learning, which may motivate students to think through many aspects of a study assignment. The use of the library and its resources may constitute a vital part of the supervised study method.

There are several ways in which supervised study can be organised.

1. **Extra class:** The teacher may stay after class and attend to the difficulties of the students or give review or drill and practice to students lagging behind in the class. However, not all teachers are so motivated.

2. **A special teacher plan:** A special teacher is employed by the school to sit with students and clarify their doubts.
3. **Double period plan:** The school time table is organised in such a way that each subject has two successive periods where one can be used for theoretical work and the other for review and drill or related practical work.
4. **Divided period plan:** One period may be divided into two parts: one used for theoretical explanations and the other for practical work. This would require that a laboratory be close to the class.
5. **Library period plan:** In this period, students may work in the library on work assigned to them by the teacher. The students should be able to use references, prepare bibliographies and evaluate the relative importance of printed materials during a supervised study period. This activity can lead to creative thinking.
6. **Extra period plan:** An extra period is planned every day where the teacher assigns to each student a list of questions on an assignment sheet which they have to answer and submit.

Advantages of Supervised Study as a Method

The advantages of supervised study are as follows:

1. Increased instructional time is available to pupils.
2. Discipline problems can be avoided with less time in transit for students.
3. A fifty-minute period of time is too short to motivate and teach pupils. Supervised study gives ample time to grasp the topic well.
4. Supervised study can lead gifted and promising students to independent study.
5. The ability to think independently and creatively can be developed.
6. Supervised study helps the below average student to make up the gap.
7. Development of reference skills besides broadening the knowledge base is an outgrowth of supervised study.
8. The teacher can give individual attention to the students, thus catering to the differential needs of the class.

EXAMPLES OF INSTRUCTIONAL APPROACHES

The goal of instructional approaches was to improve the instructional experience for the individual learner. Some of the most historically notable approaches are discussed below:

1. **Personalized system of instruction** was introduced in 1964 by Fred Keller. The Personalized System of Instruction, or the Keller Plan, is perhaps one of the first comprehensive systems of individualised instruction. Keller based his system on ten accepted educational principles.
    1. Active responding
    2. Positive conditions and consequences
    3. Specification of objectives
    4. Organisation of material
    5. Mastery before advancement
    6. Evaluation/objectives congruence
    7. Frequent evaluation
    8. Immediate feedback
    9. Self-pacing
    10. Personalisation
2. **Self-directed materials:** In this type of programme, students and teachers cooperate in establishing the outcomes of learning. The students are free to select the materials and methods to achieve the goals. This approach is generally useful with above average learners.
3. **Independent study:** In this approach, the student selects her own objectives as well as the topic. She also decides the method of achieving the objectives. This approach is usually successful for above average students.

THE DALTON PLAN

A school cannot reflect the social experience, which is the fruit of community life unless all its parts, or groups, develop those intimate relations one with the other and that interdependence which, outside of school, binds men and nations together."

—*Helen Parkhurst in Education on the Dalton Plan, 1922*

Students work at their own speed, choose the laboratory appropriate for the work in hand, and enjoy the freedom to come and go, to use books, and to consult with teachers and other students. In some Dalton schools, group activities such as debates, dramatics, and other such activities are scheduled as well.

Students at Dalton begin using the Dalton Plan from a very young age. At the First Programme, students are presented with opportunities to make educational choices about their learning and in the process discover how to identify their interests and take responsibility for pursuing them. Over the years, Dalton students learn how to take responsibility for their own education. The task of developing good human beings and responsible social citizens requires empathy, deliberative reasoning, and the moral imagination of all members of the Dalton community. The Dalton schools remain committed to Helen Parkhurst's original goals to create not only academically strong graduates but also those who will become informed, intuitive, and responsible citizens.

The face of the Indian classroom is changing. Technology is transforming the traditional methods of teaching and learning in the classrooms of the 21st century. The goal is to create students who can become active, independent and life-long learners rather than passive recipients of information. This new approach to education takes the student beyond the traditional textbook and requires them to develop a combination of skills in computer technology, critical thinking and information-seeking strategies. Although advances have been made in seeking to provide the beginning teachers with the skills, knowledge and attitudes necessary to infuse technology into the instructional process, technology is not central to teacher preparation. Technology instruction in colleges of education should be teaching both use of technology as a separate subject and teaching with technology across the curriculum. Recognising that changing teacher education is a key requirement for changing teacher practices, the NCTE has developed a challenging curriculum in keeping with international norms.

NEP2020 stress the importance of digital literacy. Meeting this challenge requires new models of faculty development in teacher education that deal with the barriers that have been identified as inhibiting past efforts in changing practice through training.

NEED FOR ENTHUSING THE RELUCTANT TEACHER COMMUNITY

Even as schools and teacher education institutions are busily filling classrooms with computers, a large percentage of teachers and teacher educators remain reluctant and skeptical. The deluge of computers and educational technology into their classrooms has left a large percentage of teacher educators at the crossroads, reluctant to embrace new technologies and to incorporate these tools into their curriculum. In order to work effectively in tomorrow's colleges of education and schools, college faculty and teachers must be literate and confident in using technologies, as well as in developing strategies for implanting the technology.

Preparing teachers proficient in the use of technology will require expanding technology use among teacher educators. This is dodged by the following problems:

- Limited availability of equipment
- Lack of faculty training
- No clear expectation that faculty will incorporate technology in academic activities
- Lack of funds
- Lack of time to develop facility in using equipment and software
- Doubt about the pedagogical validity of using some of the newer technologies
- Lack of technical support, lack of appropriate materials, particularly integrated media materials suitable for teacher education institutions
- Absence of clear programmatic goals for the teacher education program as a whole
- Inability of the faculty to remain up-to-date
- Logistics of integration of technology into curriculum
- Lack of time to fit more classes into the present curriculum

Most teacher training institutions have computer literacy courses, which expose the preservice teachers to computer applications use of Word, PowerPoint, and the like. Instead, a better approach would be integrating computer instruction into existing methods and foundation courses. There is a need to infuse technology across the whole curriculum, so that student teachers acquire core subject area skills and knowledge as well.

A cursory look at the population of teacher educators indicates that there are teachers who have not yet embraced new technologies and have not yet blended these tools into their daily classroom learning activities. It appears that teacher educators need proof of results before they buy. They have little tolerance for change and are unwilling to shift time-tested behaviours unless there is compelling evidence that the investment of time and effort will pay big dividends. Though schools have bought computers and got hooked onto the Internet, teachers and teacher educators are doubtful how effective these new fangled toys are.

An ideal situation for embedding technology into the teaching scenario would involve teacher educators, practicing teachers and teacher trainees (Figure 10.2).

The characteristics of those teacher educators who perform best in an online learning environment are:

- Tolerance for discovery learning
- Familiarity and comfort with technology
- Initiative
- Independent learning
- Curiosity
- Strong writing skills

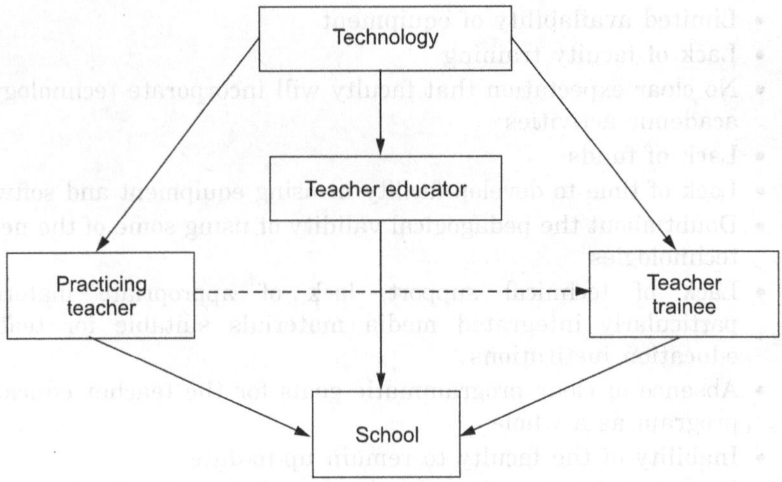

FIGURE 10.2 Technology transfer in the teaching community.

STRATEGIES RELATING TO E-LEARNING AND INNOVATIVE TECHNOLOGIES

Teacher educators should be made more enthusiastic about e-learning and new technologies.

1. **Analysis of the opportunities and constraints in using technological resources including selection of appropriate multimedia resources to the learning situation chosen:** For this, the teacher educator should be able to:
   (a) Carry out an audit to identify resource availability.
   (b) Identify the constraints within the training college.
   (c) Study the learning needs of students regarding the use of selected resources.
2. **Clarify the bottom line in terms of gains in student/ teacher trainee performance:** Most teacher educators have trouble relating to the inflated hard sell of technology enthusiasts. They want to know that their work will result in better teaching performance as measured by employability. For example, a teacher trainee should, at the end of the B.Ed. course, be capable of critically reflecting on her teaching. A teacher educator should be in a position to assess the product—teacher trainee's employability as well as capacity to reflectively think on her teaching—leading to continuous improvement. A teacher educator would need research proof of instructional technology leading to enhanced teacher trainee performance.
3. **Deliver a complete package:** Every teacher educator, teacher and trainee should be aware of the kind of resources, which

could be effective for teaching a particular unit. Conservative teacher educators are looking for excellent packages that have been tested, refined and perfected.

4. **Eliminate risk and surprise:** Reluctant teacher educators do not enjoy surprises, disappointments and adventures, especially when they occur during class time.

   Making sure that a resource is worth the effort and serves a definite educational purpose is vital. For example, downloading from the Internet during classtime can be a waste of time.

   Evaluation of software available as well as created is a necessary skill the teacher educator, teacher and trainee should cultivate. There are several checklists to facilitate assessing readymade software as well as teacher developed software.
5. **Speak their language:** The teacher educator can be put off by high tech jargon. The trainer should use simple language and build up the confidence of the teacher educator, so that the use of multimedia resources does not become a painful chore.
6. **Offer continual support:** Ongoing support gives comfort to the nervous teacher educator. The emotional nightmare of networks crashing keeps many a teacher educator away from technological inventions.
7. **Emphasise teams:** Teacher educators should be encouraged to work in teams of mixed abilities and styles. This will help build up the confidence of the reluctant teacher educator to experiment with new instructional technologies.
8. **Provide venues for rewards and recognition:** Teacher educators should be encouraged to take part in programmes like INTEL's school projects, Microsoft's programmes for teacher trainees.

LEVELS IN EMBEDDING TECHNOLOGY INTO TEACHER EDUCATION

Hall, et. al. (1975) in their study concluded that adaptation to innovation takes place at different levels. Each level is characterised by observing different behaviours related to the user's development in acquiring new skills and level of using the innovation. Sandholtz, Ringstaff and Dwyer (1990) discovered that levels of use are also characteristic of adapatation of computer technologies by teachers in their classroom.

Based on the review of literature, the following step-wise model can be considered, for infusing technology in teacher education. Figure 10.3 shows the sequential levels involved in embedding technology in teacher education.

The five sequential levels are:

1. **Entry level:** Here the focus is on acquisition of basic computer skills. Technology fluency is a basic requirement before the teacher educator can move ahead.

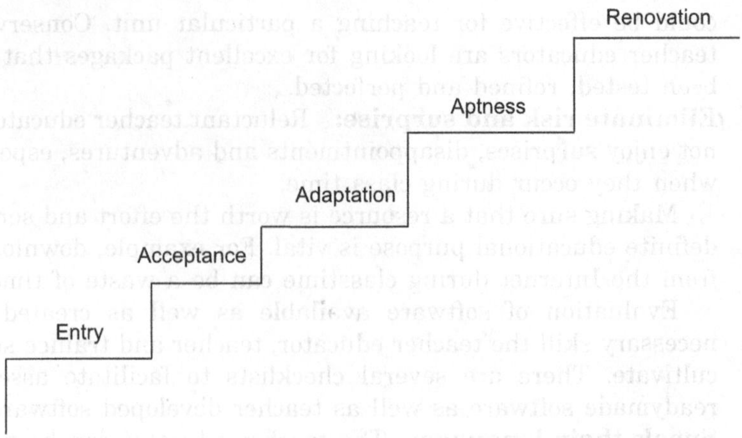

FIGURE 10.3 Levels in embedding technology in teacher education.

2. **Acceptance:** At this level, the teacher educator has developed enough computer skills and confidence to think of integrating it into the teacher education programme.
3. **Adaptation:** In the third level, the teacher educator can critically think of the various technological tools available, adapting them to the teacher education curriculum where possible. At this level, technology is thoroughly integrated into existing practices.
4. **Aptness:** The technological tools are used as a catalyst at this level. The teacher educator integrates reflective thinking into use of relevant and appropriate technological tools, leading to significant changes in the teaching learning process.
5. **Renovation:** This last level involves using the technology in a supported environment leading to professional development and networking with colleagues to determine best practices.

To enable faculty to use technology at a suitable level requires reallocating resources and providing time and support to learn the technology that will enable them to systematically redesign programmes, curriculum, and teaching learning experiences that capitalise on the power of these tools. The gradual shift from entry level to renovation level indicates the need to separate the use of technology for professional productivity by the faculty member and modelling instruction to promote new learning outcomes that employ technology.

The Rapidly Changing Model of Learning and Teaching

The easy availability of digital and networked tools has drastically changed the teaching and learning process. The Technological Pedagogical Content Knowledge (TPACK) framework put forth by Koehler & Mishra

(2008) describes the kind of teacher knowledge needed for teaching using technology in the classroom. The TPACK framework provides a set of guidelines for teachers and teacher-educators for integrating appropriate technology. Teachers, according to Shulman (1986), need to understand the interaction between pedagogy and content in order to apply suitable strategies for students to understand content.

The three major knowledge components of TPACK are:

- Content knowledge (CK) refers to the subject matter the teacher teaches
- Pedagogical knowledge (PK) refers to the teacher's knowledge of pedagogical practices, like methods and techniques of teaching and evaluation
- Technology knowledge (TK) refers to the teacher's understanding of how to integrate technology into the curriculum judiciously.

Teachers thus need a sound understanding of the interrelationship of technology, pedagogy, and content.

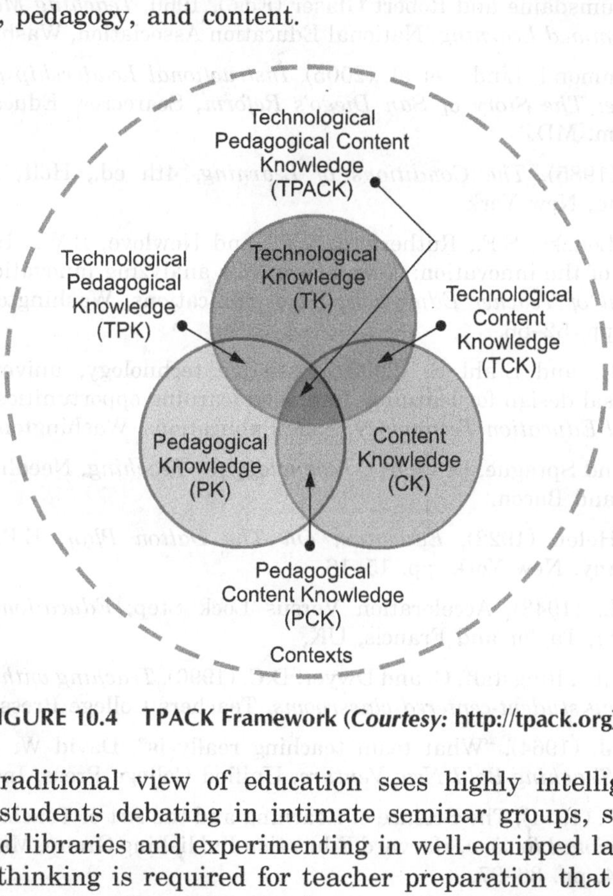

FIGURE 10.4 TPACK Framework (*Courtesy:* http://tpack.org).

The traditional view of education sees highly intelligent, well-motivated students debating in intimate seminar groups, studying in well stocked libraries and experimenting in well-equipped laboratories. A shift in thinking is required for teacher preparation that is in tune with today's needs. Preservice teachers must routinely encounter the effective infusion of technology in the normal course of their learning at the college and in their teaching practice in schools. As educators seek viable ways to use technology to enhance teaching and learning experiences, colleges must also prepare future teachers to plan for effective technology use. Teacher preparation programs should not only integrate technology throughout the curriculum, but should also provide opportunities for the students to manage problems within the actual school setting as they integrate various tools of technology.

REFERENCES

Barker, B.O. (1993), Using Instructional Technologies in the Preparation of Teachers for the 21st century, Paper presented at the National Conference on Creating the Quality School, Oklahoma City, OK. (ERIC Document Reproduction Service No. ED 367659).

Crowder, Norman (1969), Automatic Tutoring by Intrinsic Programming, in A.A. Lumsdaine and Robert Glaser (Eds.), 1960, *Teaching Machines and Programmed Learning*, National Education Association, Washington, D.C.

Darling Hammond, Linda, et al. (2005), *Instructional Leadership for Systemic Change: The Story of San Diego's Reform*, Scarecrow Education Press, Lanham, MD.

Gagne, R. (1985), *The Conditions of Learning,* 4th ed., Holt, Rinehart & Winston, New York.

Hall, G.E., Loucks, S.F., Rutherford, W.L, and Newlove, B.W. (1975), Levels of use of the innovation: A framework for analyzing innovation adoption, *Journal of Teacher Education*, Sage publications, Washington D.C. Vol. 26(1), pp. 52–56.

Hitchcock, C. and Stahl S. (2003), Assistive technology, universal design, universal design for learning: Improved learning opportunities, *Journal of Special Education Technology*, Sage Publications, Washington D.C. 18(A).

Norton, P. and Sprague, D. (2001), *Technology for Teaching*, Needham Heights, Allyn and Bacon.

Parkhurst Helen (1922), *Education On The Dalton Plan*, E.P. Dutton & Company, New York, pp. 15–16.

Pressey, S.L. (1943), Acceleration Versus Lock Step, *Educational Research Bulletin*, Taylor and Francis, UK.

Sandholtz, J.H., Ringstaff, C, and Dwyer, D.C. (1990). *Teaching with Technology: Creating student-centered classrooms*, Teachers College Press, New York.

Singer, Ira J. (1964), "What team teaching really is", David W. Beggs (Ed.), *Team Teaching-Bold New Venture*, Unified College Press, Indianpolis.

Skinner, B.F. (1954), The Science of Learning and the Art of Teaching, *Harvard Educational Review*, Harvard Education Publishing Group, Massachusetts, Vol. 24, pp. 86–97.

Terry Page, G. and Thomas, J.B. and Marshall, A.R. (1977), *International Dictionary of Education*, Kogan Page, Nichols, New York.

Thorsen, C. (2006), *Tech Tactics: Technology for Teachers*, 2nd ed., Pearson Education, Inc., Boston, M.A.

Web References

Britannica online encyclopedia. http://www.britannica.com.

The Technological Pedagogical Content Knowledge Framework for Teachers and Teacher Educators. Matthew J. Koehler Punya Mishra Mete Akcaoglu Joshua M. Rosenberg.

http://www.cemca.org.in/ckfinder/userfiles/files/ICT%20teacher%20 education%20Module%201%20Final_May%2020.pdf

Kolb, Liz. (2017) Learning First, Technology Second: The Educator's Guide to Designing Authentic Lessons. International Society for Technology in EducationMerriam Webster's Online Dictionary. http://www.merrian-webster.com.

Parkhurst Helen (1922), Education On The Dalton Plan, E.P. Dutton & Company, New York, pp. 15–16. http://www.archive.org/details/educationontheda028244mbp. Retrieved 2007-12-01.

Using the TPACK Image http://tpack.org/

Part V

PERFORMANCE AND EVALUATION

CHAPTER 11

Evaluation in Teacher Education

Evaluate teachers because teachers bridge the past, the present, and the future.

—Anonymous

INTRODUCTION

There is no ready formula to ensure change and innovations in teacher education. Nor can any one design uniform mechanisms to improve the quality of teacher education across the country. The efforts have to be more localised depending on the environment in which the teacher education programme functions and the school system it serves. Every institution has to become the base for change and quality improvement. This also highlights the need for decentralising the system of teacher education. This is particularly relevant in the case of the primary stage, which is made uniform throughout the state with no regard for local variables in the school conditions.

India is a multi-lingual, multi-cultural society. Any single form of training cannot be good for all levels, all places and all requirements. For example, whereas in most of the states the challenge is retention of primary school children, the problem in Kerala is improvement of quality. Can the training requirements of Kerala and Uttar Pradesh be same? What is required, then, is a flexible framework of training strategy that can be adopted and adapted to suit the local needs.

This module has been divided into three sections:

1. Macrolevel management of evaluation, which encompasses the interests of the various stakeholders in educational ventures discussed in this chapter.

2. Microlevel management of evaluation of education which includes pre-service and in-service training discussed in this chapter.
3. Evaluation processes in India–NAAC (discussed in Chapter 12).

MACROLEVEL MANAGEMENT OF EVALUATION

What facilitates management of change and quality at the institutional level? Research has indicated the following trends:

1. Need to create more transparency in the functioning of the curriculum, transaction processes and evaluation methods.
2. Need to create a system of social accountability. The teacher education institutions cannot remain an island, isolated from the mainstream. The stakeholders of the education system have all to be accounted to regarding the success or failure of the school system.
3. Need to initiate planned change and innovations.
4. Need to be subjected to periodic evaluation against planned quality improvement measures which are designed and implemented by the teacher educators, central agencies like NAAC.
5. Need to provide opportunities for continuous professional development of teacher educators through research and development activities.

Concept of Stakeholders

Rea-Dickins (1994) includes the concept of stakeholders in her definition of evaluation, maintaining that the evaluations are stakeholder-oriented-unlike most other educational research. The term 'stakeholder' is now widely used in many fields, particularly in business and management studies. Aspinwall et al. (1992) provide a comprehensive analysis of the concept of stakeholders in the context of educational evaluations and state that "A stakeholder is any group or individual who is affected by, or can affect the future of the organisation, programme or activity.... Stakeholders can be both internal (e.g. staff) and external (e.g. parents) to the school". The stakeholders in any given programme will thus be determined by the nature and context of the programme.

Peterson (2000) states that "an important part of the new approaches to evaluation is the increasingly felt need to incorporate *the viewpoint of stakeholders ...*".

General Frameworks for Programme Evaluation

Works on educational programme evaluation in the 1990s provide useful frameworks of criteria that those involved in organising an evaluation should consider. Rea-Dickins, 1994; Rea-Dickins and Germaine, 1992;

Aspinwall et al., 1992; Alderson, 1992, all provide similar checklists or procedures to consider when conducting an evaluation. Box 11.1 gives a synthesis of the main points that are covered.

BOX 11.1 Checklist to Consider During Evaluation

1. What is the aim of the evaluation?
2. Who is the evaluation for?
3. What is to be evaluated?
4. What criteria are going to be used in the evaluation?
5. Who should conduct the evaluation?
6. When should the evaluation take place?
7. What are the sources of data?
8. What methods of data collection are to be used?
9. How is the evaluation to be managed?
10. How is the data to be processed?
11. How are the findings to be validated?
12. What conclusions can be drawn from the evaluation?
13. How are the results to be reported?
14. What action is expected to follow?
15. How is the evaluation to be evaluated?

By focusing on the context, the players or stakeholders in the programme assume a more central role in the framework. Rea-Dickins and Germaine (1992) developed a model called a context for evaluation, which places a course within its context and illustrates the complexity involved in doing this. Their context includes the school and those within it who influence decisions made about classroom practice, such as the Head; it also looks at factors outside the school, including parents, local education authorities and society at large. Gaining an understanding of such factors and how they influence classrooms is the only way in which evaluators can gain the necessary depth of understanding of a programme.

The most comprehensive consideration of context in relation to evaluations is developed by Lynch in his 'context-adaptive model' outlined in 1990 and slightly refined in 1996. He presents a seven-step model for evaluators to consider, which involves a detailed analysis at each of the following stages:

- Determining the audience and goals of the evaluation.
- Carrying out a 'context inventory', which is an audit of the programme and the planned evaluation.
- Establishing a 'preliminary thematic framework', which focuses the evaluation in terms of what it will attempt to achieve.
- Designing data collection procedures.
- Collecting data.
- Analysing the data.
- Writing the evaluation report.

Identifying Stakeholders

The model of stakeholder identification presented by Savage and colleagues includes all the organisation's stakeholders and not just those involved in a particular area of business or programme and is too broad a model for the context that we are considering now. They do, however, make the important point that the identification process should be ongoing. A clear overview that applies the concept of stakeholders to educational evaluation is provided by Aspinwall et al. (1992), who claim that in both planning and evaluation it is important to consider the stakeholders and their expectations. They argue that their stakeholder analysis "allows us to think critically about the 'who' dimension and asks us to go a step further to examine what the stakeholders' expectations might be with regard to the institution, development or programme". The model (Figure 11.1) is used for mapping stakeholders.

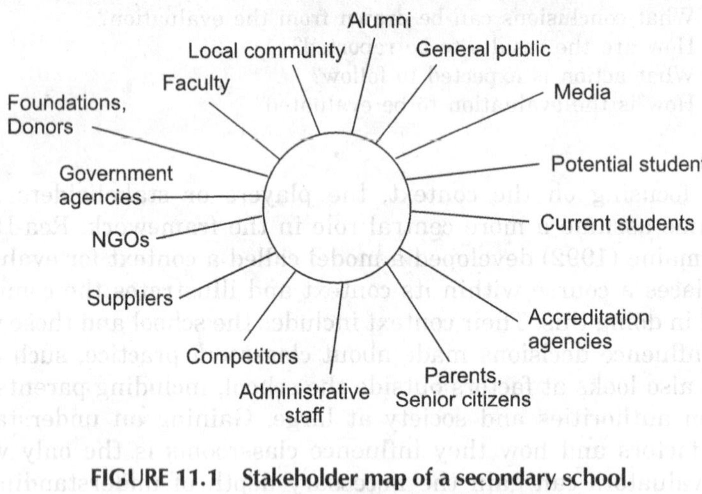

FIGURE 11.1 Stakeholder map of a secondary school.
(*Source:* Aspinwall et al. 1991:86).

Aspinwall et al. state that: "[t]he institution is placed at the centre and the perceived importance of each group is indicated by the length of the arrows, the more important stakeholders placed nearer the centre" (p. 85). *This model is useful, although it is designed for institutional evaluation and needs adapting for programme evaluation placing the programme in the centre.* Rea-Dickins and Germaine's model (1992) of the context of evaluation is useful for such refocusing.

Jonston and Peterson (1994) with their 'programme matrix' model (Figure 11.2), firstly, distinguish between 'processes', the stages of the programme and the 'elements', the people and materials involved in the programme. In this model, evaluation is only part of the matrix. They do, however, see the identification of stakeholders as essential in

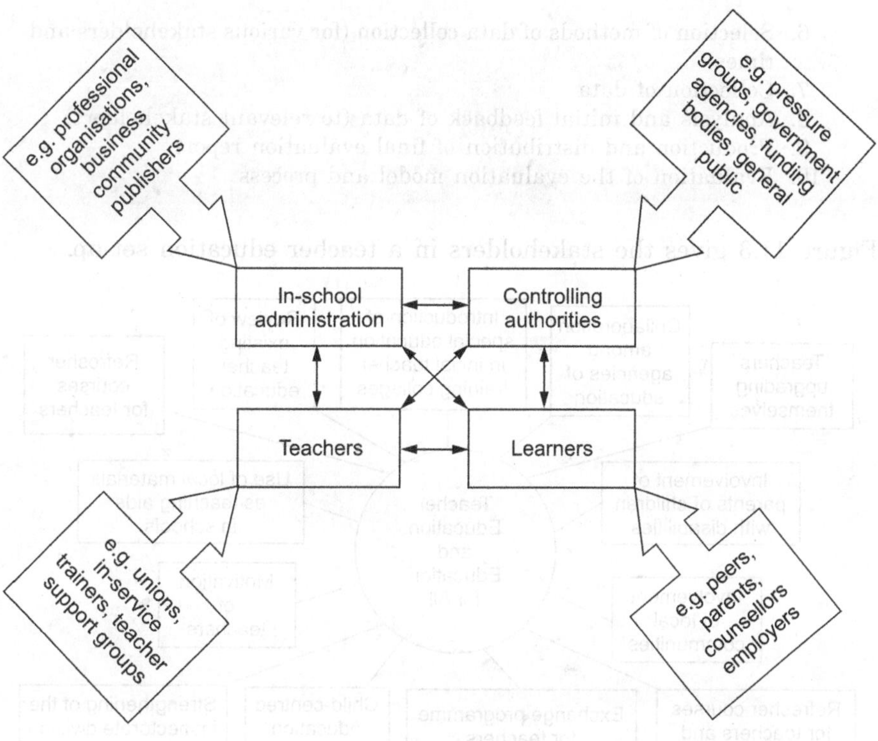

FIGURE 11.2 Influences on main stakeholders.
(*Source:* Johnston and Peterson, 1994:73).

any framework for describing or analysing language programmes. They identify four major groups of stakeholders:

1. Learners
2. Teachers
3. Administrators
4. Controlling authorities like governments, managements ....

Conducting the Stakeholder Evaluation

The steps for conducting the stakeholder evaluation are given in Box 11.2.

BOX 11.2 Steps for Conducting Stakeholder Evaluation

1. Establishment of the evaluation aims
2. Selection of a suitable evaluator
3. Evaluator gains background knowledge of the programme (if an outsider)
4. Identification of stakeholders by evaluator and central stakeholder(s)
5. Establishment of evaluation timeframe (dependent on contextual constraints)

6. Selection of methods of data collection (for various stakeholders and times)
7. Collection of data
8. Analysis and initial feedback of data (to relevant stakeholders)
9. Production and distribution of final evaluation report
10. Evaluation of the evaluation model and process.

Figure 11.3 gives the stakeholders in a teacher education set-up.

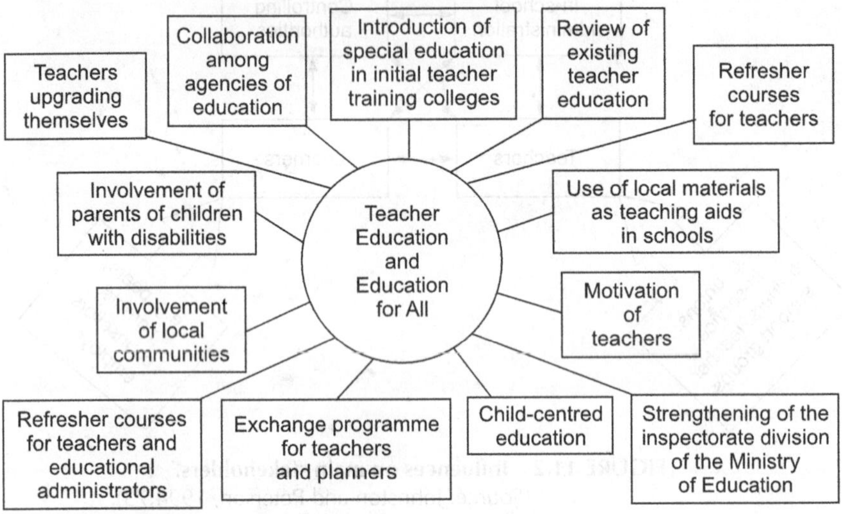

FIGURE 11.3 The stakeholders in a teacher education set-up.

Faculty: Faculty who have taught courses were considered to be principal stakeholders.

Support staff: Non-faculty staff who serve freshmen were also considered to be important stakeholders.

Students: Students are clearly important stakeholders who have expectations and can report on their experiences with the institution.

Parents: Parents of students associated with Freshman Academy are key audiences with expectations of the institution.

Others: Wider audiences with related interests are anticipated as recipients.

The evaluation of teacher education, when viewed at the macro-level, will involve looking into the functioning of the teacher training institutions in the context of the national policy requirements (NCFTE 2010) as well as the expectations of the stakeholders.

The macro level approach takes a broad perspective on the nature of most kinds of evaluands (things being evaluated), ranging from organisations to instructional products and from their conception to their completion, as first proposed by Stufflebeam (1971) in his CIPP (context, input, process, product) approach as shown in Figure 11.4.

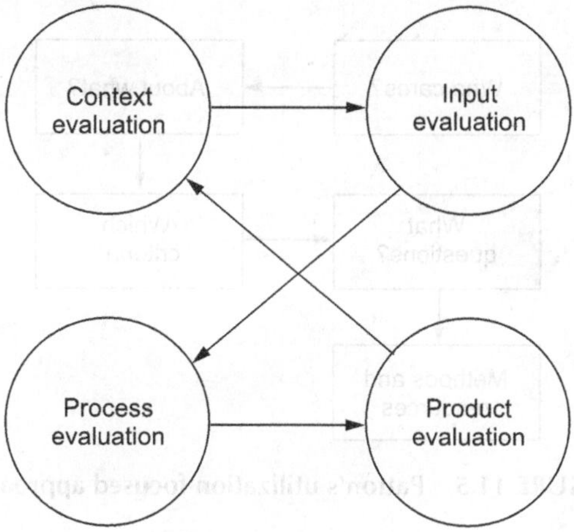

FIGURE 11.4 Context, input, process, product model.
(*Source:* Stufflebeam, 1971)

The CIPP approach assumes that anything that might be evaluated could be usefully evaluated at various stages in its development. The proposed evaluation framework organises the interests, questions, values, and participation of potential evaluation users and stakeholders around four types of evaluation which parallel four stages of development:

1. Context evaluations that investigate the socio-political, organisational, and other contextual variables associated with the need for courses, programmes, and support efforts.
2. Input evaluations that compare alternative inputs or means for meeting the needs identified in context evaluations, including but not limited to particular programmes.
3. Process evaluations that formatively assess the planning, design, development, and implementation of programmes and associated efforts to use them.
4. Product evaluations that allow summative judgements to be made regarding the quality, utility, and value of programmes and infrastructures that support them.

Ideally, evaluations of all four types will occur simultaneously and repeatedly throughout the life of an organisation such as a university (at the macro level) that has multiple projects, programmes, initiatives, and courses, and throughout the life of a particular programme, such as a school or training college (at the micro level).

The participant-oriented approach presented here combines Stufflebeam's approach with Patton's utilisation-focused approach (Patton, 1997) is illustrated in Figure 11.5. A comprehensive model-CIPP and utilisation-focused evaluation combined is presented in Figure 11.6.

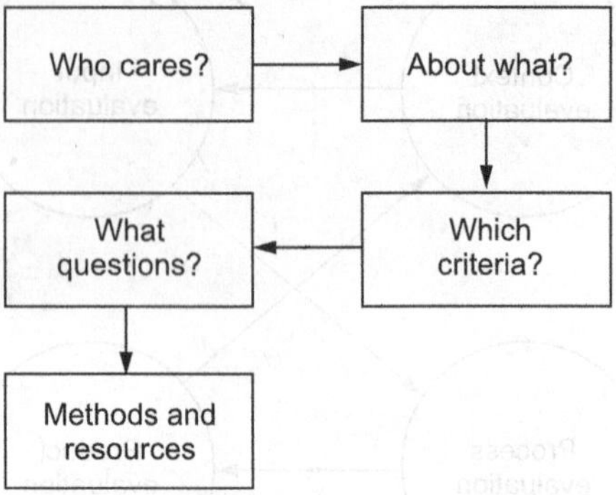

FIGURE 11.5 Patton's utilization-focused approach.

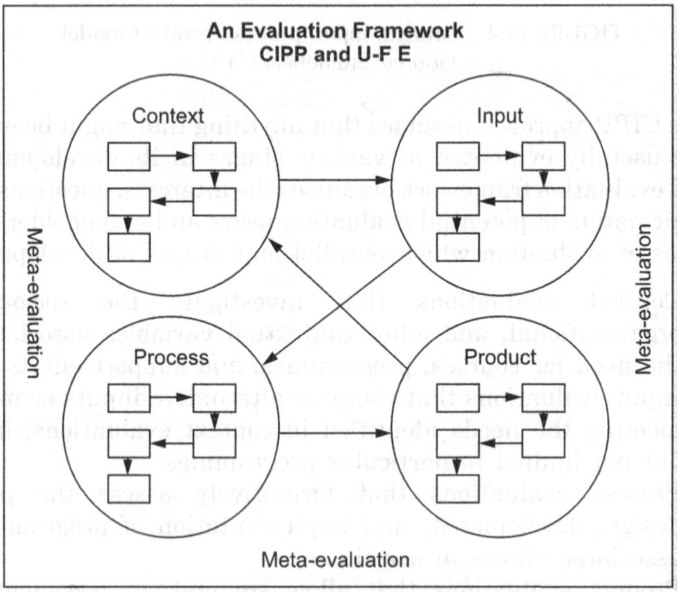

FIGURE 11.6 CIPP and utilisation-focused evaluation combined.

As represented in Figure 11.5, Patton argues that the key to evaluation utility is to identify people who are disposed to learning from evaluations. He outlines several procedures for identifying these users and then working with them to clarify what they want to know and what they are likely to do with information gathered by an evaluation.

As shown in Figure 11.6, CIPP and utilisation-focused evaluation combined, combining Stufflebeam's and Patton's approaches suggest that different users with different questions, criteria, and information needs may be more or less crucial at different stages in the life of an evaluand.

Questions Based on Stakeholders Expectations

A key dimension of both broader and programmatic issues is the understanding and management of stakeholder expectations. Questions should include:

Relevance

How relevant is the programme to national needs, priorities and expectations?

How coherent is it in relation to the needs and objectives of other stakeholders in the system?

To what extent is the programme working in synergy with and contributing to the implementation of the National goals and vision as outlined in NCTEF 2009?

Efficiency

Have programme delivery mechanisms been appropriately resourced, cost effective and timely?

Have the roles and responsibilities of society, university, cooperating schools, NGOs and employers and Institutions been clear and effectively coordinated?

Have capacities/support provided been sufficient and appropriate?

Effectiveness and impact

Have target objectives been met?

If so, how effectively?

How effectively has the programme mobilised multilateral partners, additional funding, and how effectively has it worked in coherence with other stakeholders?

What have been the unanticipated outcomes?

Is there evidence of medium and longer term impacts?

Sustainability

In what way are activities planned and implemented to support sustainability?

What are the practices as well as key lessons emerging?

Responses to those key questions should lead to recommendations concerning the resources, priorities, and model of implementation.

Teacher Evaluation—In-service Teacher Evaluation

As the most significant resource in schools, teachers are critical to raise education standards. Improving the efficiency and equity of schooling depends, in large measure, on ensuring that teachers are highly skilled,

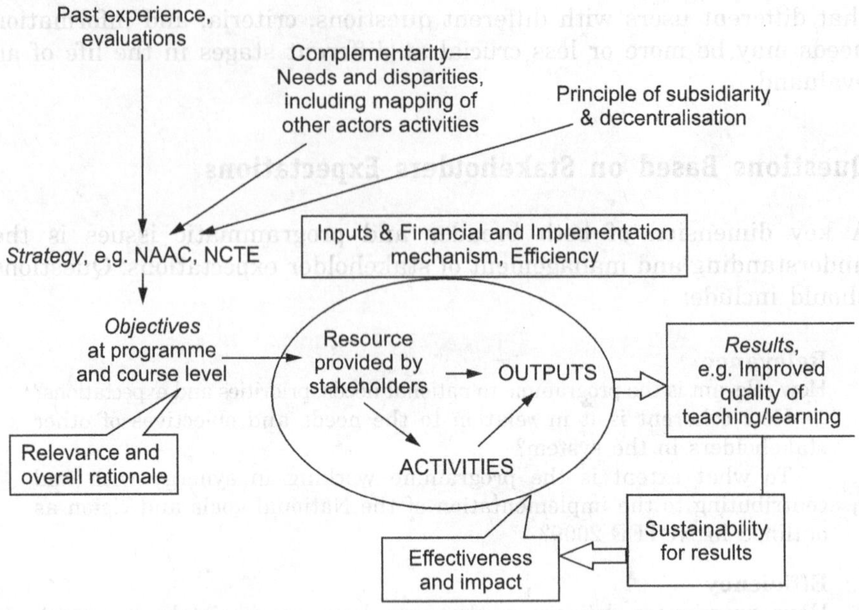

FIGURE 11.7 Overview of evaluation approach.

well resourced, and motivated to perform at their best. Raising teaching performance will lead to substantial gains in student learning. This in turn, will require effective monitoring and evaluation of teaching for the continuous improvement of the effectiveness of teaching in a school. It is essential to know the strengths of teachers and those aspects of their practice which could be further developed. From this perspective, the institution of teacher evaluation is a vital step in the drive to improve the effectiveness of teaching and learning and raise educational standards.

Since systems of school evaluation and teacher appraisal and feedback have the objective of maintaining standards to improve student performance, there are likely to be great benefits from the synergies between school evaluation and teacher evaluation. To achieve the greatest impact, the focus of school evaluation should either be linked to or have an effect on the focus of teacher evaluation, which in turn should be linked to pre-service teacher evaluation. Hence, the school strategy and the school self-evaluation results ensure a continuous monitoring and improving of colleges of education, school and teacher quality.

Teacher evaluation may be interlinked with school arrangements to improve teaching quality in a range of ways. First, teacher evaluation can serve the direct purpose of improving the teaching process within the school when teacher evaluation is carried out as part of school internal evaluation, and distinct from the formal individual assessment of teachers. Teacher evaluation for improvement purposes as part of internal school evaluation is usually carried out by the school head or the school management team.

Conceptual Framework to Analyse Teacher Evaluation (Figure 11.8)

Teacher evaluation issues cannot be studied in isolation. There is a need to consider the impact on and of the various stakeholders involved in the school education systems. Responsibilities for teacher evaluation are typically shared between educational authorities, including quality assurance agencies such as inspectorates, schools and their leadership, and teachers themselves.

Teacher evaluation procedures require setting up evaluation criteria to determine the level of performance of individual teachers for each of the aspects assessed. This typically implies the development of indicators and/or standardised forms to record teacher performance. An additional criterion is the weightage given to different aspects assessed in order to compute an overall quantitative rating, in case it is part of the teacher evaluation model.

Role of Stakeholders

1. **Educational authorities:** Educational authorities play a major role in the conception and application of teacher evaluation, since they set the national learning outcome objectives, agree standards for the teaching profession and establish the norms that regulate teacher evaluation. This might include the design of specific evaluation tools and instruments, the determination of evaluation criteria, the distribution of evaluation duties, and the follow-up on evaluation results.
2. **Inspectorates:** In India education inspectorates take full responsibility for teacher evaluation. This includes developing teacher evaluation procedures and undertaking individual teacher evaluations with school inspectors taking the role of evaluators.
3. **Schools and school leadership:** The effective operation of teacher evaluation depends to a great extent on the way the concept and practice of school leadership is established in schools.
4. **Teachers:** In some systems, teacher evaluation is based on reviews by peers, often more experienced and with more responsibilities. This is more typical of evaluation for improvement purposes.
5. **Community:** Teacher evaluation can play a critical role in helping stakeholders start discussing sustainability early

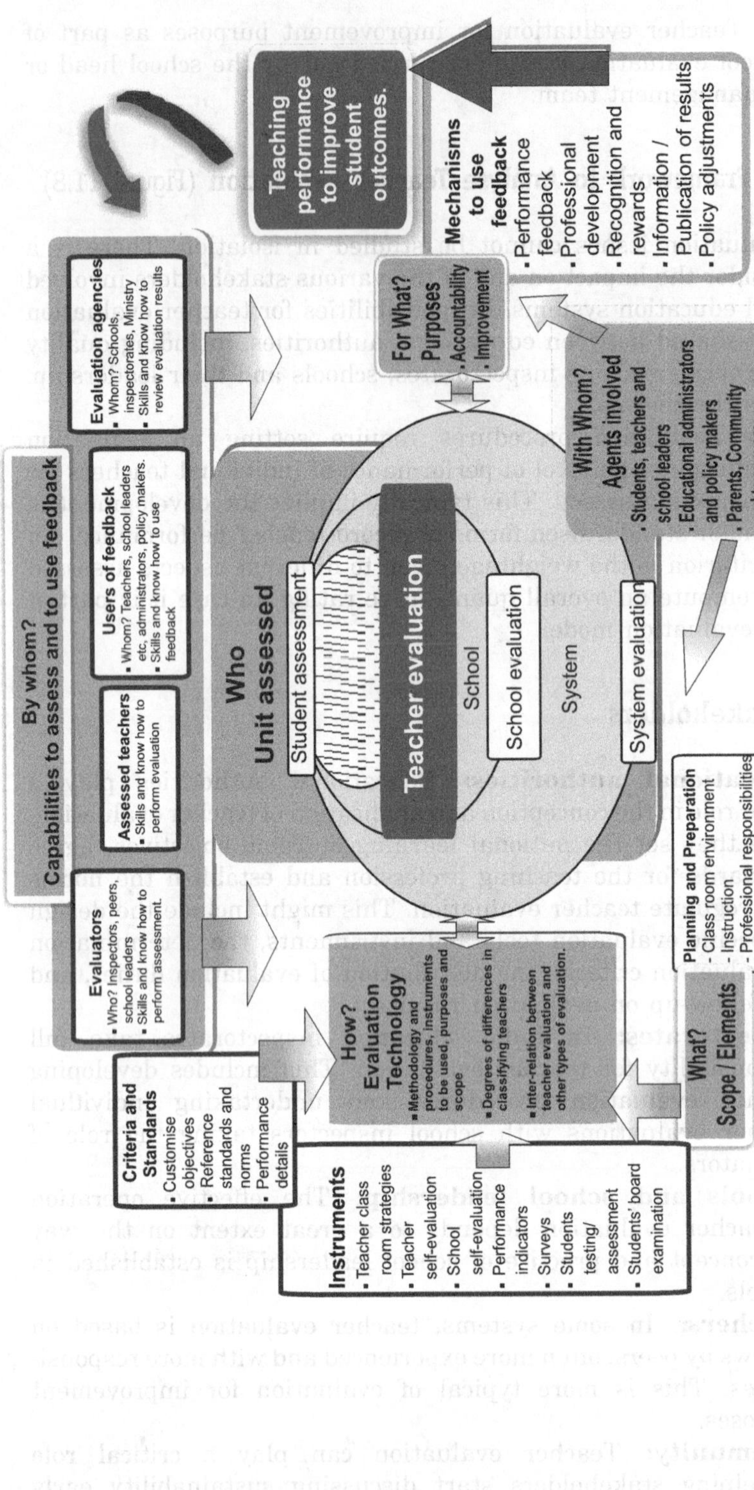

FIGURE 11.8 Conceptual model of teacher evaluation.
(*Source*: Adapted from OECD Review an Evaluation and Assessment Frameworks for Improving School Outcomes).

enough and maintain that discussion over time. The community will set the norms as well as the expectations to be met by the school. Frequent interaction between school and community, parent-teacher associations, alumni associations, will help match community expectations with school functioning. Evaluation can support sustainability by tracking progress and regularly feeding back information that can be used to ensure that sustainability is on course.

6. **Placement agencies:** Schools should cater to the needs of the nation in general and the local community in particular. The evaluation of all the aspects of the education system will show how effectively each aspect of the school system is functioning. The stakeholders with their varied expectations and feedback help in promoting viable placement in schools.

The conceptual framework has six main interrelated aspects as given in Table 11.1.

TABLE 11.1 Aspects of conceptual framework

Aspects	*Question raised*	*Action*
Unit assessed	Who?	The subject of the evaluation is the individual teacher. The teacher evaluation is to be analysed as part of an evaluation and assessment framework which **includes** other components such as student assess-ment, school evaluation and system evaluation based on other stakeholders.
Capabilities to assess and to use feedback	By Whom?	The issues involved are: Choice of the evaluators. The role of the evaluator is typically played by: **Teachers**, either internal or external to the school of the evaluated teacher. **External inspectors**. These can take responsibility for the evaluation of individual teachers, the evaluation of teachers playing the role of evaluators, or school leaders. **School leaders**. In some instances school leaders evaluate both pedagogic competencies and skills for other duties within the school. In others, school leaders evaluate non-pedagogical competencies only.

(Contd.)

TABLE 11.1 Aspects of conceptual framework (Contd.)

Aspects	*Question raised*	*Action*
		• Training in skills for assessment of a teacher • Preparation by teachers to be the subject of an evaluation • Skill to analyse the results of an evaluation for the improvement of teaching practices • Empowering agencies to review teacher evaluation results and use effectively
Aspects assessed	What?	Focus on • the core activity of teaching, typically covering areas such as planning and preparation, the classroom environment and instruction itself. • the remaining responsibilities of teachers such as their contribution to school development, links to the surrounding community and professional-stakeholders.
Evaluation methods	How?	The mix of instruments, criteria and standards, purposes, knowledge and skills used in a specific teacher evaluation model.
Purposes	For what?	The objectives of a particular teacher evaluation process and the mechanisms designed to ensure that evaluation results are used in a way such objectives are reached. Accountability and improvement are key factors here. *Teacher evaluation for improvement* focuses on the provision of feedback useful for the improvement of teaching practices. *The accountability function* of teacher evaluation focuses on holding teachers accountable for their performance associating it to a range of consequences for their career.
Agents involved	With whom?	This mostly deals with the implementation aspects of teacher evaluation procedures. It relates to the involvement of a range of stakeholders such as parents, students, teachers, school leaders, teacher unions, educational administrators and policy makers in the development and implementation of teacher evaluation and assessment processes.

Teacher evaluation for ***improvement*** purposes is likely to benefit from conditions such as:

1. A non-threatening evaluation context
2. A culture of mutually providing and receiving feedback
3. Clear individual and collective objectives with regard to improving teaching within the school as well as a sharing of school objectives
4. Simple evaluation instruments such as self-evaluation forms, classroom observation, and structured interviews
5. A supportive school leadership

Examples of ***school system factors*** are:

1. Distribution of responsibilities across educational authorities
2. School governance and autonomy
3. Structure of schooling
4. Curriculum, academic standards, learning time
5. Market mechanisms/school choice
6. Allocation of resources within school system
7. Career and reward/incentive structures for teachers and school leaders
8. Teacher education and certification policies
9. Roles and views of stakeholder groups

Examples of ***school level factors*** are:

1. Socio-economic context of schools
2. Management, leadership and distribution of responsibilities within school
3. Professional activities of teachers and other school personnel
4. Teaching and learning arrangements
5. Community and family involvement
6. Learning conditions, support structures
7. Opportunities to enhance competencies as well as resources and means to improve practice
8. Teacher evaluation integrated in a system of school self-evaluation and quality assurance.

In turn, teacher evaluation for ***accountability*** is likely to benefit from conditions such as:

1. An independent and objective assessment of the teacher's performance
2. National-level standards and criteria across schools
3. An evaluation component external to the school and more formal processes
4. Well-established rules regarding the consequences of the evaluation

5. Clear individual objectives with regard to all aspects of a teacher's performance
6. Well-trained, competent evaluators of teaching performance
7. Impact on professional development plan
8. Possibilities for appeal for teachers who feel they have not been treated fairly.

Promoting teacher evaluation is clearly in the national interest as well as serving students and their families and communities. Teachers need feedback on their performance to help them identify how to better shape and improve their teaching practice and, with the support of effective school leadership, to develop schools as professional learning communities. At the same time, teachers should be accountable for their performance and progress in their careers on the basis of demonstrated effective teaching practice.

MICROLEVEL EVALUATION

Teacher Education Programmes

At the microlevel, there is the evaluation of pre-service teacher training, in-service training, and its relevance to societal needs.

Pre-service Education

The broad goals of the teacher preparation are to prepare entry-level teachers and advanced in-service teachers and school personnel who:

1. are capable of teaching and guiding students of varying backgrounds, strengths, and needs;
2. are competent decision makers;
3. are skilled in planning, implementing, and evaluating learning experience for students;
4. view decision making as a reflective process;
5. understand and are committed to the moral dimensions of teaching;
6. select and apply technology appropriately; and
7. accept the view that professional growth and development is an ongoing, never-ending process.

Conceptual Framework—Pre-service Teacher Preparation

The four major elements of the conceptual framework are supported in both pre-service and in-service assessments.

1. **Planning:** While planning, the teacher/teacher trainee must make decisions regarding areas such as goals and objectives, the degree of background building required, specific materials and methods to use.
2. **Implementation:** The implementation function is that which requires the teacher/teacher trainee to carry out the plans that have been made. During the actual teaching phase, numerous decisions need to be made. Often, they need to be made quickly as the teacher responds to students' reactions, comments, and instructional needs. As a result, modification of prepared plans becomes the rule rather than the exception.
3. **Evaluation:** During the evaluation phase of decision-making, the teacher/teacher trainee needs to determine the degree to which the instructional objectives were attained. Determining the degree of re-teaching that is needed, recording information, and reporting progress are some of the areas within the evaluation phase of decision-making.
4. **Reflection:** The teacher/teacher trainee plans, implements and evaluates by using feedback in a reflective manner. During the entire process, it is essential for the teacher to realise that professional growth and development is continuous.

Pre-service Teacher Evaluation—Teacher Education Domains

The pre-service teacher education programme has four major domains. Figure 11.9 gives the skills to be evaluated in each of the four domains to make for effective reflection and decision making as pre-service teachers.

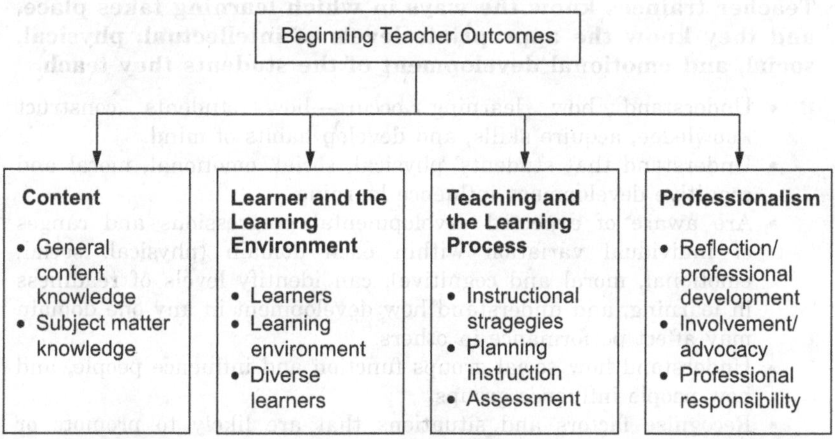

FIGURE 11.9 Four domains—Evaluation of pre-service teacher trainees.

Domain I—Content

The essence of content in domain one is the acquisition of content knowledge, pedagogical knowledge and the development of creative and critical thinking skills for beginning educators.

Teachers/trainees have broad knowledge of their subjects.

- Have background in basic subject areas: the arts, humanities, mathematics, and sciences, and have a broad understanding of the major cultures, religions, geography, political systems, philosophies, and economic systems by which people organise their lives.
- Know and appreciate the great creative works of world cultures.

Teacher trainees know the content appropriate to their teaching specialty and the relevant applications of this content.

- Know their subjects considerably beyond the content they are expected to teach, and know how professionals in their field think and analyse the world.
- Have a strong background in the subjects related to their specialty area.
- Understand major concepts, assumptions, debates, processes of inquiry, and ways of knowing that are central to the discipline they teach.
- Know how to apply information from their discipline to real-world situations.

Teacher trainees understand the ways in which their teaching area connects to the broad curriculum.

- Know the links between the grade or subject they teach and what comes before and after their course or grade.
- Can relate disciplinary knowledge to other subject areas.

Teacher trainees know the ways in which learning takes place, and they know the appropriate levels of intellectual, physical, social, and emotional development of the students they teach.

- Understand how learning occurs—how students construct knowledge, acquire skills, and develop habits of mind.
- Understand that students' physical, social, emotional, moral and cognitive development influence learning.
- Are aware of expected developmental progressions and ranges of individual variation within each domain (physical, social, emotional, moral and cognitive), can identify levels of readiness in learning, and understand how development in any one domain may affect performance in others.
- Understand how social groups function and influence people, and how people influence groups.
- Recognise factors and situations that are likely to promote or diminish intrinsic motivation.

Teachers recognise the impact of cultural, economic, political, and social environments upon their discipline.

- Know the history of their discipline.
- Know the contributions that diverse cultural groups have made to their discipline.

Teachers know the specific uses of technology in their discipline.

- Understand how technological advances affect their discipline.
- Know where to find technological resources specific to their discipline.

Domain II—The learning and the learner environment

The learning and the learner environment, domain two, focuses on the ability of the teacher trainees to define characteristics of their learners and create pro-social behaviours that engage learners in their classes.

Effective classroom management: Teacher trainees practice effective classroom management.

- Exercise leadership by taking personal responsibility for the progress of all students.
- Organise and motivate students to act in ways that meet the needs of both the individual student and the class as a whole.
- Maximise efficiency, maintain discipline and morale, promote team-work, plan, communicate, focus on results, evaluate progress, and make constant adjustments.
- Work to minimise disruptions in student learning and take advantage of unexpected events to teach students.
- Are skilled at facilitating consensus and mediating conflict.
- Use a range of strategies to promote positive relationships, cooperation, and purposeful learning in the classroom.
- Engage students in individual and cooperative learning activities that help them develop the motivation to achieve.
- Organise, allocate, and manage the resources of time, space, activities, and attention to provide active and equitable engagement of students in productive tasks.
- Help the group to develop shared values and expectations for student interactions, academic discussions, and individual and group responsibility that create a positive classroom climate of openness, mutual respect, support, and inquiry.

Effective teaching practices: Teacher trainees use a variety of methods to teach students, including cooperative learning techniques, to promote content knowledge, critical thinking, and problem-solving skills.

- Teach students how to live and work together productively and in a positive manner.
- Effectively use multiple representations and explanations of disciplinary concepts that capture key ideas and link them to students' prior understandings.

- Represent and use differing viewpoints, theories, "ways of knowing" and methods of inquiry in the teaching of subject matter concepts.
- Integrate interdisciplinary learning experiences that allow students to integrate knowledge, skills, and methods of inquiry from several subject areas.
- Use multiple teaching and learning strategies to engage students in active learning opportunities that promote the development of critical thinking, problem solving, and performance capabilities and that help students assume responsibility for identifying and using learning resources.
- Constantly monitor and adjust strategies in response to learner feedback.
- Engage students in individual and cooperative learning activities that help them develop the motivation to achieve
- Model effective communication strategies in conveying ideas and information and in asking questions.

Domain III—Teaching and the learning process

The core of domain three, teaching and the learning process, is the ability of the beginning educator to plan, implement and assess instruction that is congruent with identified outcomes.

Effective assessment: Teacher trainees use a variety of methods to assess what students have learned.

- Use formal tests, responses to quizzes, evaluation of class assignments, student performances and projects, and standardised achievement tests to understand what students know.
- Evaluate informal measures of student understanding, such as the questions asked in class and the level of student enthusiasm.
- Use assessment strategies to involve learners in self-assessment activities, to help them become aware of their strengths and needs, and to encourage them to set personal goals for learning.
- Modify teaching strategies and behaviour in relation to student success, modifying plans and instructional approaches accordingly.
- Maintain useful records of student work and performance and communicate student progress knowledgeably and responsibly, based on appropriate indicators, to students, parents, and other colleagues.

Curriculum alignment: Teacher trainees align their instruction with the required curriculum.

- Develop and apply strategies to make the local curriculum framework, and content standards by professional organisations in their speciality area significant to the students they teach.
- Meet the requirements of the entire curriculum, while recognising and focusing on those concepts in the curriculum which are fundamental to student understanding.

- Diversified instruction. Teachers plan instruction that is appropriate for a diverse student population, including students with special needs.
- Develop short- and long-range plans for instruction, which reflect understanding of how students learn, and allow for students who learn at a faster or slower pace than others to be successful and engaged in learning.
- Understand that plans are general guidelines and must be constantly monitored and modified to enhance the learning that is occurring in the classroom.
- Make inclusion of special needs students in the regular classroom a positive experience for each student in the class and collaborate with the range of support specialists to help them meet the needs of all students.
- Identify and design instruction appropriate to students' stages of development, learning styles, strengths, and needs.
- Bring multiple perspectives to the discussion of subject matter, including attention to students' personal, family, and community experiences and cultural norms.
- Know how to take contextual considerations (instructional materials, individual student interests, needs and aptitudes, and community resources) into curriculum goals and students' experiences.
- Know when and how to adjust plans based on student responses and other contingencies.

Technology skills: Teacher trainees have strong and current technology skills.

- Know when and how to use current educational technology.
- Understand the most appropriate type and level of technology to use to maximise student learning.

Domain IV—Professionalism

In domain four, professionalism relates to the collaboration, reflection and the ethical behaviours of the beginning educator.

Belief that all students can learn: Teacher trainees believe that all students can learn.

- Instill a love of learning and self-confidence based on achievement.
- Treat students as individuals.
- Enjoy spending time in the company of children and young adults learn all they can about each of their students; maintain the dignity of each student; express pride in their students' accomplishments.
- Believe that all children can learn at high levels and persist in helping all children achieve success.

Respect for diversity: Teacher trainees know and respect the influence of race, ethnicity, gender, religion and other aspects of culture on a child's development and personality.

- Demonstrate the belief that diversity in the classroom, in the school, and in society is a strength and show this commitment by daily conduct.
- Do not allow subtle or overt intolerance to bigotry in classrooms or schools, and actively select materials and develop lessons that counteract stereotypes.
- Strive to understand how an individual child's culture and background influence her school performance.

Professional development and ethics: Teacher trainees meet high ethical standards of practice and engage in professional development activities, including development in the area of technology.

- Keep the needs of students at the centre of professional thoughts and actions.
- Live up to universal ethical principles of honesty, truthfulness, integrity, fair treatment, and respect for others.
- Maintain a clear distinction between personal values and professional ethics.
- Advocate for teacher professionalism, for school conditions that encourage teaching and learning, and for decision-making structures that take advantage of the expertise of teachers.
- Recognise that life-long learning is an integral part of the profession.
- Recognise the professional responsibility for engaging in and suppor-ting appropriate professional practices for self and colleagues.
- Reflective practice. Teachers are reflective about their practice.
- Think systematically about what happens in the classroom and school, why it happens, and what can be done to improve student achievement.
- Study educational literature and interpret research and apply it to classroom and school.
- Value critical thinking and self-directed learning as habits of mind.

Community and school collaboration: Teacher trainees work collaboratively with colleagues, families, and the community to support the learning environment.

- Reach out beyond the school to promote trust and understanding, to build partnerships with all segments of the school community, and to overcome obstacles that stand in the way of effective family and community involvement in the education of children.
- Are informed about policy issues and initiate or assist in implementing initiatives to improve the education of children.
- Are respected members of the community who play key roles in helping improve communication and collaboration between the members of the community and educators in the school and school system.

- Realise that everything that happens in the community, between individual students, with families, or with colleagues has an impact in the classroom, and work to minimise disruptions in student learning and take advantage of unexpected events to teach students.
- Value and learn from the expertise of other educators.

Details of the practicum component of the B.Ed. syllabus of the Tamil Nadu Teacher Education University can be viewed at this website: http://www.tnteu.ac.in/pdf/BEd_2016_2017.pdf.

Using a Quality Function Deployment Approach for Measuring Customer Satisfaction in Teacher Education Institutions

The two-year integrated B.Ed. curriculum by the NCTE, necessitates teacher-training colleges to have a clear strategy for process improvement. Quality function deployment (QFD) provides a simple and systematic way to upgrade the quality of teacher education programs based on educational quality indicators. QFD will facilitiate addressing the education system in its entirety, based on the requirements of the schools, their vision and mission statements, matching them with the training provided to the teacher trainees facilitating enhancement in the B.Ed. curriculum meeting the needs of the coming generations.

The NCTE document on Curriculum Framework: Two Year B.Ed. Programme points to the need for the use of a variety of approaches for the transaction of courses. How effective are these approaches to meeting the needs of the 21st-century schools?

QFD is hence a structured approach for integrating the 'voice of the customer' with both the product and the transaction process. Here the customer is the school while the design is the curriculum framed by NCTE. QFD will give an insight into the effectiveness of the new B.Ed. curriculum in meeting the needs of current schools who have appointed the teachers who have undergone this two-year curriculum. The process group and NCTE own the responsibility for building a high-quality product, the teacher, which is equal to defining an effective quality management system in the Indian education sector.

CONCLUSION

The expectation is that teachers, whether in-service or pre-service, engaging in reflective practice, studying their own methods of teaching and sharing their experiences with their peers in schools, are a regular feature of professional life.

REFERENCES

Aspinwall, K. et al. (1992), *Managing Evaluation in Education*, Routledge, London.

Lynch, B.K. (1990), A Context Adaptive Model for Programme Valuation, *TESOL Quarterly,* Wiley, USA, Vol. 24, No. 1.

Mohan, Radha (2018), Effectiveness of Two-Year B.Ed. Curriculum in Meeting Schools Requirements: A Quality Function Deployment Approach, EduTracks, Neelkamal Publications, New Delhi, Vol 18, No. 1.

Myint Swe Khine (Editor), and Yang Liu (Editor) (2022), Handbook of Research on Teacher Education: Innovations and Practices in Asia, Springer, Singapore. 1st ed.

Patton, Michael Quinn. (2008), Utilization-Focused Evaluation, Sage, Thousand Oaks, USA.

Stufflebeam, D.L. (1971), The Relevance of the CIPP Evaluation Model for Educational Accountability, *Journal of Research and Development in Education*, Vol. 5, No. 1, pp. 19–25.

Web References

Details of the agencies in India monitoring teacher education.

http://www.naac.giv.in/

http://www.ncte.gov.in

OECD Review on Evaluation and Assessment Frameworks for Improving School Outcomes www.oecd.org/edu/evaluationpolicy.

CHAPTER 12

Central Agency for Accreditation

Quality means doing it right when no one is looking.

—Henry Ford

CURRENT PRACTICES AND TRENDS IN ACCREDITATION IN TEACHER EDUCATION

With increased evidence that the quality of teachers is the most important educational resource for our country, attention needs to be given to quality indicators. This will include the capacity of teacher education colleges to attract able students and to prepare them well to meet the demands of teaching.

Accreditation refers to an endorsement by an independent external agency that a professional preparation course is adequate for the purpose of a particular profession: that the course is able to produce graduates who meet standards for entry to the profession and are competent to teach. It is a key mechanism for assuring the quality of preparation courses in the professions. Accreditation is also an important mechanism for engaging members of a profession in decisions relating to standards expected of those entering their profession.

NEED FOR QUALITY ASSURANCE

1. The expansion of higher education in the past fifty years indicates that university standards can no longer be maintained.
2. Globalisation has made it difficult for countries to restrict the activities of online providers of higher education.
3. The very rapid expansion of new technologies and new modes of delivery have necessitated the need for new forms of quality assurance.

4. There is a need for recognition and harmonisation of foreign degrees and diplomas with the advent of globalisation. This is to ensure the equivalence of qualifications and competencies across countries. Can the B.Ed. obtained from any of the training colleges in India be considered comparable to a European teaching qualification and equivalent for entry to a Masters programme in US?
5. In general, countries that have a national accreditation framework.
6. Establish nationally agreed standards for accrediting teacher education programmes that are based on agreed profession wide standards for graduate teachers.
7. Establish processes for accrediting teacher education programmes based on the standards.

The literature points to the existence of two models of quality assurance in teacher education. They are:

1. University affiliation
2. Accreditation by an independent body.

University Affiliation Model

The university affiliation model indicates that teacher training colleges are affiliated to parent universities. These universities supervise the progression towards eventual independence. The B.Ed. students of these colleges are awarded a qualification, which is accredited by the university. This model has the advantage of fostering collegiality between colleges and affiliating universities. The university has the advisory role of setting criteria and standards and awarding degrees.

However, in today's global scenario, universities themselves are being subjected to evaluation by external agencies. Quality assurance and teacher education qualifications are being managed more by state agencies and other bodies. There is, hence, a shift towards a model of accreditation by an independent body all over the world.

Accreditation by an Independent Body

The American or European model for quality assurance and accreditation usully has a national body comprising independent local bodies as well as defined set of national standards and local standards for accrediting teacher training institutions. Figure 12.1 illustrates the range of bodies and procedures involved in quality assurance and accreditation processes across the European Union.

	Exeternal evaluations	*Internal evaluations*
Bodies responsible	Inspectorate for school education An education agency The ministry of education An evaluation agency or committee	Management Government board of the institution Evaluation committee within the institution Council of acadedmic staff respresentatives
Profile/participants	Peers Experts in evaluation Inspectors with a teaching background Students Foreign experts	Management Academic staff Students Evaluation experts working on behalf of the principal or board Evaluation experts offering staff support
Official documents used to establish criteria	Legislation on higher education Regulations/guidelines for initial teacher education Qualification standards for prospective teachers Internal/external evaluation criteria National indicators (on trainer/student ratios, student performance, etc.)	
Scope	Contents of the teacher education curriculum Teaching methods Assessment practices Balance between professional training and general education School placements Partnerships with schools Human resources management Trainer/student ratios Student performance Student attitudes/motivation Student opinions on the training they receive Infrastructure (libraries, computers, etc.)	
Procedures and mechanisms	Site visit that includes: – interviews with the management, or surveys – interviews with academic and admin staff, or surveys – interviews with students, or surveys – classroom observation	

FIGURE 12.1 Bodies, scope, documents and procedures involved in teacher preparation in Europe.
(*Source:* Adapted from Eurydice European Univ. Brussels, 2006).

The process of accreditation generally involves three steps:

1. A self-evaluation carried out by the staff of the institution or programme according to the criteria set by the accrediting body, and the submission of a written report.
2. A peer review study visit by a team of peers selected by the accrediting body who submit an assessment report based on site visits, interviews, etc.
3. Examination by the accrediting body of both self-evaluation and peer review, leading to a formal decision on recognition for a fixed period of time. The accrediting agency grades and ranks the institution so that the public are aware of the best.

These three steps emphasise that that both internal and external evaluation processes are equally important. The two processes tend to overlap. The university is now not solely responsible for setting the norms and criteria. National indicators play a key role now.

Figure 12.2 is adapted from Quality Assurance in Teacher Education in Europe. It looks at the bodies, scope, documents and procedures involved in teacher preparation in Europe.

	Analysis of internal/External evaluation findings	
Consequences of evaluation	Accreditation or re-accreditation De-accreditation Impact on funding Implementation of a plan for improvement	Implementation of a plan for improvement

FIGURE 12.2 Consequences of this evaluation in Europe.
(*Source:* Adapted and summarised from: Eurydice European Unit., 2006, Quality Assurance in Teacher Education in Europe, Brussels, Eurydice).

Figure 12.3 gives the details of the Australian Universities Quality Agency. In general quality assurance frameworks for education are independent, not-for-profit national agencies, established to monitor, audit and report on higher education. This provides public assurance of the quality of higher education besides assisting in enhancing the academic quality of these institutions.

NATIONAL ASSESSMENT AND ACCREDITATION COUNCIL (NAAC)

The National Assessment and Accreditation Council (NAAC) is an autonomous body, established by the University Grants Commission (UGC) of India to assess and accredit institutions of higher education

Australian Universities Quality Agency (AUQA)	• Independent, not-for-profit national agency • Promotes audits, reports on quality assurance in higher education	• Higher education institutions accountable for adherence to the institution's internally defined mission and objectives • Operates at the institutional level	• Assess the institution's success in maintaining standards consistent with university education
External accreditation by State and Territory statutory authorities		Holds specific professional preparation progra-mme and courses to account against external standards for graduate knowledge and capability and programme quality	

FIGURE 12.3 Teacher accreditation in Australia.

in the country. It is an outcome of the recommendations of the National Policy on Education (1986) that laid special emphasis on upholding the quality of higher education in India.

The system of higher education in India has expanded rapidly during the last fifty years. In spite of the built-in regulatory mechanisms that ensure satisfactory levels of quality in the functioning of higher education institutions, there have been criticisms that the country has permitted the mushrooming of institutions of higher education with fancy programme and substandard facilities and consequent dilution of standards. To address the issues of deterioration in quality, the National Policy on Education (1986) and the Plan of Action (POA-1992) which spelt out the strategic plans for the policies, advocated the establishment of an independent national accreditation body. Consequently, the NAAC was established in 1994 with its headquarters at Bangalore.

Governance

The NAAC functions through its General Council (GC) and Executive Committee (EC), where educational administrators, policy makers and senior academicians from a cross-section of the system of higher education are represented. The Chairperson of the UGC is the President of the GC of the NAAC. The Chairperson of the EC is an eminent academician in the area of relevance to the NAAC. The Director of the

NAAC is its academic and administrative head, and is the member-secretary of both GC and EC. The NAAC also has many advisory and consultative committees to guide its practices, in addition to the statutory bodies that steer its policies. The NAAC has a core staff and consultants to support its activities. It also receives assistance from a large number of external resource persons from across the countries who are not full time staff of the NAAC.

Vision and Mission

The activities and future plans of the NAAC are guided by its vision and mission that focus on making quality assurance, an integral part of the functioning of higher education institutions.

> The vision of the NAAC is:
>
> To make quality the defining element of higher education in India through a combination of self and external quality evaluation, promotion and sustenance initiatives.
>
> The mission statements of the NAAC aim at translating the NAAC's vision into reality, defining the following key tasks of the organisation:
>
> 1. To arrange for periodic assessment and accreditation of institutions of higher education or units thereof, or specific academic programme or projects.
> 2. To stimulate the academic environment for promotion of quality of teaching-learning and research in higher education institutions.
> 3. To encourage self-evaluation, accountability, autonomy and innovations in higher education.
> 4. To undertake quality-related research studies, consultancy and training programme.
> 5. To collaborate with other stakeholders of higher education for quality evaluation, promotion and sustenance.

Guided by its vision and striving to achieve its mission, the NAAC primarily assesses the quality of institutions of higher education that volunteer for the process, through an internationally accepted methodology.

Methodology

For the assessment of a unit, the NAAC follows a three-stage process, which is a combination of self-study and peer review. The three stages are:

1. The preparation and submission of a self-study report by the unit of assessment.

2. The on-site visit of the peer team for validation of the self-study report and for recommending the assessment outcome to the NAAC.
3. The final decision by the Executive Committee of the NAAC.

The self-study report to be validated by peers is the backbone of the whole exercise. Manuals have been developed to suit different units of higher education, with detailed guidelines on the preparation of the self-study report and the other aspects of assessment and accreditation.

The New Methodology of Institutional Assessment and Accreditation of NAAC, in practice since April 2007, has been designed with a view to overcoming some of the limitations of its earlier methodology, and to enhance its rigour, reliability and validity. Besides envisaging significant reduction in inter-team assessment variations, the New Methodology, which is user-friendly, is also expected to enable NAAC to conduct the assessment of large numbers of institutions effectively and in a short time.

Why Accreditation

Education plays a vital role in the development of any nation. Therefore, there is a premium on both quantity (increased access) and quality (relevance and excellence of academic programmes offered) of higher education.

Like in any other domain, the method to improve quality remains the same—finding and recognising new needs and satisfying them with products and services of international standards.

The NAAC has been set up to help all participating institutions assess their performance vis-a-vis set parameters. It is a rating agency for academic excellence across India, and the country's first such effort.

Benefits of Accreditation

The following are the benefits of accreditation:

1. Helps the institution to know its strengths, weaknesses and opportunities through an informed review process.
2. To identify internal areas of planning and resource allocation. Enhances collegiality on the campus.
3. Provides funding agencies objective data for performance finding. Initiates institutions into innovative and modern methods of pedagogy.
4. Gives institutions a new sense of direction and identity.
5. Provides society with reliable information on quality of education offered.

6. Employers have access to information on the quality of education offered to potential recruitees.
7. Promotes intra and inter-institutional interactions.

Criteria for Assessment

Any assessment and subsequent accreditation is made with reference to a set of parameters so that the standing of an institution can be compared with that of other similar institutions.

NAAC has identified the following seven criteria to serve as the basis of its assessment procedures:

1. Curricular aspects
2. Teaching-learning and Evaluation
3. Research, Innovations and Extension
4. Infrastructure and learning resources
5. Student support and progression
6. Governance, Leadership and Management
7. Institutional Values and Best Practices.

Each criterion has a few key indicators identified which are delineated as metrics.

Units of Assessment

To assess and grade the institutions of higher education using the three-step process for accreditation and make the outcome as objective as possible, NAAC has developed an instrument. Though the methodology and the broad framework of the instrument are the same, there is a slight difference in the focus of the instrument depending on the unit of accreditation.

Institutional accreditation

- University: University central governance structure along with all the undergraduate and postgraduate departments.
- College: Any college—affiliated, constituent or autonomous—with all its departments of studies.

Department accreditation

Taking cognizance of differences in the unit of assessment, NAAC has made changes in the focus of the instrument. Thus, separate instruments have been developed to suit different units of higher education. The manuals give details of the criteria on which value judgment on institutional accreditation will be taken by the peer, as well as operational suggestions to get ready for the process. Separate manuals and criterion-wise aspects are being developed by Expert Committees in each subject for this purpose.

New Assessment Instrument

The Assessment Instrument has been redesigned to provide a two-step approach for such institutions. However, a single step approach will continue to be applicable to universities, autonomous colleges and colleges with potential for excellence, as before.

The Assessment Instrument has also been fine-tuned for greater objectivity and validity, for a more effective assessment by the following processes:

1. Identification of key aspects under each criterion and appropriate assessment indicators under each key aspect.
2. Provision of key aspect-wise differential weightages under each criterion.
3. Shifting the institutional overall scoring pattern from the earlier percentages to the cumulative grade point average (CGPA) system on a 4-point scale.

The new Instrument has been designed to bring into operation the **seven assessment criteria** into **criterion-wise key aspects**.

1. Each key aspect is further differentiated into assessment indicators, to be used as guidelines/probes by assessors to capture the micro-level quality pointers.
2. The key aspect-wise grade points yield criterion-wise grades, by making use of key-aspect-wise and criterion-wise weightages. This can lead to a more accurate measurement of the quality of an institution.

The process is shown in the Flow Chart 12.1.

1. *First step: Institutional eligibility for quality assessment (IEQA).* In the first step, IEQA is required to be obtained by an applicant institution at the beginning, while it is still in the planning stage for assessment.
2. *Second step: Assessment and accreditation of affiliated/constituent colleges.* Each category of these institutions shall prepare their appropriate documents for Assessment and Accreditation, by following the institution—specific NAAC Manuals.

Value Framework

A value framework is required to promote the following core values among the higher educational institutions of India.

1. Contributing to national development
2. Fostering global competencies among students
3. Inculcating a value system in students
4. Promoting the use of technology

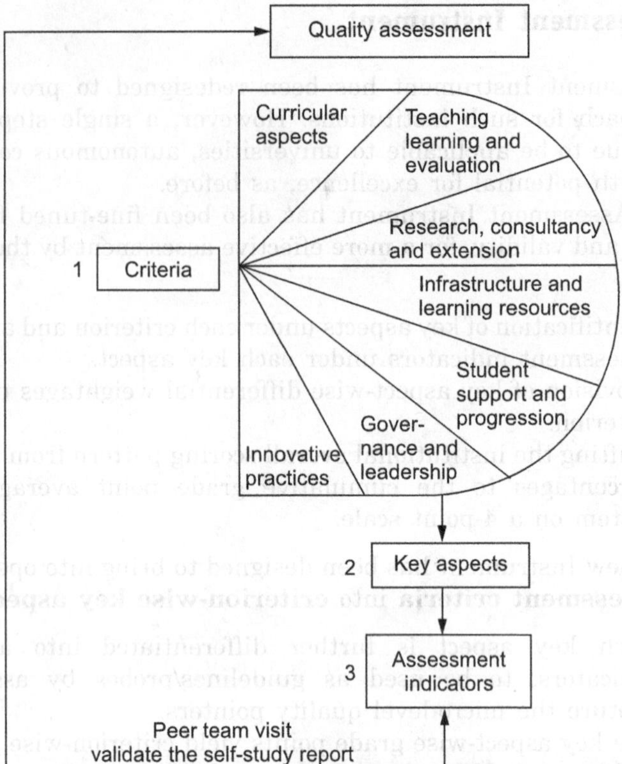

FLOW CHART 12.1: The process of new assessment instrument.
(*Source:* Adapted from NAAC website http://www.naac.gov.in/).

The criteria for University Autonomous Affiliated/College Constituent College

1. Curricular aspects
2. Teaching-learning and evaluation
3. Research, consultancy and extension
4. Infrastructure and learning resources
5. Student support and progression
6. Governance and leadership
7. Innovative practices

New Grading System

In the new methodology, the institutions will be graded for each key aspect under four categories, viz. A, B, C and D, denoting very good, good, satisfactory and unsatisfactory levels, respectively. Table 12.1 highlights the new assessment instrument used by NAAC in India.

TABLE 12.1 The new assessment instrument in India

Two steps: Affiliated/constituent colleges			*Assessment and Accreditation of Affiliated and Constituent Colleges* Institutional Eligibility for Quality Assessment (IEQA) is required to be obtained by an applicant institution
		First step	*The Methodology for First-step* Format to be filled by the applicant institution: Organisational profile, providing specific quantitative information about the institution Filled-in format is received by NAAC The scores obtained: Presented to the appropriate committee of NAAC for deciding on its eligibility for the next step The minimum scores: Given the IEQA status for undergoing the second step (Demonstrate basic compliance with the minimum requirements necessary for the teaching-learning processes, to achieve the educational outcome)
	One step: Universities, autonomous colleges, colleges with potential for excellence		*Assessment and accreditation* (similar to as practiced by NAAC hitherto) Affiliated colleges and constituent colleges (which earned the IEQA status through the first step process), universities, autonomous colleges with potential for excellence (CPEs) The institutions prepare their appropriate documents for assessment and accreditation, by following specific NAAC manuals.
		Second step	*The new instrument: Seven assessment criteria* (Differential weightages for some criteria according to the type of each institution) Curricular aspects – Teaching-learning and evaluation – Research, consultancy and extension – Infrastructure and learning resources – Student support and progression – Governance and leadership (new) – Innovative practices (new)
			Assessment indicators Used as guidelines/probes by the peer teams (their visit to the institution), to arrive at key aspect-wise grade points (KR-GPs) and criterion-wise grade point average (CR-GPAs)
			The new grading system Each institutions will be graded for each key aspect under four categories: A (point average 3.01–4.00, very good/accredited), B(2.01–3.00, good/accredited), V(1.51–2.00, satisfactory/accredited) or D(0–1.50, unsatisfactory-not accredited)

CONCLUSION

In general, most systems of teacher education make use of an external system of approval and/or accreditation of the programmes of teacher education and/or of an external system of certification of the professional qualifications of (prospective) teachers. These external systems aim at giving public assurance of the adequacy of programmes of initial teacher education and their suitability to prepare for the professional tasks and roles of the teaching profession.

Systems of accreditation and/or certification have to meet the following criteria:

1. They must be governed by institutions comprising of various recognised social partners where teachers and teacher educators have to play a decisive role.
2. They have to follow methodologies that build on social consensus in the elaboration of the definitions of the roles and tasks of teachers, as well as concerning standards of evaluation of teacher education programmes and of professional qualifications.
3. Accreditation and certification given by these institutions have to be renewed periodically, taking into consideration changes in the context.
4. They have to consider the entire process of teachers' professional development.
5. The standards that these systems approve have to be defined as general guidelines that provide space for a variety of individual solutions to be found and built by particular teacher education institutions.

REFERENCES

Harford, Judith, Niemi,Hannele, and Hudson, Brian. (2012), Quality assurance and teacher education international challenges and expectations, Lang, New York, Wien, Oxford, 2012.

Yamazumi, K. (2016), Quality Assurance in Teacher Education: Implications for Promoting Student Learning, In: Ng, Ch., Fox, R., Nakano, M. (eds) Reforming Learning and Teaching in Asia-Pacific Universities. Education in the Asia-Pacific Region: Issues, Concerns and Prospects, vol. 33, Springer, Singapore.

Web References

Eurydice European Unit, Brussels, 2006.

http://eacea.ec.eeuropa.eu/education/eurydice/thematic_studies_en.php.

National Assessment and Accreditation Council (NAAC) http://naac.gov.in/.

National Education Policy 2020

https://www.education.gov.in/sites/upload_files/mhrd/files/NEP_Final_English_0.pdf.

National Policy on Education, 1986

http://www.education.nic.in/policy/npe86-mod92.pdftional Policy in Education 1986.

Part VI

PROFESSIONAL PRACTICE AND ETHICS

CHAPTER 13

Characteristics of a Profession

People in this country have been slow to recognise that education is a profession for which intensive preparation is necessary as it is in any other profession.

— UNIVERSITY EDUCATION COMMISSION, 1949

Teaching is the profession that teaches all the other professions.

TEACHING

Good teaching is one of the best ways to create and develop critical thinking among citizens and workers. Enthusiastic, intelligent and well-educated teachers inspire and prepare students for the technological world. It is mainly through their devotion that a great number of students develop enduring scientific interests and perseverance and learn to appreciate and understand the nature of science.

QUALIFICATIONS OF A TEACHER

A teacher should first and foremost possess the following basic qualities:

T—Truthfulness/Tolerance
E—Enthusiasm
A—Accuracy/Aptitude
C—Confidence/Commitment
H—Honesty/Hardwork/Humour
E—Empathy
R—Rational thinking

Each teacher should have the following characteristics:

1. *The basic academic qualifications* laid down by the State Education Departments. Thus for high schools, teachers should have a B.A./B.Sc. degree, and for the higher secondary, M.A./M.Sc. degree.

2. *Professionally trained in modern methods of teaching*. A teacher should have a B.Ed. from a recognised university. This entails that a teacher is well-versed in:

(i) the various teaching methods in use today
(ii) lesson and unit planning
(iii) laboratory management and organisation
(iv) if a science teacher improvising apparatus and developing teaching aids when necessary
(v) organising and managing co-curricular activities
(vi) maintenance and use of libraries
(vii) preparation of instructional materials
(viii) use of evaluation techniques
(ix) confident use of ICT.

3. *Practical knowledge of child psychology and the process of learning*. The teacher should be able to cater to individual differences in her class. She should be able to guide the students according to their interests, capabilities and help them whenever necessary.

Besides these, a teacher should be of a scientific temper, rational in approach to problems, free of bias and superstitions, innovative, and inquisitive about the world around. A teacher should regularly evaluate her teaching, so that she can keep improving, and besides identifying weak areas, using a checklist or rating scale.

Appendix 13.1 is a sample of a well thought out reflective scale. This instrument was developed by the Measurement and Research Division of the Office of Instructional Resources at the University of Illinois Urbana. It may be used in whole or part if credit is given to this source. Directions and scoring instructions have been revised by The Instructional Development Program at The Pennsylvania State University.

QUALITIES OF A GOOD TEACHER

A good teacher:

- Is confident.
- Has belief in herself, despite setbacks.
  (Teachers encounter situations all the time that could be considered setbacks.)
- Has true compassion for students.
- Is a true friend to the students.
- Has a never ending willingness to ensure that all students reach their maximum potential.
- Exemplifies what she teaches.

- Has the ability to look at life in a different way and to explain a topic in a different way.
- Is dedicated to excellence.
(Good teachers want the best from their students and themselves.)
- Offers unwavering support.
(The best teachers know that everyone is able to do well if they have the right teacher. They do not accept that a student is a lost cause.)
- Strives to develop the students into self-learners.
- Is a subject expert with good presentation skills.
- Is aware of what the students do and do not know.
- Is a life-long learner and committed to the profession.
- Strives to develop the students into ethical individuals.
- Is ethical herself.
- Endeavours to develop the students into self-motivated and self-disciplined individuals.
- Attempts to develop scientific attitude in the students.
- Is flexible.
- Has a great sense of humour.
- Is tactful and patient.
- Is willing to help student achieve.
(The best teachers are those that do not stop teaching when the bell rings. They hold extra sessions for board exam preparation and reach out to students after class.)
- Is honest
- Is impartial and free of bias.
- Is a good team player.
(The best teacher works with others to accomplish goals, other teachers and students, parents, etc.)
- Has a passion for life.
(The best teachers are passionate about it. They are also passionate about many other things. They praise good weather and smile when they take a few minutes to discuss last night's episode of a popular TV show.)
- Takes pride in student's accomplishments.
(The best teachers let the student know how glad they are about their students' good performance.)
- Caters as much as possible to each student's individual needs.
- Realises that she is a finite human being.
- Thrives on challenge, can easily build relationships with students and their parents.
- Constantly strives to 'reach and teach' every student under her care.
- Teaches lessons and sequences of lessons across the age and ability range for which she is trained in which she:
  - Uses a range of teaching strategies and resources, including e-learning, taking practical account of diversity and promoting equality and inclusion.

- Builds on prior knowledge, develop concepts and processes, enable learners to apply new knowledge, understanding and skills and meet learning objectives.
- Adapts her language to suit the learners she teaches, introducing new ideas and concepts clearly, and using explanations, questions, discussions effectively.

A professional teacher needs to be confident without being arrogant. Nobody can expect to have all the answers. So, if a student asks a tough doubt, the professional teacher should be able to admit not knowing the answer and offer to find out more for the student. The ideal teacher should have special qualities in addition to those necessary for success in teaching in general. In particular, she should have wide knowledge of her subject—far wider than the limits of the actual syllabus since a teacher is always exposed to investigation, analysis, experimentation and a sea of bewildering questions in the field. Absolute honesty, a passionate love of truth for its own sake, and an enthusiasm for the work of experimental investigation that will not grudge many hours spent in the laboratory beyond those for which she is paid are some of traits she should possess. The teacher should keep reading, to remain in touch with the latest development. Devising of new experiments and improvement of old ones will furnish her with subjects for research of a modest kind. Interaction with the group needs professional standards of behaviour: polite, firm and fair just. Managing the class, the teacher must give everyone their chance to contribute and should be flexible enough to modify lessons if they are obviously not going to plan. Manipulative skill is a valuable asset to the teacher of subject who should try and develop a few workshop skills. Lastly, she could attend in-service training programmes whereby she can remain in-tune with the world around.

Box 13.1 stresses the need to strengthen the teaching community qualitatively.

BOX 13.1 National Knowledge Commission—Teaching Profession

Revitalise the teaching profession to attract and retain quality teachers—The working condition of teachers needs to be drastically improved. Rewards and recognition should be publicised and given at all levels. Teachers at the school and college levels should be encouraged to develop innovative teaching methods. Research should be promoted in colleges by building linkages between colleges and research institutions. Academic autonomy and flexibility should be encouraged. Further, a mentoring programme for young faculty members should be started in universities and colleges. Many reserved faculty posts remain vacant in the absence of innovative or flexible appointment modes to fill these posts, creating enormous practical difficulties in teaching. There is a need to start a systematic affirmative campaign 2 to rectify this situation.

Young students who can eventually fill these posts could be selected from an early age and nurtured and trained carefully to induct them into a career in teaching.

National Knowledge Commission (2nd May 2008), Government of India. http://www.knowledgecommission.gov.in/recommendations/math&science.asp

Box 13.2 gives the common important qualities of a good teacher.

BOX 13.2 Qualities of a Good Teacher

Empathy: You have the ability to bond with students, to understand and resonate with their feelings and emotions. To communicate on their level. To be compassionate with them when they are down and to celebrate with them when they are up.

Positive mental attitude: You are able to think more on the positive and a little less on the negative. To keep a smile on your face when things get tough. To see the bright side of things. To seek to find the positives in every negative situation. To be philosophical.

Open to change: You are able to acknowledge that the only real constant in life is change. You know there is a place for tradition but there is also a place for new ways, new ideas, new systems, and new approaches. You don't put obstacles in your way by being blinkered and are always open and willing to listen to others' ideas.

Creative: You are able to motivate your students by using creative and inspirational methods of teaching. You are different in your approach and that makes you stand out from the crowd. Hence, the reason why students enjoy your classes and seek you out for new ideas.

Sense of humour: You know that a great sense of humour reduces barriers and lightens the atmosphere, especially during heavy periods. An ability to make your students laugh will carry you far and gain you more respect. It also increases your popularity.

Presentation skills: You know that your students are visual, auditory or kinaesthetic learners. You are adept at creating presentation styles for all three. Your body language is your main communicator and you keep it positive at all times. Like a great orator you are passionate when you speak. But at the same time you know that discussion and not lecturing stimulates greater feedback.

Calmness: You know that the aggression, negative attitudes and behaviour that you see in some of your students have a root cause. You know that they are really scared young people who have come through some bad experiences in life. This keeps you calm and in control of you, of them and the situation. You are good at helping your students de-stress.

Respectful: You know that no one is more important in the world than anyone else. You know that everyone has a place in the world. You respect your peers and your students. Having that respect for others gets you the respect back from others.

Inspirational: You know that you can change a young person's life by helping them to realise their potential, helping them to grow, helping them to find their talent, skills and abilities.

https://tewhakatipurangahouictpdcluster.wikispaces.com/file/view/Qualities.png

WHO IS A PROFESSIONAL TEACHER?

A professional teacher, that is, a teacher possessing high degree of 'professionalism', approaches each of her professional tasks and responsibilities in a planned and systematic manner with high level of efficiency. More specifically, a professional teacher:

1. Possesses reasonably sufficient level of mastery over the content knowledge of the subject she teaches to her students. She validates or invalidates the 'given' knowledge and constructs new knowledge on the basis of her own experiences, observations and reflections and encourages her students to do the same.
2. Continuously strives to update her knowledge through self-study, reflections, discussion with colleagues and participation in orientation or training programmes.
3. Is a keen observer of children's behaviour in different settings inside or outside the school. She examines the prevalent concepts related to children's development through her own studies.
4. Is sincerely committed to the students and always keeps their interests above everything else including her own personal interests.
5. Is committed to the teaching profession, strives to contribute towards its further development and does nothing to lower its reputation in the society.
6. Is well aware of her social obligations and does nothing to violate the basic principles of our Constitution and to loosen the moral and social fabric of society.
7. Is well-versed in providing guidance and counselling to students and is always willing to help them in solving their problems.
8. Possesses a fair amount of expertise in various professional tasks such as teaching, testing, curriculum making, textbook writing, preparing teaching aids, etc.

Dimensions of a Professional

Figure 13.1 represents the two major dimensions—career and professional elements—which provide guidance to the professional expectations of practicing teachers.

Career Dimensions

Teachers develop their knowledge, skills and practices throughout their professional lives. However, teacher development is not a simple linear process. They enter the profession with varying levels of prior learning, work experience and professional preparation, and work in a range of

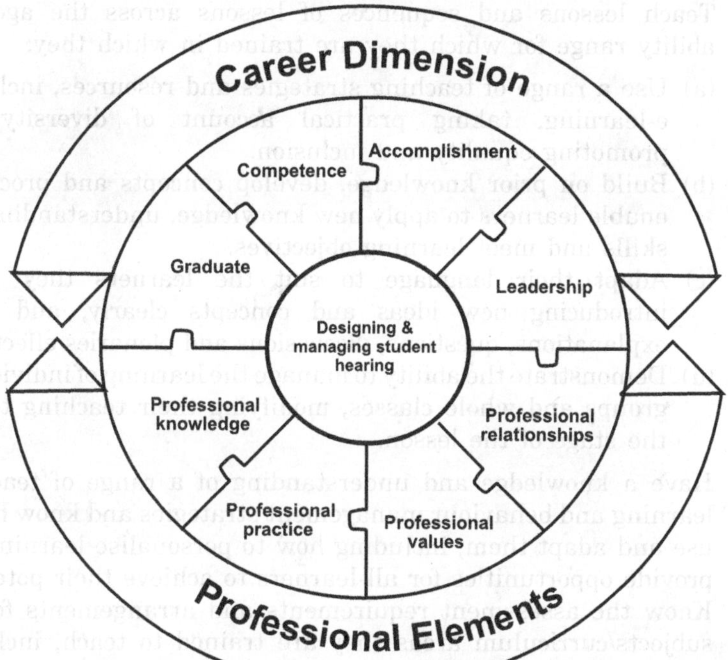

FIGURE 13.1 Dimensions of a professional.

different contexts. Individual teachers display a profile pattern along a continuum of practice related to their competence and confidence in particular aspects of their role over the period of a career.

The components of this dimension are:

- Academic achievement
- Competence
- Accomplishment
- Leadership

Professional Elements

The components under this dimension are discussed in detail in the following sections:

Professional knowledge

Professional knowledge requires the teachers to:

1. Have a secure knowledge and understanding of their subjects/ curriculum areas and related pedagogy to enable them to teach effectively across the age and ability range for which they are trained.

2. Teach lessons and sequences of lessons across the age and ability range for which they are trained in which they:
   (a) Use a range of teaching strategies and resources, including e-learning, taking practical account of diversity and promoting equality and inclusion.
   (b) Build on prior knowledge, develop concepts and processes, enable learners to apply new knowledge, understanding and skills and meet learning objectives.
   (c) Adapt their language to suit the learners they teach, introducing new ideas and concepts clearly, and using explanations, questions, discussions and plenaries effectively.
   (d) Demonstrate the ability to manage the learning of individuals, groups and whole classes, modifying their teaching to suit the stage of the lesson.
3. Have a knowledge and understanding of a range of teaching, learning and behaviour management strategies and know how to use and adapt them, including how to personalise learning and provide opportunities for all learners to achieve their potential.
4. Know the assessment requirements and arrangements for the subjects/curriculum areas they are trained to teach, including those relating to public examinations and qualifications.
5. Provide timely, accurate and constructive feedback on learners' attainment, progress and areas for development.
6. Support and guide learners to reflect on their learning, identify the progress they have made and identify their emerging learning needs.
7. Establish a purposeful and safe learning environment conducive to learning and identify opportunities for learners to learn in out-of-school contexts.

Professional practice

Professional practice requires the teachers to:

1. Know and understand the relevant statutory and non-statutory curricula and frameworks, including those provided through the National Curriculum Framework for their subjects/curriculum areas, and other relevant initiatives applicable to the age and ability range for which they are trained.
2. Plan homework or other out-of-class work to sustain learners' progress and to extend and consolidate their learning.
3. Know a range of approaches to assessment, including the importance of formative assessment.
4. Know how to use local and national statistical information to evaluate the effectiveness of their teaching, to monitor the progress of those they teach and to raise levels of attainment.

5. Be aware of the current legal requirements, national policies and guidance on the safeguarding and promotion of the well-being of children and young people.
6. Know how to identify and support children and young people whose progress, development or well-being is affected by changes or difficulties in their personal circumstances, and when to refer them to colleagues for specialist support.

Professional values

Professional values require the teachers to:

1. Plan for progression across the age and ability range for which they are trained, designing effective learning sequences within lessons and across series of lessons and demonstrating secure subject/curriculum knowledge.
2. Understand how children and young people develop and that the progress and well-being of learners are affected by a range of developmental, social, religious, ethnic, cultural and linguistic influences.
3. Establish a clear framework for classroom discipline to manage learners' behaviour constructively and promote their self-control and independence.

Professional relationships—Team working and collaboration

Professional relationships require the teachers to:

1. Work as team members and identify opportunities for working with colleagues, sharing the development of effective practice with them.
2. Ensure that colleagues working with them are appropriately involved in supporting learning and understand the roles they are expected to fulfill.
3. Know and understand the roles of colleagues with specific responsibilities, including those with responsibility for learners with special educational needs and disabilities and other individual learning needs.
4. Maintain a cordial relationship with all stakeholders of the education system—management, parents, society and community.

CHARACTERISTICS OF A PROFESSION

The fact that professionals, including teachers, do normally get paid for what they do, is important. The receipt of payment is one side of the contract. The other side is the performance of the services contracted for. A professional teacher is not simply one who does teach, but also one who has a duty to teach. Since the duty arises out of a contract, it is primarily a legal duty.

Many occupational groups claim a "professional" identity for their practitioners and some groups endorse a "code of ethics" as evidence of their professionalism. However, forms of occupational control, within either professional or other work groups, may influence the manner in which ethical standards function. It is clear that a professional is defined differently than an average worker. While not every professional will possess every quality of a perfect professional, they do possess most of the traits as defined.

In the past, defined traits of a professional group were based on the analysis of education in the health care field (Flexner, 1915). The essence of professional practice centered on key common values and behaviours.

Some elements considered critical to professional practice include:

- Independent thinking applied to understanding and resolving problems
- Development of ongoing, systematic knowledge
- Transfer of knowledge and techniques through education using specialised symbols
- Autonomous decision-making with responsibility and, therefore, inherent risk
- Code of ethics with ideal of service for social good
- Public trust with social contract for self-governance

Wickenden (1949) lists the six characteristics of a profession as one who:

1. Renders a specialised service based upon advanced specialised knowledge and skill, and dealing with its problems primarily on an intellectual plane rather than on a physical or a manual labour plane.
2. Involves a confidential relationship between a practitioner and a client or an employer.
3. Is charged with a substantial degree of public obligation by virtue of its profession of specialised knowledge.
4. Enjoys a common heritage of knowledge, skill, and status to the cumulative store of which professional men are bound to contribute through their individual and collective efforts.
5. Performs its services to a substantial degree in the general public interest, receiving its compensation through limited fees rather than through direct profit from the improvement in goods, services, or knowledge, which it accomplishes.
6. Is bound by a distinctive ethical code in its relationships with clients, colleagues, and the public.

GENERAL CHARACTERISTICS OF A PROFESSIONAL

In general, a professional, in any particular field, will have the following characteristics.

1. **Specialised knowledge based on extensive preparation:** Being a professional does not happen overnight. It requires many hours of study and preparation. Professionals are expected to maintain a high knowledge level and expertise.
2. **Participates in ongoing training and development:** A professional firmly believes in staying current in their field. This means that a professional is committed to continued training and development.
3. **Accepts responsibility:** Professionals seek and accept responsibility. They can be trusted and given high levels of responsibility within the organisation. A professional is handed tasks at such a high level that poor performance can reflect poorly on the entire organisation, not just the individual.
4. **Have a sense of ownership of their work:** Professionals feel a sense of ownership and pride in everything they do. They work not to just meet organisation standards, but also most importantly, meet the standards of their own pride in their work. Professionals work for the organisation as if they were working in their own business.
5. **Maintains a collective networking spirit outside of the organisation:** Professionals understand that their work is not limited to their organisation. They understand the importance of professional relationships outside of work with others in the same field.
6. **Maintains high standards of ethics and integrity:** Professionals are driven by a code of ethics. They have a strong sense of right and wrong. Their integrity ensures that they adhere strongly to a set of values about how they do their work.
7. **Maintains high standards of performance:** Professionals have high levels of expectations both of themselves and others. They are determined to always do the right thing and do it well. Doing a job well is more important to a professional than the number of hours that they work by the clock. A true professional is unsatisfied with poor performance. While money may be important, it is not the driving force behind the professional's desire to put forth exemplary work. Teaching as a profession fulfils all these criteria.

PROFESSIONALISATION OF TEACHER EDUCATION

Teaching is a profession and teacher education is a process of professional preparation of teachers. Preparing one for a profession is an arduous task and it involves action from multiple fronts and perspectives. A profession is characterised by a sufficiently long period of academic training, an organised body of knowledge on which the undertaking is

> based, an appropriate duration of formal and rigorous professional training in tandem with practical experience in the field and a code of professional ethics that binds its members into a fraternity. These dimensions acquire critical importance in view of several factors.
>
> —NCFTE, 2010

There is, first of all, the traditional idealism, the esteem and importance attached to the role of the school teachers and very high societal expectations from them. Teachers are concerned, in an important way, with the total development of human beings—physical, intellectual, emotional, social, moral and spiritual. While the dimensions of teaching other than the informational and cognitive may have suffered neglect in modern times due to a variety of factors, one cannot deny that they constitute an integral part of the teachers' role and functions. The implication of this is to give due emphasis to developing reflective teachers with positive attitudes, values and perspective, along with skills for the craft of teaching.

AIMS OF PROFESSIONAL DEVELOPMENT

The aims of continuing professional development programmes for teachers are to:

1. Explore, reflect on and develop one's own practice.
2. Deepen one's knowledge of and update oneself about one's academic discipline or other areas of school curriculum.
3. Research and reflect on learners and their education.
4. Understand and update oneself on educational and social issues.
5. Prepare for other roles professionally linked to education/ teaching, such as teacher education, curriculum development or counselling.
6. Break out of intellectual isolation and share experiences and insights with others in the field, both teachers and academics working in the area of specific disciplines as well as intellectuals in the immediate and wider society.
7. Enable teachers to work towards prioritised goals in education such as universalisation and inclusion.
8. Influence social attitudes and generate greater commitment to constitutional values and overcoming discrimination in the classroom.
9. Transform existing practices towards more learner-friendly methods and methods suited to strengthening conceptual learning and understanding rather than rote learning.
10. Enable teachers to implement and achieve specific targeted aspects in the curriculum, such as the use of a type of technology, or the addition of topics such as AIDS and adolescent education.

11. Prepare teachers to play enhanced roles in the education system as resource persons, or principals, etc.

ACTIVITIES FOR PROFESSIONAL DEVELOPMENT

All teachers should have a professional responsibility to be engaged in effective, sustained and relevant professional development throughout their careers and all teachers should have a contractual entitlement to effective, sustained and relevant professional development throughout their careers.

When a teacher begins her career, the knowledge and skills acquired by her in college serve only as basic necessities or minimal requirements to launch her work. The first few years of teaching will lead the new teacher to identify, re-examine and evaluate her goals of subject teaching methods, the nature of the content and one's own personal aspirations. An excellent education for subject content teaching can merely provide the basic tools for the creative teacher to implement, supplement, and modify knowledge to meet the everyday challenges of young people in a subject content classroom.

The subject teacher, like any other professional, does not commence her career with a complete understanding of methodology of teaching subject content to students. It is necessary that she continues to learn not only from day-to-day teaching experience but also from the many opportunities that are available. The continual learning of subject and of 'how to teach subject content creatively' are development processes that never end.

Professional development for a teacher would require teachers to:

1. Become members of associations which have from time to time, taken up academic activities and organised conventions and meetings to discuss professionally important developments.
2. Be involved in textbook preparation and indeed even in the preparation of training modules.
3. Work in the block and cluster resource centres as well as to contribute to training as resource persons.
4. Act as members of committees formulating educational policies.
5. Participate in NGO initiatives in several parts of the country that have developed and implemented models of teacher professional development and support in ways that directly impact the classroom practices.
6. Attend seminars, workshops, conferences.
7. Pursue higher qualifications like M.A., M.Sc., M.Ed., etc.
8. Exchange teaching position, either in the same school or through exchange programmes.
9. Visit other schools to study different methods of teaching, the facilities, etc.

10. Write articles, etc. for professional journals like *School Science, Indian Educational Review*.
11. Participate in refresher courses to get acquainted with the latest developments in the field.
12. Participate in the national integration camps which are being introduced for primary school teachers organised in different parts of the country. Each camp is attended by primary school teachers drawn from different states and regions.

PRINCIPLES OF DESIGNING IN-SERVICE PROGRAMMES FOR TEACHERS

The NCFTE 2010 has highlighted the principles for designing relevant in-service programmes for teachers.

Content and Pedagogic Approach

- Principle of space—space to think and develop one's own ideas
- Clarity of aims and objectives
- Principle of choice—needs of the teacher, time and utility
- Principle of interactivity—with colleagues and resource persons
- Related to real life experiences—activities in keeping with teacher's day-to-day activities.

Addressing Teachers as Learners

1. Principle of acknowledging what the teacher already knows.
2. Principle of respect of the teacher as a professional. Programmes must build on and strengthen the teacher's own identity as a professional teacher and, in many cases, also establish and nurture the linkage with the academic disciplines of their interest
3. Principle of freedom to assess quality and the extent to which it relates to their needs.
4. Principle of balance. Over-training, routinised and superficial training leads to cynicism and training fatigue.

Short- and Long-term Courses

Courses of short and long duration designed to develop either specific skills or areas of interest could be developed and offered to teachers to attend over the year. For example, a DIET could design and offer courses in specific topics such as 'teaching decimals', 'developing honesty among children' or 'AIDS education'. Some of these could be of a short duration, say 4 to 5 days, while others may even be for a longer period of time, from 1 to 3 months, to enable teachers to develop a specific core area in which they need to strengthen their knowledge-base and professional skills, e.g. using puppets in the English classroom, organising and managing group activities.

Use of Distance Media

ICT including TV, radio, telephony and internet are useful as resources and providing access to ideas or for the wider dissemination of information.

Sabbatical for Study and Research

Teachers could be provided with the option of taking a year off (paid or unpaid) to pursue a course or spend time at another school, university or NGO in order to learn and study. Such sabbaticals could be tied to a report or even a publication for wider dissemination that is produced at the end. Such sabbaticals could also be linked up with an appropriate mentor on the site to guide the teacher during this period.

Professional Conferences and Meetings

Attending meetings and conferences connected to the profession. Teachers could be permitted to avail of duty leave, 3–4 days a year, to attend such meetings.

Professional Fora, Resource Rooms and Materials

Providing professional fora such as meetings in the school and in the cluster to discuss and review one's practice, to plan for annual work calendars, and on a weekly and monthly basis to plan for one's teaching as well as to discuss with colleagues, the school academic head and resource persons at the cluster or block level, is an essential aspect of the teaching profession.

Faculty Exchange Visits and Fellowships

A few exchange teacher fellowships could be provided for each district to enable selected teachers to go for a period of three months to one academic year to a school in another state within the country or even outside the country, to teach and learn there.

CONCLUSION

Staff development activities have traditionally been packaged into short-term, discrete, in-service sessions or workshops. Most of these workshops tend to follow a somewhat standardised format, with an outside expert interacting with teachers while teachers are expected to passively receive and then try to make use of it in their teaching practice. Training-based discrete in-service workshops may be useful for delivering certain types of information such as methods for organising portfolio assessment of students' work (Little, 1993) or teaching specific skills such as the use of a particular computer software package (Grant, 1997). However, their usefulness as the dominant channel of professional development in diverse contexts has been widely criticised.

New guidelines have emerged for the professional development of science teachers in order to facilitate the desired reform. Accordingly, the standards encompass shift in several areas of emphases in the professional development of science teachers, which reflect the changing conception of the role of professional development in educational reform as well as the role of teachers in the professional development and reform process.

REFERENCES

Falloon, G. (2020), From digital literacy to digital competence: The teacher digital competency (TDC) framework, Educational Technology Research and Development, Springer, Germany, 68, 2449–2472.

Government of India (2010), *National Curriculum Framework for Teacher Educators 2009*, Ministry of Human Resource Development, New Delhi.

Web References

Bates, A.W. (2019) Teaching in a Digital Age: Guidelines for designing teaching and learning-2nd Edition., University of British Columbia. BCCampus https://open.umn.edu/opentextbooks/textbooks/221.

Calvin College-Instructor self-evaluation instructorself-eval.doc (live.com).

Guidelines For 50 Hours Of Continuous Professional Development For Teachers, Head Teachers And Teacher Educators Based On National Education Policy 2020. Ncert. https://ncert.nic.in/pdf/Guidelines50HoursCpd.pdf.

New Vision for Education Unlocking the Potential of Technology. World Economic Forum. https://www3.weforum.org/docs/WEFUSA_NewVisionforEducation_Report2015.pdf.

RISE-Indiana Department of Education Evaluation Model https://www.in.gov/doe/files/rise-handbook-30.pdf.

Teaching Effectiveness
https://resources.depaul.edu/teaching-commons/teaching-guides/reflective-practice/Pages/teaching-effectiveness.aspx

Technology Use for Teacher Professional Development in Low- and Middle-Income Countries: A systematic review.
https://www.sciencedirect.com/science/article/pii/S2666557322000088?via%3Dihub

APPENDIX 13.1

instructorself-eval.doc (live.com)

Instructor Self-Evaluation

Calvin College
Teaching Development Forms
Committee On Faculty Teaching

PURPOSE:

This instrument aims to provoke instructor reflection about assumptions and priorities that affect teaching. No set "right" answers exist nor are value judgments attached to a particular score. The goal is to encourage encounters with ideas and assumptions that inform the practice of instruction.

ADMINISTRATION:

Instructors can complete this form at almost any juncture. Answers may be determined in terms of instructional activities in a given class or based on the general approach taken to teaching. The objective here is self-evaluation. The results need to be shared. For that reason, honesty is encouraged and no risk is involved.

INTERPRETATION:

The last page of the instrument contains scoring instructions, which ought to be consulted when the instrument has been completed. These interpretive suggestions should also be read then as well. **Do not read further if you intend to use the instrument.**

Scored results on this instrument identify areas of priority ascribed to one's teaching. The nature of the questions force you to think about your priorities even though you may perceive your instruction to be balanced. Results should stimulate reflections and introspection. Are they what you anticipated or were you surprised by the results? Given a predilection towards a priority area, consider the instructional strategies and activities commonly included in your course. Do they communicate and reinforce this priority? What about the area on this instrument that represents the lowest priority? Should that area assume a greater importance? Are there instructional alterations that might increase your effectiveness in the area? Can they be implemented efficiently and without compromising your focus in other areas?

SOURCE:

This instrument was developed by the Measurement and Research Division of the Office of Instructional Resources at the University of Illinois Urbana. It may be used in whole or part if credit is given to this source. Directions and scoring instructions have been revised by The Instructional Development Program at The Pennsylvania State University.

INSTRUCTOR SELF-EVALUATION

DIRECTIONS:

Following are a number of statements describing aspects of college teaching. Examine the items in each set and rank them from 1 to 4 according to the degree to which they apply to your beliefs about teaching generally or your attitudes towards a course specifically. While responding, first examine the set and find the item that describes you or your course MOST, and assign a rank of 1 to that statement. Then decide which statement describes you or your course second best, assign a rank of 2 to that item. Do likewise with the two remaining statements, assigning to them ranks of 3 and 4, respectively. If you find some items difficult to rank, show what your choice would be if you had to choose. It is important that you assign a different rank to each item and complete all sets in order to score the instrument.

SET 1

_______ a. I present thought-provoking ideas.
_______ b. I am sympathetic towards and considerate of my students.
_______ c. I assist students in appreciating things they did not appreciate before.
_______ d. I am interested in and concerned with the quality of my teaching.

SET 2

_______ a. My students feel efforts made by them in the course are worthwhile.
_______ b. I am aware of students' needs.
_______ c. I raise challenging questions or problems in class.
_______ d. I make every effort to improve the quality of students' achievement in my course.

SET 3

_______ a. I encourage students to share in class their knowledge, opinions, and experiences.
_______ b. I help students become aware of the implications of the course's subject matter in their life.
_______ c. I remind students to come to me for help whenever it is needed.
_______ d. I analyze previous classroom experience to improve my teaching.

SET 4

_______ a. I take an active, personal interest in improving my instruction.
_______ b. I stimulate and answer questions in class.
_______ c. I relate to students easily.
_______ d. I help students to develop the ability to marshal or identify main points or central issues.

SET 5

_______ a. I organise my course well.
_______ b. I am knowledgeable about related areas aside from my own.

_______ c. I stimulate students' appreciation for the subject.
_______ d. I get along well with students.

SET 6

_______ a. I restate questions or comments to clarify for the entire class.
_______ b. I try to make every course the best every time.
_______ c. I am sensitive to students' feelings.
_______ d. I promote students' satisfaction in learning the subject matter.

SET 7

_______ a. My students gain new viewpoints and appreciation.
_______ b. I have zest and enthusiasm for teaching.
_______ c. I develop a sense of mutual respect with students.
_______ d. I present clear and relevant examples in class.

SET 8

_______ a. I find teaching intellectually stimulating.
_______ b. I make students feel at ease in conversation with me.
_______ c. I stimulate students' interest in the subject.
_______ d. I answer questions as thoroughly and precisely as possible.

SET 9

_______ a. I coordinate different activities of my course well.
_______ b. I look forward to class meetings.
_______ c. I enjoy having students come to me for consultation.
_______ d. My students feel that they can recognize good and poor reasoning or arguments in the field.

SET 10

_______ a. I try to function creatively in teaching my course.
_______ b. I encourage students to participate in class.
_______ c. I actively help students who are having difficulties.
_______ d. I stimulate students' intellectual curiosity.

SET 11

_______ a. I meet with students informally out of class when necessary.
_______ b. I make the objectives of the course clear.
_______ c. I try to make every course the best every time.
_______ d. My students become motivated to study and learn.

SCORING THE INSTRUCTOR SELF-EVALUTION FORM

The form has four scales. One statement from each set is associated with each scale.

Adequacy of Classroom Procedures.
Enthusiasm for Teaching and Knowledge of Subject Matter.
Stimulation of Cognitive and Affective Gains in Students.
Relations with Students.

STEP 1 – Record the score assigned each individual item in each of the four areas.

STEP 2 – Total each scale's scores. (see next page)

STEP 3 – To interpret the results, consider the lowest total score to represent the area in this course or in your teaching generally to which you ascribe the highest priority. The cover sheet on the instrument contains some pointer on interpreting the results.

SCORING SHEET

Adequacy Scale			**Enthusiasm Scale**	
	Score			Score
Set			Set	
1-a	_______		1-d	_______
2-c	_______		2-d	_______
3-a	_______		3-d	_______
4-b	_______		4-a	_______
5-a	_______		5-b	_______
6-a	_______		6-b	_______
7-d	_______		7-b	_______
8-d	_______		8-a	_______
9-a	_______		9-b	_______
10-b	_______		10-a	_______
11-b	_______		11-c	_______
TOTAL	_______		TOTAL	_______
Stimulation Scale			**Relations Scale**	
	Score			Score
Set			Set	
1-c	_______		1-b	_______
2-a	_______		2-b	_______
3-b	_______		3-c	_______
4-d	_______		4-c	_______

(Contd.)

Stimulation Scale			Relations Scale	
	Score			Score
5-c	______		5-d	______
6-d	______		6-c	______
7-a	______		7-c	______
8-c	______		8-b	______
9-d	______		9-c	______
10-d	______		10-c	______
11-d	______		11-a	______
TOTAL	______		TOTAL	______

CHAPTER 14
Professionalism in Teacher Education

Professionalism means consistency of quality.

— Frank Tyger

INTRODUCTION

High quality teaching is essential to improving student outcomes and reducing gaps in student achievement. The Teacher Performance Appraisal System provides teachers with meaningful appraisals that encourage professional learning and growth. The system is designed to foster teacher development and identify opportunities for additional support where required. By helping teachers achieve their full potential, the performance appraisal process represents a method of achieving high levels of student performance. Performance appraisals in the field of education refer to the process of a supervising educator observing and evaluating the performance of a teacher. Supervising educators are usually department heads or administrative faculty—principals or vice principals. Performance appraisals are usually structured in such a way that the teachers being observed receives valuable feedback on both strengths and weaknesses in their teaching approach, allowing them to increase their effectiveness.

PERFORMANCE APPRAISAL OF A TEACHER (Figure 14.1)

Performance appraisals follow a set pattern determined by the school board. The district develops a way of evaluating teachers based on the state teaching objectives and standards. This provides an external, neutral and objective measure by which to evaluate teachers. The staff members responsible for observing teachers are usually individuals who

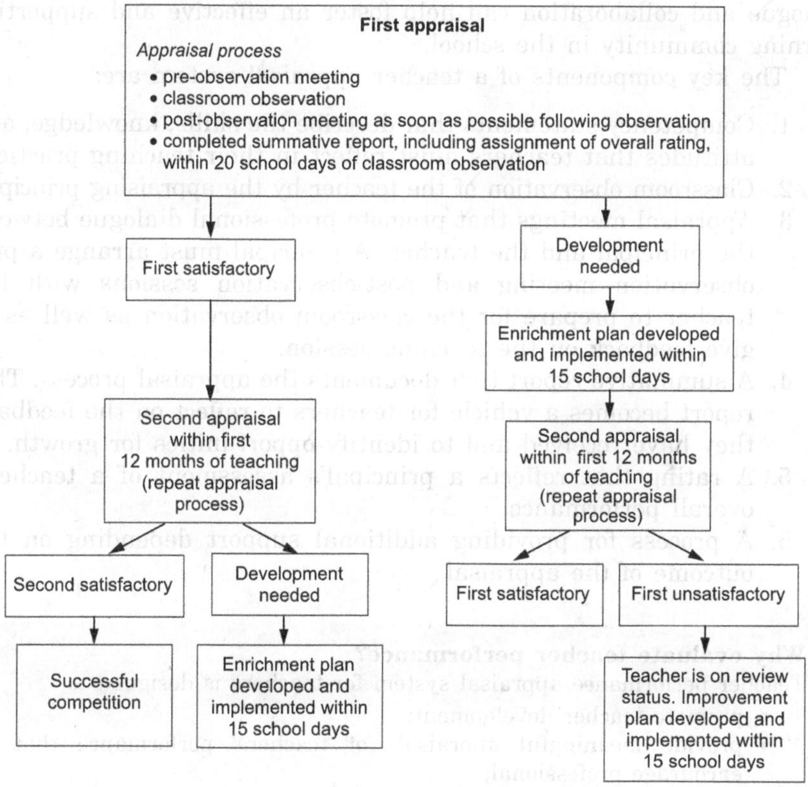

FIGURE 14.1 Procedure for appraisal.

have demonstrated proficiency in teaching and who have a thorough knowledge of the appraisal criteria.

Performance appraisals are an integral part of a continuum of professional learning that supports effective teaching, learning, and assessment practices by building on and complementing previous learning in pre-service teacher education programmes as well as learning acquired throughout each individual's teaching career. It helps strengthen schools as learning communities where teachers have the chance to engage in professional exchanges and collaborative inquiries that foster continuous growth and development. Professional dialogue and collaboration are essential to the creation and maintenance of a healthy school culture. An appraisal system in which both teachers and principals are actively engaged provides a framework for assessing teachers' practices in a way that meets their professional learning needs. Appraisals engage principals and teachers in professional dialogue that deepens their understanding of what it means to be a teacher.

Through this inquiry process, principals and teachers move closer to the shared vision they have established for the school. A growth-focused appraisal process that emphasises the importance of professional dialogue and collaboration can help foster an effective and supportive learning community in the school.

The key components of a teacher appraisal system are:

1. Competency statements that describe the skills, knowledge, and attitudes that teachers must reflect in their teaching practice.
2. Classroom observation of the teacher by the appraising principal.
3. Appraisal meetings that promote professional dialogue between the principal and the teacher. A principal must arrange a pre-observation meeting and post-observation sessions with the teacher to prepare for the classroom observation as well as to give feedback on the teaching session.
4. A summative report that documents the appraisal process. This report becomes a vehicle for teachers to reflect on the feedback they have received and to identify opportunities for growth.
5. A rating that reflects a principal's assessment of a teacher's overall performance.
6. A process for providing additional support depending on the outcome of the appraisal.

Why evaluate teacher performance?

Teacher performance appraisal system for teachers is designed to:

- promote teacher development;
- provide meaningful appraisals of teachers' performance that encourage professional;
- learning and growth;
- identify opportunities for additional support where required; and
- provide a measure of accountability to the public.

PROCEDURE FOR APPRAISAL

Principals, vice-principals, teachers, and supervisory officers are key players in the performance appraisal process.

Principals

- Principals are responsible for conducting performance appraisals of all teachers assigned to their school.
- Teachers actively participating in each appraisal are vital to a teacher's ongoing growth and development.
- School boards must make every effort to ensure that all teachers have documented evidence of their competency.

Teacher performance appraisal often takes the shape of a formal observation of the teacher in the classroom. This involves the supervising teacher or administrator scheduling an observation ahead of time. The observer sits in the class and takes notes on teacher behaviour, student response and flow of lesson. Another appraisal technique takes place outside of the classroom in the form of a portfolio review. An appointed individual will read and evaluate a portfolio of lessons and assessments the teacher has created as well as student work. These two techniques together can provide a comprehensive view of the teacher's work in and outside of the classroom.

Feedback

After the appraisal has been completed, the individual reviewing the teacher will create a formal set of observations complete with feedback and suggestions. This is often formally presented in writing to the teacher being observed.

Professional Development

The supervising teacher or administrator in charge of evaluating the teacher usually reports on strengths and weaknesses, as well as actionable suggestions for development. Weaknesses are analysed for growth opportunities, and the evaluator will often help the teacher develop a specific action plan for personal professional development. This is often called a personal growth plan, or teacher improvement plan.

Code of Conduct for Appraisers

The reviewer should operate at the highest ethical standard in all aspects of the performance appraisal process to ensure that the report is not compromised. The principles of *objectivity, transparency, honesty* and *consistency* should be upheld. Using the process effectively requires an investment of time and energy from both principal/team leader and teacher. The following principles must be maintained:

1. Confidentiality in handling and storing all information.
2. Awareness that performance is being assessed, i.e. the way the individual works, and not the individual himself or herself.
3. Awareness that ratings should reflect the teacher's performance in relation to the goals and action plan agreed on during the earlier part of the school year and not in comparison to other individuals.
4. Comments should provide clear evidence and measurements to support the rating given.

5. Respect and courtesy should be displayed by and to all who are involved in the evaluation process.
6. Sensitivity should be demonstrated towards the context, circumstances and conditions in which the teacher works.
7. While special recognition may be given to teachers who use their initiative in overcoming deficiencies in the system, a teacher should not be penalised where the necessary materials, equipment, etc. are not provided by the school.
8. The interest and welfare of the students are paramount in executing the performance appraisal process.

FIVE DOMAINS—TEACHER COMPETENCY ASSESSMENT

1. **Commitment to students and student learning:** Teachers are dedicated in their care and commitment to students. They treat students equitably and with respect and are sensitive to factors that influence individual student learning.
2. **Professional knowledge:** Teachers strive to be current in their professional knowledge and recognise its relationship to practice. They understand and reflect on student development, learning theory, pedagogy, curriculum, ethics, educational research, and related policies and legislation to inform professional judgment in practice.
3. **Professional practice:** Teachers apply professional knowledge and experience to promote student learning. They use appropriate pedagogy, assessment and evaluation, resources, and technology in planning for and responding to the needs of individual students and learning communities. Teachers refine their professional practice through ongoing inquiry, dialogue, and reflection.
4. **Leadership in learning communities:** Teachers promote and participate in the creation of collaborative, safe, and supportive learning communities. They recognise their shared responsibilities and their leadership roles in order to facilitate student success. Teachers maintain and uphold the principles of the ethical standards in these learning communities.
5. **Ongoing professional learning:** Teachers recognise that a commitment to ongoing professional learning is integral to effective practice and to student learning. Professional practice and self-directed learning are informed by experience, research, collaboration, and knowledge.

Table 14.1 sets out the 16 competency statements within the five domains in a tabular form.

TABLE 14.1 The 16 competency statements within the five domains.

Domain	*Competency*
Commitment to pupils and pupil learning	• Teachers demonstrate commitment to the well-being and development of all pupils. • Teachers are dedicated in their efforts to teach and support pupil learning and achievement. • Teachers treat all pupils equitably and with respect. • Teachers provide an environment for learning that encourages pupils to be problem solvers, decision makers, lifelong learners, and contributing to a changing society.
Professional knowledge	• Teachers know their subject matter, the Ontario curriculum, and education related legislation. • Teachers know a variety of effective teaching and assessment practices. • Teachers know a variety of effective classroom management strategies. • Teachers know how pupils learn and the factors that influence pupil learning and achievement.
Teaching practice	• Teachers use their professional knowledge and understanding of pupils, curriculum, legislation, teaching practices, and classroom management strategies to promote the learning and achievement of their pupils. • Teachers communicate effectively with pupils, parents, and colleagues. • Teachers conduct ongoing assessment of pupils' progress, evaluate their achievement, and report results to pupils and their parents regularly. • Teachers adapt and refine their teaching practices through continuous learning and reflection, using a variety of sources and resources. • Teachers use appropriate technology in their teaching practices and related professional responsibilities.
Leadership and community	• Teachers collaborate with other teachers and school colleagues to create and sustain learning communities in their classrooms and in their schools. • Teachers work with professionals, parents, and teachers of the community to enhance pupil learning, pupil achievement, and school programmes.
Ongoing professional learning	Teachers engage in ongoing professional learning and apply it to improve their teaching practices.

(*Source:* Adapted from Ontario College of Teachers' Standards of Practice for the teaching profession)

PROFESSIONAL ETHICS

"Scientific statements of facts and revelations, indeed, cannot produce ethical directives. However, ethical directives can be made rational and coherent by logical thinking and empirical knowledge" (Einstein, 1953).

Ethics is the term that encompasses a variety of approaches to the understanding and examination of moral living. Morality is the distinction and content of right and wrong. Common morality is based on social codes or rules which can be erroneous and incomplete. Thus, morality can be viewed as the end result of ethical deliberation about problems that need decisions and require action

In education, conflicts about morality may arise during the development of scientific knowledge and during application of learned knowledge in practice. Differences in the concepts of education and morality interface among individuals or groups of people, for example, between an education professional and a religious bigot, or among education researchers and a cultural or community group.

Professional Code of Ethics

Professional associations have accepted the role of identifying and espousing the key values of their members based on the social contract and public trust. This role includes activities such as ongoing reform of the profession, serving as a vehicle for communicating professional standards, and integrating the ethics of the profession into the values of society at large. The method commonly used by professional organisations to communicate ethical standards to professional members and to society is the "code of ethics."

The two key attributes are confidentiality and loyalty.

1. **Confidentiality:** Maintain confidences despite vital interest to others.
2. **Loyalty:** Exhibit allegiance to either an employer or to the broader community.

The ethical standards for the teaching profession represent a vision of professional practice. At the heart of a strong and effective teaching profession is a commitment to students and their learning. Teachers in their position of trust demonstrate responsibility in their relationships with students, parents, guardians, colleagues, educational partners, other professionals, the environment and the public—all stakeholders of the educational community.

The purposes of the ethical standards for the teaching profession are to:

1. Inspire members to reflect and uphold the honour and dignity of the teaching profession.

2. Identify the ethical responsibilities and commitments in the teaching profession.
3. Guide ethical decisions and actions in the teaching profession.
4. Promote public trust and confidence in the teaching profession.

The ethical standards for the teaching profession are (Figure 14.2):

1. **Care:** The ethical standard of care includes compassion, acceptance, interest and insight for developing students' potential. Teachers express their commitment to students' well-being and learning through positive influence, professional judgment and empathy in practice.

2. **Respect:** Intrinsic to the ethical standard of respect are trust and fair-mindedness. Teachers honour human dignity, emotional wellness and cognitive development. In their professional practice, they show respect for spiritual and cultural values, social justice, confidentiality, freedom, democracy and the environment.

3. **Trust:** The ethical standard of trust embodies fairness, openness and honesty. Teachers' professional relationships with students, colleagues, parents, guardians and the public are based on trust.

4. **Integrity:** Honesty, reliability and moral action are embodied in the ethical standard of integrity. Continual reflection assists teachers in exercising integrity in their professional commitments and responsibilities.

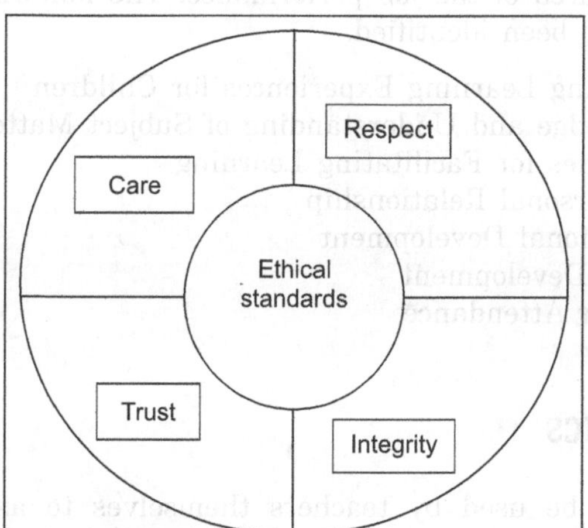

FIGURE 14.2 Components of ethical standards in teaching profession.

Ethics of Professional Practice and Educational Research

Professional groups strive to establish standards of practice that ensure high quality of services to the public. Professional codes of ethics are guidelines that attempt to assure the moral behaviour of professionals within acceptable ethical conduct and defined standards of professional practice. To maintain scientific integrity, research studies investigating education issues must be designed to comply with basic standards of professional practice, including ethical behaviour. In education research, professional practice standards, codes of ethics, and guidelines for scientific integrity must all interact with sound practices of scientific inquiry.

Performance Indicators (PINDICS) are used to assess the performance and progress of teachers. It consists of performance standards (PS), specific standards and performance indicators. Performance standards are the areas in which teachers perform their tasks and responsibilities. Under performance standards, there are some specific tasks which are expected to be performed by the teachers. These are termed as specific standards. From specific standards performance indicators have been derived.

PINDICS is based on the provisions in sections 24, and 29 and the schedule specifying norms and standards for schools in the RTE Act 2009, NCF-2005 and SSA Framework-2011. It has been further fine-tuned using the feedback received from the NCERT Study- 'In-service Education for Teachers (INSET) impact on classroom transaction' conducted in 2010-11, try out with primary and upper primary school teachers and comments received from state-level officers from SCERT and SPO, and teacher education professionals.

Performance Standards (PS) communicate expectations for each responsibility area of the job performance. The following performance standards have been identified.

- Designing Learning Experiences for Children
- Knowledge and Understanding of Subject Matter
- Strategies for Facilitating Learning
- Interpersonal Relationship
- Professional Development
- School Development
- Teacher Attendance

Use of PINDICS

PINDICS can be used by teachers themselves to assess their own performance and to make continuous efforts to reach the highest level. These can also be used for teacher appraisal by the supervisory staff/ mentor to assess and provide constructive feedback for the improvement of teacher performance. Each performance indicator is rated on a 4-point scale ranging from 1 to 4 indicating the levels of performance.

The rating points are:

1. Not meeting the expected standard
2. Approaching the expected standard

3. Approached the expected standard
4. Beyond the expected standard

If the teacher innovatively performs tasks and makes extra efforts to improve student performance, he/she can be rated as beyond the expected standard.

The details of the tool can be obtained from https://ncert.nic.in/dte/pdf/PINDICS.pdf.

CONCLUSION—THE FUTURE OF PROFESSIONAL ETHICS IN TEACHING

A generation ago, Sockett (1990, p. 243) argued that a code of ethics was "something to be hammered out as professionalism develops... as we discover what best practice is..." Clearly, it is time for an attempt to be made. A code of ethics can encourage discussion on the issues and improve how people deal with ethical dilemmas. On the other hand, if this code can encourage professional bodies to adopt their own codes, perhaps largely based on this design, then perhaps it has accomplished more than it would as a free-standing set of rules.

REFERENCES

Danielson, C. and McGreal, T. (2000), Teacher Evaluation to Enhance Professional Practice, Association for Supervision and Curriculum Development, Alexandria, VA.

Einstein, Albert (1953), Correspondence 1903–1955, as quoted by D.H.J. Hermann, 1972, University of Kentucky, College of Law.

Nigro, F.A. and Nigro, L.G. (Eds.) (1984), *Modern Public Administration*, 6th ed., Harper & Row, New York.

Sockett, H. (1990), Accountability, Trust, and Ethical Codes of Practice, in J.I. Goodland, R. Soder & K.A. Sirotnik (Eds.), *The Moral Dimensions of Teaching*, Jossey-Bass Publishers, San Francisco.

Web References

Murphy, J. and Swenson, W. (2003), 20 Questions to Ask about Your Code of Conduct, *Ethikos* 17(1). Retrieved January 1, 2006 from http://www.ethikosjournal.com/html/20questions.html.

National Education Association (1975), Code of Ethics of the Education Profession, Retrieved December 20, 2005 from http://www.nea.org/aboutnea/code.html.

National Education Association (2020), Code of Ethics of the Education Profession, Retrieved December 20, 2005 from https://www.nea.org/resource-library/code-ethics-educators.

UNESCO document -Draft of NCTE (2010)

https://etico.iiep.unesco.org/sites/default/files/2019-02/india_2010_code_of_professional_ethics_for_school_teachers.pdf.

Part VII

RESEARCH AND ACTION

CHAPTER 15

Research in Teacher Education

Somewhere, something incredible is waiting to be known.

—Carl Sagan

INTRODUCTION

The well-established tradition of teaching and learning in India has retained its inherent strength even under adverse circumstances. The paradigm shift from the *gurukula* system of ancient times to the post-independence period was characterised by major efforts being made to mould teacher education to meet the changing needs. Pre-service education has come under considerable pressure as a result of the expansion and growth of school education, through efforts to universalise elementary education. Having inherited a foreign model of teacher preparation at the time of independence from Britain in 1946, major efforts have been made to adapt and update the teacher education curriculum to local needs, to make it more context based, responsive and dynamic to India's rapidly changing needs. The current system of teacher education is supported by a network of national, state and district level resource institutions, like NCERT, NCTE, SCERT, DIET, IASE and others working together to enhance the quality and effectiveness of teacher preparation programmes at the pre-service level and also through in-service programmes for serving teachers throughout the country.

NEED FOR RESEARCH

Teacher education is an important field for research since the quality of teacher education has been regularly questioned by governments at the same time as teacher quality is increasingly being identified as crucial to educational outcomes and pupil gains. Consequently, teacher education researchers need to work together in order to:

1. Share emerging research findings.
2. Develop innovative research methodologies within teacher education.
3. Disseminate innovative pedagogical methods within teacher education.
4. Find new publishing outlets within an overcrowded academic field.
5. Support colleagues in institutions with underdeveloped research profiles.

Research in teacher education can be categorised into several areas. Researching teacher education in changing times and with current national policies is the need of the day. In the light of National Curriculum Framework for Teacher Education 2010, the innovations to be incorporated into teacher education provide an excellent basis for research.

> Teacher education today is an integral part of any educational system. Teaching, being both a skill and an art, was found amenable to transmission in the early years of the 19th century. If, for ages, teacher education, per se, was a caste or family affair, it could not afford to remain so after education became a mass movement. Mass literacy goals as well as the emergence of technology transformed the very character of teacher training and its philosophy. The National Policy on Education, 1986, reflects precisely this change in its concept and practice. Now, teacher education is no longer limited to primary or secondary levels of teachers but extends far beyond. The creation of the Academic Staff College under the aegis of the UGC is a case in point. No wonder then that teacher education has emerged as an important area of educational research.
>
> *Research in Teacher Education: A Trend Report: L.C. Singh, S.P. Malhotra*

In the first four surveys, 410 studies have been identified as belonging to the area of teacher education. Researchers working in this area have brought into their study a wide spectrum of variables. This was because teacher education is a vast subject covering a range of disciplines. The institution, the process of admission, training climate, administrative set-up, the student—teacher, the personal characteristics of teachers, practice schools—these factors, and quite a few more, are constantly at work in the teaching learning scenario.

Figure 15.1 gives the overall general areas in teacher education which can be researched. The areas are:

1. Research and teacher education—context and goals
2. Researching teacher education in changing times: policies and paradigms

3. Teachers' characteristics:
   (i) Research on the demographic profile
   (ii) Research on the indicators of quality
4. Teacher education programmes—pre-service and in-service
   (i) Research on the effects of coursework in the foundations of education
   (ii) Research on methods: courses and field experiences
   (iii) Research in preparing general education teachers to work with students with disabilities
   (iv) Research on pedagogical approaches in teacher education
   (v) Research on accountability in teacher education
5. A research agenda for teacher education.

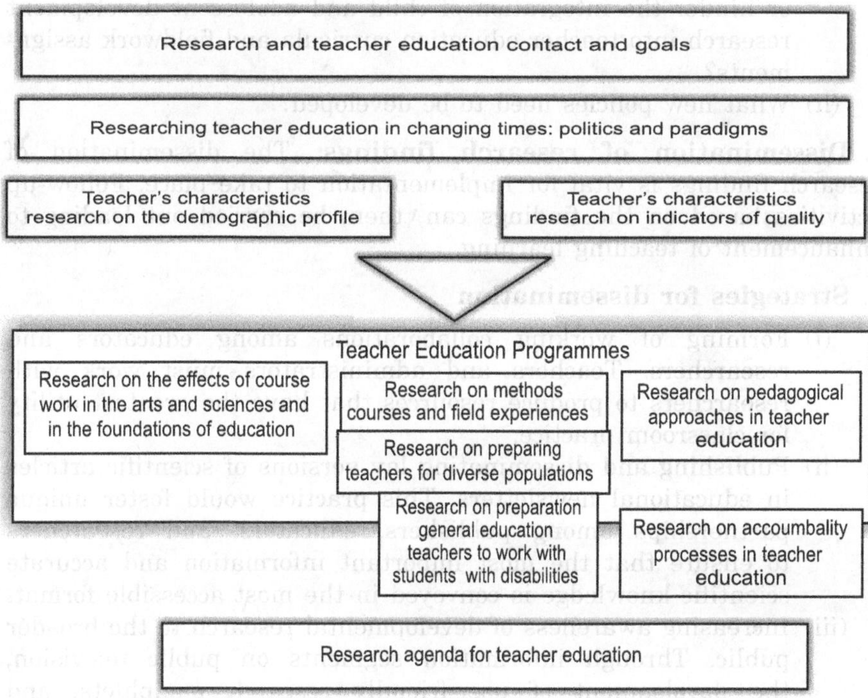

FIGURE 15.1 Overall general areas in teacher education.

Questions which need answers in determining some of the most important areas of knowledge and practice in teacher education that could be examined in greater depth are:

1. **Pre-service, induction and in-service teacher education**
   (i) What are the current best practices in teacher education and preparation and to what extent are these practices supported by scientific evidence?

(ii) What new standards regarding student development need to be developed and incorporated into the current standards of practice for teacher education programmes?

2. **Teaching, learning and adolescence**

(i) What is the current state of teaching and learning with respect to the development of the student (child or adolescent)?

(ii) What are the gaps in the research base?

(iii) Where are the areas of convergence in the research base?

3. **Implications of research in teacher education for policy building**

(i) What are the current policies (local, state, national) that support or hinder the integration of child and adolescent development research into teacher education curricula and fieldwork assignments?

(ii) What new policies need to be developed?

4. **Dissemination of research findings:** The dissemination of research findings is vital for implementation to take place. Follow-up activities based on the findings can, then, be carried out leading to enhancement of teaching learning.

5. **Strategies for dissemination**

(i) Forming of working collaborations among educators and researchers. Teachers and administrators must work with researchers to produce resources that have the greatest utility for classroom practice.

(ii) Publishing and disseminating lay versions of scientific articles in educational newsletters. This practice would foster unique partnerships among publishers, educators, and researchers to ensure that the most important information and accurate scientific knowledge is conveyed in the most accessible format.

(iii) Increasing awareness of developmental research to the broader public. Through information segments on public television, the development of user-friendly research pamphlets, and interdisciplinary clearing houses, child and adolescent development research could be made available to a broader base of consumers.

TEACHER EDUCATION RESEARCH IN HISTORICAL CONTEXT

Research on teacher education has evolved through various phases since the beginning of the 20th century within the overall context of the history of teacher education. Although the body of research on the history of teacher education is relatively small, major works by

Borrowman (1956) and Labaree (1995) have revealed significant factors that have framed subsequent research efforts. Much of research in teacher education was dominated by surveys of practices in the field (e.g. Conant, 1963), by studies of changes in student teacher attitudes during practice teaching, and by studies that sought to indirectly identify the characteristics of good teachers by surveying those in the field about what traits and abilities those teachers identified as good possessed (Barr, 1929; Charters and Waples, 1929). The sixties and seventies saw a new emphasis in teacher education research on training teachers to perform behaviours that were thought to be effective based on research correlating teacher behaviour with student achievement test scores (Gage, 1978).

Reviews of studies in the area of teacher education have been attempted by Lulla and Singh (1974), Mehrotra (1979), Das and Jangira (1983), Bhatnagar (1980), and Pillay (1987). A synoptic overview of the nature of these reviews would help one to take stock of the researches completed in the area. Lulla and Singh (1974), in their trend report in 'A Survey of Research in Education' (Buch, 1974), classified teacher education research into six areas, namely, *selection criteria; abilities and qualities of the teacher; pre-service and in-service training of teachers; workload, job satisfaction and difficulties experienced by the teachers; procedures and practices of teacher education in India;* and *personality variables of teachers.*

In his trend report in the Second Survey of Research in Education, Mehrotra (1979) did the classification differently. Here, the variables were clustered under *contextual, input, process* and *output categories.*

In the Third Survey, Jangira (1986) adopted a systems model of classifying (as per Sage, 1974) variables under context-presage-process-product categories.

The trend report by L.C. Singh, S.P. Malhotra is based on the studies abstracted in the three earlier surveys (Buch 1974, Buch 1979 and Buch 1986) and also 150 additional studies identified for the area in this volume. All these 410 studies done at Ph.D. and project levels have been taken together for identifying emerging trends. No separate classification has been thus worked out for the additional studies separately. This had been done with a view to avoiding overlapping and to present a comprehensive view of trends in the area over a substantial period. The studies have been viewed from three points of view—*their nature, methodology of research,* and *a systems approach to teacher education.*

1. **Nature of studies:** 276 studies at Ph.D. level and 134 at project level were examined. The most explored area in teacher education is pre-service education, having 248 studies, while 110 studies have been done in in-service education. Thirty six studies have tried to probe both pre-service and in-service education. The levels (pre-primary,

primary, secondary, higher secondary, technical) at which teacher education is organised provide another frame of reference for clustering the studies.

2. **Methodology:** Different researchers followed different research procedures according to the nature of the problem selected by them. Cross-cultural studies constitute 40 per cent and longitudinal studies six per cent of the total. Among the different methods of research followed, nearly 49 per cent can be classified as survey studies, 26 per cent as experimental, eight per cent as case studies, nine per cent as historical, and six per cent as exploratory studies. In most of the studies, students of different courses and teachers formed the controlled factors studied under higher education. *Researchers have paid little attention to developmental and evaluation studies. There is a need to go in for such studies so as to provide guidelines for future teacher-education programmes.*

3. **Systems approach to teacher education:** Teacher education has been viewed by them from a systems approach point of view and the studies have been categorised as context-presage-process-product studies.

GAPS IN TEACHER EDUCATION RESEARCH

Several questions need to be answered in the context of teacher education and school education. Are the demands of teachers' need and classroom concerns met? How can teachers be made more independent, motivated and critical thinking oriented regarding the teaching profession? How can teaching practice be made more effective, interactive, vibrant and meaningful with use of e-resource material in teacher education? How can the gap between teacher education curriculum and school curriculum be bridged?

Shamsha Emanuel, S. Gaythri and Hitarth Panchal (2005) has identified pitfalls in teacher education curriculum. There is a wide gap between the 'phraseology' and the 'implementation'.

Poonam Batra's Voice and Agency of Teacher' (2005: 4352) has found some gaps in the vision of teacher education envisaged by the NCF 2005. 'First viewing the teacher as one who needs to be persuaded and trained… oriented to be empowered to evolve pedagogy that fosters critical thinking within a consciously created democratic environment of learning for all children irrespective of class, religion, region, community and gender.' Secondly, it is assumed that teachers (typically constructed as homogenous category) exist in isolation of socio-political context that actively discriminates between people and children from different background and that they can be 'oriented' successfully to 'implement' the articulated new perspective of NCF.

Bansal (2005) has observed some gaps between teacher education curriculum and school education curriculum. He considers the following points lacking in the teacher education curriculum

1. Lack of knowledge of school subjects
2. Pedagogical weakness
3. Lack of coordination between technocratic culture and cultural heritage
4. Lack of research on problems of schools and education
5. Scarcity of resources in schools and training institutions.

Volumes I and II on Research Abstracts of the studies conducted by Teacher Education Institutions in India 1998 onwards consisted of 216 studies differentiated into 19 areas. These volumes are available on the INTEL website, www.educationinindia.net. Goel, Goel and Madhavi of M.S. University, Baroda have compiled abstracts of research studies conducted by teacher education institutions in India. The present volume attempts to abstract and classify educational research conducted by Teacher Education Institutions in India mostly 2005 onwards. It presents abstracts of the 120 Research Studies categorised into 23 areas. This is available at http://www.educationinindia.net/download/Research_Abstracts_Volume_3.pdf

In the Section 15 on Teacher Education, the studies listed are shown in Table 15.1.

TABLE 15.1 Survey of selected studies in teacher education—2000 onwards

No.	*Topic*	*Researcher/s*	*University*	*Year*
1.	Educational Innovations in the Primary Schools of Gujarat State: A Status Survey	Ashwin Kumar D. Trivedi	South Gujarat University, Surat	2003
2.	To Study the Effect of Creativity Appreciation Training Programme (CATP) on the Teachers	Madhumita Roy	Nagaland University, Kohima	2004
3.	Evaluation of Teachers by Students	Shrirang Baburao Kshisagar	University of Pune, Pune	2006
4.	Study of Personality Traits and Academic Achievement in Relation to Socio-metric Status of Tribal Students in Varying School Settings	Ashok Kumar Parida	Kurukshetra University, Kurukshetra	2007
5.	Teacher Education in Portuguese Goa (1841–1961): A Historical Perspective	Richard Cabral,	University of Pune, Pune	2007

(*Contd.*)

TABLE 15.1 Survey of selected studies in teacher education—2000 onwards (Contd.)

No.	*Topic*	*Researcher/s*	*University*	*Year*
6.	A Study of the Academic Accountability of Teacher Educators as indicated by the Performance appraisal system prevailing in Teacher Education Institutions in Mumbai	Raju Talreja	University of Mumbai, Mumbai	2008
7.	Designing, Developing and Implementing an Educational Programme for Enhancing Emotional Maturity of Student-Teachers	Archana Dutta	M.S. University of Baroda, Vadodara	2009
8.	Evolving Competency based Curriculum in Science Education for in-service Primary School Teachers	Gyanendra Nath Tiwari	University of Allahabad, Allahabad	2009
9.	A Study of Human Resource Development Climate of DIETs in Rajasthan	G. Kamesh Rao	M.S. University of Baroda, Vadodara	2009
10.	Shbhagitapooran Adhyapak -Shiksha Karyakram Kee Kshetra Tatha Savvikas Mein Prasangikta" ("Relevance of the Participatory Teacher-Education Programme in the context of Area and Self Development")	Priya Gupta	Banasthali Vidyapeeth, Rajasthan	2009
11.	Sevapoorva Avam Sevarat Adhyapakon Ke Daitavbodh Avam Samajik Moolyon Ka Ek Samikshatmak Adhyyan	Santosh Kumar Singh, Dr. R.M.L.	Avadh University, Faizabad	2009

FUTURE DIRECTIONS FOR RESEARCH

Over the past three decades, as new research methods and methodologies have been developed in the social sciences, they have been employed in educational research in general and in teacher education in particular. Methods of research in teacher education have not yet shown the same kind of dynamic relation between the problems and contexts of the field and the kinds of research methods that are being developed.

The list of research topics mentioned in the website http://www.aiaer.net/pdffiles/RESEARCHTOPICSINTEACHEREDUCATION.pdf

has been developed for perusal of teacher educators and researchers in teacher education. The areas in which suggested topics have been listed are as follows: 1. Student teachers and school teachers; 2. Teacher educators; 3. Teacher education courses; 4. Management of teacher education; 5. Evaluation of performance of student teachers; 6. Admission procedures; 7. Laboratory/pre-practice teaching preparation; 8. Innovations; 9. Practice teaching, Internship and field experiences; 10. Super vision; 11. Laboratory/demonstration/professional development schools; 12. Linkage of teacher education institutions and their linkage with others; 13. In-service and induction programmes; 14. Gender issues; and 15. Technology and teacher education.

TEACHING PROCESS AND TEACHER BEHAVIOUR

The research in organisation and behaviour in teacher education has centred its attention primarily on how best to teach teachers what they need to learn to do to positively affect student learning. One aspect of this line of research tries to identify teacher behaviours and techniques that can be shown to be most effective with groups of students. Although the research is not directly research on teacher education, it has formed the basis for identifying strategies that can be used to organise teacher education content and processes and the research programme that can be used to assess their effectiveness.

Figure 15.2 represents the teaching process and the points to be pondered over.

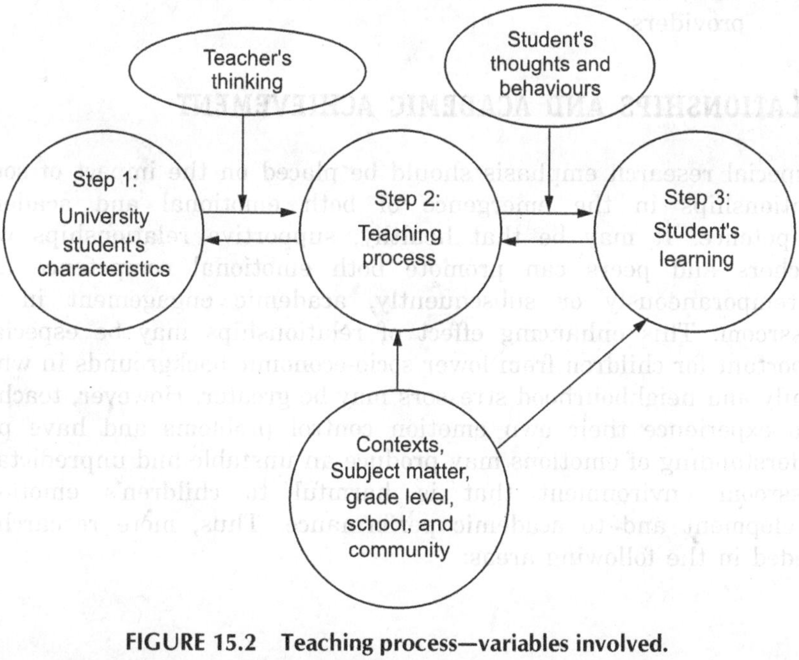

FIGURE 15.2 Teaching process—variables involved.

The following specific areas of interest could be explored in future research studies:

1. Sources of individual differences in cognitive and social functions, and how these differences affect curricular demands.
2. How to mentor teachers to be problem solvers by learning how, within the classroom context, developmental issues impact school performance and behaviour.
3. The impact of increasing demands on children and how the increasingly complex information environment affects functions such as discipline.
4. A more systemic understanding of cognitive development, for example learning to appreciate how language capabilities play out in interpersonal relationships.
5. Research related to emotional maturity; specifically studies that involve research on the role that teachers can play in helping students learn to control emotions, and that test the effectiveness of interventions designed to help teachers respond to problematic behaviour as a failure of emotion control.
6. Studies on inclusive education, addressing the ways in which special education can play an important role in facilitating a child's comfort level in school thereby improving behaviour, and in helping the child to be more engaged in the school environment and available for learning.
7. Evaluations of programmes that bring mental health services into the schools—especially those in which children have a great many stressors in their lives and little access to mental health providers.

RELATIONSHIPS AND ACADEMIC ACHIEVEMENT

A special research emphasis should be placed on the impact of social relationships in the emergence of both emotional and academic competence. It may be that healthy, supportive relationships with teachers and peers can promote both emotional competence and, contemporaneously or subsequently, academic engagement in the classroom. This enhancing effect of relationships may be especially important for children from lower socio-economic backgrounds in which family and neighbourhood stressors may be greater. However, teachers who experience their own emotion control problems and have poor understanding of emotions may produce an unstable and unpredictable classroom environment that is harmful to children's emotional development and to academic performance. Thus, more research is needed in the following areas:

1. Studies that highlight the connections between adult emotion regulation, classroom environment, and student behaviour and achievement.
2. Parent-teacher relationships that promote academic achievement; research is needed that will enable classroom teachers to provide parents with developmentally appropriate information about ways in which parents can promote their children's academic performance. Such research must address the specific parenting behaviours that enhance a child's ability in reading, writing, and mathematics. The research should be longitudinal, following students at various levels (pre-school, elementary school, middle school, and high school) over time to gather the needed in-depth information.
3. More research is needed to determine how emotional competence translates into academic success during the transition to elementary school.
4. More applied research is needed to investigate prevention programmes targeting both socio-emotional and academic competence.

Culture, Development and Achievement

1. How teachers working in urban school districts could benefit from a deeper understanding of low-income students' experiences and responsibilities at home, and how these constrain students' behaviour and achievement in school.
2. Studies that highlight variations in student experiences and outcomes within urban and rural schools, and how teachers can best be prepared to work effectively with diverse groups of students who have diverse needs and strengths.
3. Studies focus on the importance of parental involvement in children's learning as well as on efforts to improve schools. This implies paying more attention to the processes by which parents, teachers, and children can work together as a community and learn together.
4. The historical and comparative dimensions of teacher education research are in need of support. In a context of expansions of the globalisation of economy and culture, researchers need to employ research strategies that will aid in understanding the various contexts of teacher education.
5. The pedagogical focus for teacher preparation has been primarily directed towards understanding the research on child and adolescent development in order to program the behaviour of teachers. Now, given the changing scene of schooling, the current focus should shift to increasing teachers' knowledge

and understanding to inform their decisions about particular children, classes and schools. There is need to study the paradigm shift away from traditional thinking towards acknowledging the impact of interacting classroom processes on diverse student populations and their outcomes.

CONCLUSION

The lockdowns in response to COVID-19 have interrupted conventional schooling with nationwide school closure. Schools and teachers have tried valiantly to maintain learning continuity during this period. Students have had to rely more on their own resources to continue learning remotely through the Internet, smart phones, television or radio. Teachers were propelled to learn new pedagogical concepts and modes of delivery of teaching. Teachers had to cater to a diverse student population, with some learners in the most marginalized groups with no access to digital learning resources and are at risk of falling behind. Gaps of learning in all domains are evident in most school children. Research in filling these gaps is the need of the day.

The future will undoubtedly present the teaching community with so many more challenges which will have to be met. The "Learn, unlearn, relearn" cycle will definitely have to be in place.

REFERENCES

Bansal, N.K. (2005), Bridging the Gaps between School Curriculum and Teacher Education Curriculum, Quality concern in Teacher Education, CASE, Faculty of Education and Psychology, the M.S. University of Baroda, pp. 185–187.

Batra, P. (2005), Voice and Agency of Teachers: Missing Link in National Curriculum Framework 2005, *Economics EPW*, Oct. 1–7, pp. 4347–4356.

Buch, M.B. (1974), in Buch, M.B. (Ed.), *A Survey of Research in Education*, CASE, MSU, Baroda.

Charters, W. and D. Waples (1929), *The Commonwealth Teacher Training Study*, University of Chicago Press, Chicago, IL.

Das, R.C. and N.K. Jangira (1983), in Buch, M.B. (Ed.), *Third Survey of Research in Education*, CASE, MSU, Baroda.

Dorn, Emma, Hancock, Bryan, and Sarakatsannis, Jimmy, (2021), Covid and education: An emerging K-shaped recovery, McKinsey & Company. COVID-19 and the widening learning gap, McKinsey, New York.

Gage, N.L. (1978), *Handbook of Research on Teaching*, Rand McNally, Chicago, pp. 94–141.

Jangira, N.K. (1986), in Research in Teacher Education: Trend Report, in Buch, M.B. (ed.), *Third Survey of Research in Education*, CASE, MSU, Baroda.

Lulla, B.P. and L.P. Singh (1974), Teacher Education: A Trend Report in Buch, M.B. (Ed.), *A Survey of Research in Education*, CASE, MSU, Baroda.

Mehrotra, R.N. (1979), Teacher Education: A Trend Report in Buch, M.B. (Ed.), *Second Survey of Research in Education*, SERD, Baroda.

Shamsha Emanuel, S. Gaythri, and Hitarth Panchal (2005), Teacher Education Curriculum in Alignment with School Curriculum—An Introspection, Quality Concern in Teacher Education, CASE, Faculty of Education & Psychology, M.S. University of Baroda, pp. 140–146.

Singh, L.C. and S.P. Malhotra, Research in Teacher Education: A Trend Report, Buch, M.B. (Ed.), in *Fourth Survey of Research in Education, CASE, MSU, Baroda, 1983–88* (Vol. II).

Web References

Abstracts of Research Studies Conducted by Teacher Education Institutions in India Volume IV. Research Abstracts of the Studies conducted (sadbhavnapublications.org).

Goel, D.R., Goel, Chhaya and R.L. Madhavi, CASE, M.S. University of Baroda, Vadodara. http://www.educationinindia.net/download/Research_Abstracts_Volume_3.pdf.

INDIAN EDUCATIONAL ABSTRACTS Prilims (ncert.nic.in).

Research Abstracts on Education 1998–2009. Microsoft Word-Research Abstracts on Education.doc (educationforallinindia.com).

CHAPTER 16
Action Research

Any genuine philosophy leads to action and from action back again to wonder, to the enduring fact of mystery.

— HENRY MILLER

INTRODUCTION

Action research is a practical approach to professional inquiry in any social situation. Professional practice need not be teaching: it may be management or administration in a school or college, or it may be in an unrelated area, such as medicine or the social services. The context for professional inquiry might change, but the principles and processes involved in action research are the same, regardless of the nature of the practice.

Action research in education is grounded in the working lives of teachers, as they experience them. As its name suggests, action research concerns actors—those people carrying out their professional actions from day to day—and its purpose is to understand and to improve those actions. It is someone on somebody else's practice.

The notion of improvement can be problematic when viewed from the outside. One person's improvement can be another person's about trying to understand professional action from the inside; as a result, it is research that is carried out by practitioners on their own practice, not (as in other forms of research), done by deterioration. It depends on the beliefs and values underpinning the individual's perspective. Practice is contingent upon the practitioners' intentions, values and beliefs and the situation in which those elements are given form. Children, students, classrooms and colleges all vary, as do the management structures, schemes of work, course programmes and assessment procedures which impose structure on them. Educational research through action research does not produce understanding that has universal truth; it is about the here and now—understanding what can be done to improve the current teaching situation. Action research can produce generalisations about practice, but such generalisations are only part of a wider search for understanding. They are not directly applicable beyond the contingencies of the current teaching situation.

Figure 16.1 gives the steps in layman terms of action research.

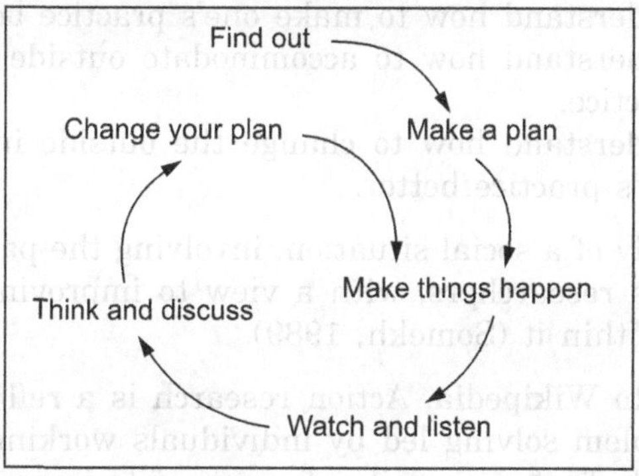

FIGURE 16.1 Steps in action research.

DEFINITIONS OF ACTION RESEARCH

Stephen Corey at Teachers College at Columbia University was among the first to use action research in the field of education. He believed that the scientific method in education would bring about change because educators would be involved in both research and application of information. The process by which practitioners attempt to study their problems scientifically in order to guide, correct and evaluate their decisions and actions is what a number of people have called *action research*.

- Action research emphasises the involvement of teachers in problems in their own classrooms and has as its primary goal the in-service training and development of the teacher rather than the acquisition of general knowledge in the field of education. (Borg, 1965, p. 313)
- Action research is a form of self-reflective enquiry undertaken by the participants [teachers, students or principals, for example] in social [including educational] situations in order to improve the rationality and justice of [a] their own social or educational practices, [b] their understanding of these practices, and [c] the situations [and institutions] in which these practices are carried out (Carr and Kemmis [1986]).

  Carr and Kemmis's (1986) description of action research is thus about the:

  (a) Improvement of practice

(b) Improvement of the understanding of practice.
(c) Improvement of the situation in which the practice takes place.

Action research can thus be used to:

(a) Understand one's own practice.
(b) Understand how to make one's practice better.
(c) Understand how to accommodate outside change in one's practice.
(d) Understand how to change the outside in order to make one's practice better.

- The study of a social situation, involving the participants themselves as researchers, with a view to improving the quality of action within it (Somekh, 1989).

According to Wikipedia, Action research is a reflective process of progressive problem solving led by individuals working with others in teams or as part of a "community of practice" to improve the way they address issues and solve problems.

Based on the uses of action research, a few definitions will prove useful.

- Action research can be used to investigate practical, everyday issues:
- Action research investigates everyday problems experienced by teachers (Elliott, 1981).
- All you need is a general idea that something might be improved (Kemmis and McTaggart, 1982).
- I experience a problem when some of my educational values are negated in my practice (Whitehead, 1985).

Action research is thus *research on action* by using *action* as a *tool for research.* It involves the careful monitoring of planned change in practice. A decision is taken that a particular action may either yield improvements or provide information as to the nature of the teaching situation. The action is thus used as a research tool. Both elements of action and research are of equal prominence in the approach.

TYPES OF ACTION RESEARCH

There are different types of action research (Figure 16.2) depending upon the participants involved. A plan of research can involve a single teacher investigating an issue in her classroom, a group of teachers working on a common problem, or a team of teachers and others focusing on a school- or district-wide issue.

	Individual teacher research	*Collaborative action research*	*School-wide action research*	*District-wide action research*
Focus	Single classroom issue	Single classroom or several classrooms with common issue	School issue, problem, or area of collective interest	District issue organisational structures
Possible support needed	Coach/mentor Access to technology Assistance with data organisation and analysis	Substitute teachers Release time Close link with administrators	School commitment Leadership Communication External partners	District commitment Facilitator Recorder Communication External partners
Potential impact	Curriculum Instruction Assessment	Curriculum Instruction Assessment policy	Potential to impact school restructuring and change Policy Parent involvement Evaluation of programmes	Allocation of resources Professional development activities Organisational structures policy
Side effects	Practice informed by data Information not always shared	Improved collegiality Formation of partnerships	Improved collegiality, collaboration and communication Team building Disagreements on process	Improved collegiality collaboration and communication Team building Disagreements on process Shared vision

FIGURE 16.2 Types of action research.

1. **Individual teacher research** usually focuses on a single issue in the classroom. The teacher may be seeking solutions to problems of classroom management, instructional strategies, use of materials, or student learning. Teachers may have support of their supervisor or principal, an instructor for a course they are taking, or parents. The problem is one that the teacher believes is evident in his or her classroom and one that can be addressed on an individual basis. The research may then be such that the teacher collects data or may involve looking at student participation. One of the drawbacks of individual research is that it may not be shared with others unless the teacher chooses to present findings at a faculty meeting, make a

formal presentation at a conference, or submit written material to a LISTSERV, journal, or newsletter.

2. **Collaborative action research** may include as few as two teachers or a group of several teachers and others interested in addressing a classroom or department issue. This issue may involve one classroom or a common problem shared by many classrooms.
3. **School-wide research** focuses on issues common to all. For example, a school may have a concern about the lack of parental involvement in activities, and is looking for a way to reach more parents to involve them in meaningful ways. Or, the school may be looking to address its organisational and decision-making structures. Teams of staff from the school work together to narrow the question, gather and analyse the data, and decide on a plan of action.
4. **District-wide research** is far more complex and utilises more resources, but the rewards can be great. Issues can be organisational, community-based, performance-based, or processes for decision-making. A district may choose to address a problem common to several schools or to only one school.

ACTION RESEARCH CYCLE

At the simplest level, therefore, action research involves a spiral or cycle of planning, action, monitoring and reflection (Figure 16.3).

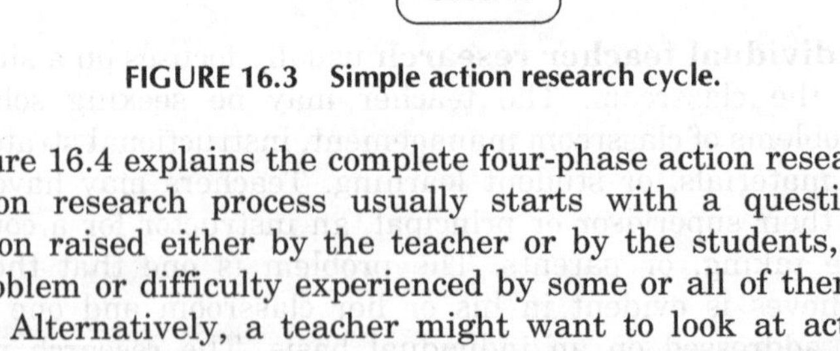

FIGURE 16.3 Simple action research cycle.

Figure 16.4 explains the complete four-phase action research cycle. The action research process usually starts with a question or an observation raised either by the teacher or by the students, about an issue, problem or difficulty experienced by some or all of them in their learning. Alternatively, a teacher might want to look at actions that are successful with some of students so that this can be extended to other students. The cycle continues as the teacher decides on methods to investigate the question. This will involve data collection either in the form of feedback from the students or by observation of their work.

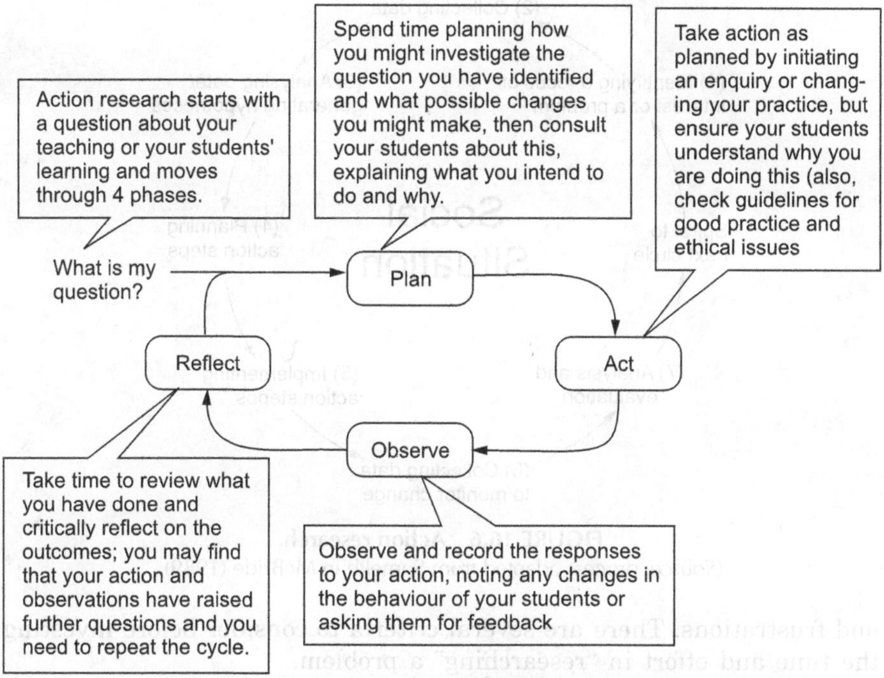

FIGURE 16.4 The four-phase action research cycle.

The process is rarely a simple cycle but more a spiral: reflection on the teacher's action and findings, leading to another question and further action, usually a change in practice, which in turn loops forward to further exploration and greater understanding of how to teach and how students learn, as represented in Figure 16.5.

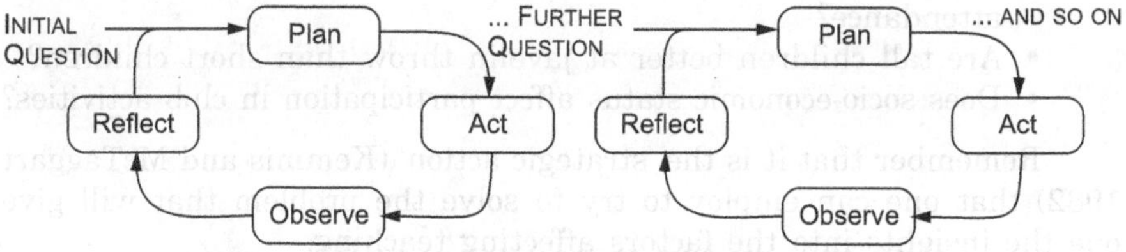

FIGURE 16.5 Action research cycle moving forward.

STEPS IN ACTION RESEARCH

Figure 16.6 illustrates that action research is not only about research but about action too.

***Step 1*—Identification of the problem:** Teachers often have several questions they wish to investigate; however, it is important to limit the question to one that is meaningful and doable in the confines of their daily work. Careful planning at this first stage will limit false starts

FIGURE 16.6 Action research.
(*Source:* process adapted from Somekh in McBride (1989).

and frustrations. There are several criteria to consider before investing the time and effort in "researching" a problem.

An important guideline in choosing a question is to ask if it is something over which the teacher has influence. Is it something of interest and worth the time and effort that will be spent?

Defining and delimiting the problem
It is important to choose an area that you can do something about. Some questions are not amenable to action research:

- Is there any relationship between single-parent families and attendance?
- Are tall children better at javelin throw than short children?
- Does socio-economic status affect participation in club activities?

Remember that it is the 'strategic action' (Kemmis and McTaggart 1982) that one can employ to try to solve the problem that will give one the insights into the factors affecting teaching.

Focusing on a topic

Golden rules for selecting a topic

- Keep it manageable—keep the focus small scale.
- It should be interesting to you—you may need some perseverance to see the inquiry through!
- It should be workable—you are not stumped for ideas, but can identify ways in which you might have a go at addressing your question.
- It is not too disruptive of normal routines. (Important here to think not just of your own, but others' that your actions might affect.)

Step 2—Collecting data: The collection of data is an important step in deciding what action needs to be taken. Multiple sources of data are used to better understand the scope of happenings in the classroom or school. There are many vehicles for collection of data:

1. Select the data that are most appropriate for the issue being researched
    - Are the data easy to collect?
    - Are these sources readily available for use?
    - How structured and systematic will the collection be?
2. Use at least three sources (triangulation) of data for the basis of actions (Figure 16.7).
3. Organise the data in a way that makes it useful to identify trends and themes.
4. Data can be arranged by gender, classroom, grade level, school, etc.

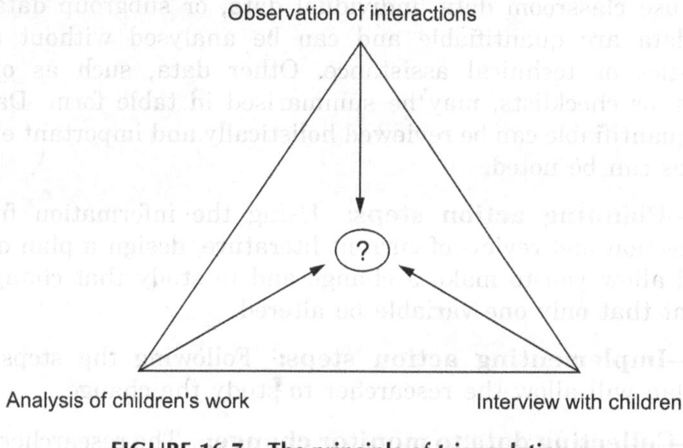

FIGURE 16.7 The principle of triangulation.

Sources of data

journals
individual files
logs of meetings
videotapes
case studies
surveys
records—tests, report cards
attendance
self-assessment
samples of student work
an analytic memo
sociometry
photography
projects, performances
interviews
portfolios
diaries
field notes
audio tapes
photos
memos
questionnaires
anecdotal records
checklist

Example: What is most important is that the researcher understands that any one method of data collection illuminates only particular aspects of a situation. None give a whole picture. In seeking evidence of her practice, or the effectiveness of a change in practice, a teacher needs to look at it from different perspectives; she needs to employ a triangulation of methods. This is a simple principle, involving the careful choice of a range of data gathering techniques, each of which might illuminate a different aspect of the same issue.

In this case, [?] in Fig. 16.7 might be children's engagement during science sessions. Each method will give access to different aspects of the situation. There will still be areas not illuminated, but more is known than if only one method is used. Also, cross-referencing of data from different methods adds to the overall reliability of the research process.

***Step 3*—Analysing data/generating hypotheses:** Analyse and identify major themes. Depending upon the question, teachers may wish to use classroom data, individual data, or subgroup data. Some of the data are quantifiable and can be analysed without the use of statistics or technical assistance. Other data, such as opinions, attitudes, or checklists, may be summarised in table form. Data that are not quantifiable can be reviewed holistically and important elements or themes can be noted.

***Step 4*—Planning action steps:** Using the information from the data collection and review of current literature, design a plan of action that will allow you to make a change and to study that change. It is important that only one variable be altered.

***Step 5*—Implementing action steps:** Following the steps in the action plan will allow the researcher to study the change.

***Step 6*—Collecting data to monitor change:** The researcher collects data using a multipronged method so that she can monitor the observed changes with the implementation of the action plan.

***Step 7*—Analysis and evaluation:** Assess the effects of the intervention to determine if improvement has occurred. If there is improvement, do the data clearly provide the supporting evidence? If no, what changes can be made to the actions to elicit better results?

CHARACTERISTICS OF ACTION RESEARCH

Based on the work of Hult and Lennung (1980), several important features of action research can be identified:

1. The goal of action research is typically increased understanding of a social process, system or situation.

2. Action research is both (a) practical (it assists in problem solving in the context of the social system that is studied), and (b) seeks to expand abstract scientific knowledge, possibly by allowing the development of useful generalisations and systems theories based on results from study of specific social problems.
3. Action research promotes collaboration between researchers and the subjects of the research.
4. Action research is particularly useful for learning about how change takes place in social systems.
5. Action research is about teachers striving to understand and to improve their practice. It may lead to collaboration and a critique of the situation in which the practice is carried out, but this does not have to be a fundamental aim.
6. Action research proceeds through a process of planning, action and reflection upon action. This can be thought of as an action-reflection 'cycle'.
7. Action research involves the gathering of evidence about practice.
8. Action research involves teachers trying to see the effects of planned change in their practice.
9. Action research strives to be systematic and rigorous.

ADVANTAGES OF ACTION RESEARCH

Action research can be a worthwhile pursuit for educators for a number of reasons. Foremost among these is simply the desire to know more. Good teachers are, after all, themselves students, and often look for ways to expand upon their existing knowledge.

1. **Focus on school issue, problem, or area of collective interest:** Research done with the teacher's students, in a setting with which the teacher is familiar helps to confer relevance and validity to a disciplined study. Often, academic research is seen as disconnected from the daily lives of educators. While this might not always be true, it can be very helpful for teachers to pick up threads suggested in academic circles, and weave them into their own classroom. It is also comforting for parents, or education administrators outside of the school, to know that a teacher is not just blindly following what the latest study seems to suggest, but is transforming the knowledge into something meaningful. Reasons for performing action research fall into three categories: to promote personal and professional growth, to improve practice to enhance student learning, and to advance the teaching profession.

2. **Form of teacher professional development:** Research and reflection allow teachers to grow and gain confidence in their work. Action research projects influence thinking skills, sense of efficacy, willingness to share and communicate, and attitudes toward the process

of change. Through action research, teachers learn about themselves, their students, their colleagues, and can determine ways to continually improve.

3. **Collegial interactions:** Isolation is one of the downsides of teaching. Teachers are often the sole adult in a room of children, and have little or no time scheduled for professional conversations with others. Action research in pairs or by teams of teachers allows time to talk with others about teaching and teaching strategies. Teachers learn what it is that they are able to influence and they make changes that produce results that show change. The process provides the opportunity to work with others and to learn from the sharing of ideas. By working on these teams, teachers must describe their own teaching styles and strategies and share their thoughts with others. As a team, they examine curricular materials used in the classroom. Through these discussions with colleagues they develop stronger relationships. As the practice of action research becomes part of the school culture, we see increased sharing and collaboration across departments, disciplines, grade levels, and schools.

4. **Potential to impact school change:** As teachers get into action research, they are more apt to look at questions that address school and district concerns rather than questions that affect the individual teacher. This process creates new patterns of collegiality, communication, and sharing. Contributions to the body of knowledge about teaching and learning may also result. Development of priorities for school-wide planning and assessment efforts arise from inquiry with potential to motivate change for improvement's sake.

5. **Reflect on own practice:** Opportunities for teachers to evaluate themselves in schools are often few, and usually happen only in an informal manner. Action research can serve as a chance to really take a look at one's own teaching in a structured manner. While the focus of action research is usually the students, educators can also investigate what effect their teaching is having on their students, how they could work better with other teachers, or ways of changing the whole school for the better. Conversations can take on a different focus from attempting to "fix" to arrive at understanding.

6. **Improved communications:** Team work within the school or district brings individuals together for a shared purpose. Educators involved in action research become more flexible in their thinking and more open to new ideas (Pine, 1981). Studies by Little (1981) suggest positive changes in patterns of collegiality, communication, and networking. Action research can improve the teaching and learning process by reinforcing, modifying, or changing perceptions based on informal data and nonsystematic observations.

ROLE OF THE ACTION RESEARCHER

The researcher's role is to implement the action research method in such a manner as to produce a mutually agreeable outcome for all participants, with the process being maintained by them afterwards. To accomplish this, it may necessitate the adoption of many different roles at various stages of the process, including those of

planner	leader
catalyst	facilitator
teacher	designer
listener	observer
synthesiser	reporter

The main role, however, is to nurture local leaders to the point where they can take responsibility for the process. This point is reached when they understand the methods and are able to carry on when the initiating researcher leaves. In many action research situations, the hired researcher's role is primarily to take the time to facilitate dialogue and foster reflective analysis among the participants, provide them with periodic reports, and write a final report when the researcher's involvement has ended.

Guidelines for good practice—for the action researcher

1. Decide, in consultation with colleagues and students where possible, what question you want to explore.
2. Work out the details of your methodology (with colleagues if appropriate) and discuss with your students what you are planning to do and why.
3. Make sure that whatever enquiry you plan to undertake is with your own students and with those of any colleague with whom you are working.
4. Make sure your enquiry methods do not disrupt your students' study in any way. If possible, what you plan to do should enhance it.
5. Make sure your students know that you will preserve their anonymity and that you will quote from their responses only with their permission.
6. Make it quite clear that involvement in any enquiry is voluntary and any student who wishes to opt out of the activity is perfectly at liberty to do so.
7. When you have collected evidence from your students, share your findings with them and explain the implications of these, both for them and for future cohorts of students.
8. You may want to check your plans with your staff tutor who may know if other tutors in your region are engaging in similar enquiries.
9. Talk to colleagues about their experiences or read some reports of action research carried out by others.

Example

Action Plan

- http://www.sagepub.com/mertler2study/pdf/Sample%20Action%20Research%20Report%201.pdf Effect of Technology on Enthusiasm for Learning Science, Jane L. Hollis Lake City Middle School Lake City, Florida.

REFERENCES

Elliott, J. (1981), *Action Research: A Framework for Self-evaluation in Schools. TIQL working paper no.1.*, Cambridge Institute of Education, Cambridge.

Forster, Colin and Eperjesi, Rachel (2021), Action Research for Student Teachers, Sage, UK, 2nd Edition.

Hult, M. and Lennung, S. (1980), Towards a Definition of Action Research: A Note and Bibliography, *Journal of Management Studies*, Wiley, USA. Vol. 17, No. 2, pp. 242–250.

Kemmi's S. and McTaggart, R. (1982), The Action Research Planner, Deakin University Press, Victoria.

McAteer, Mary (2013), Action Research in Education Series, BERA/SAGE Research Methods in Education, UK.

Mertler, Craig A, (2019), Action Research (6th ed.) Improving Schools and Empowering Educators, SAGE Publications, UK.

Pine, G.J. (1981), *Collaborative Action Research: The Integration of Research and Service*, Paper presented at the annual meeting of the American Association of Colleges for Teacher Education, Detroit, MI.

Part VIII

WAY FORWARD

CHAPTER 17

Current Issues and Problems in Teacher Education

....putting in the groundwork now, with an eye on the future and the trends that are driving technology and society, will give us the best chance of ensuring it will be something meaningful and rewarding.

—Bernard Marr

INTRODUCTION

Education is the backbone of a developing nation like India. It is the standard of education that determines a citizen's progress and the country's development. To sustain growth and development requires provision of quality education at all levels—primary, secondary as well as higher education, including teacher education.

The various institutions affiliated to Indian Universities and recognised by the NCTE providing teacher education are commencing their restructured mandates after repeated inspections. Many of these institutions fail to provide acceptable levels of teacher education.

Various studies and reports have already been undertaken to look into teachers' professional development in India. All of them have cited that teacher performance and quality is most notably affected by: educational qualification of teachers; recruitment on merit; adequate teacher performance monitoring system; incentives, upgradation of teacher skills and growth oriented career structure With the issues being identified both at the macro and micro level and solutions also proposed, what remains to be done is the implementation of these corrective actions, which will ultimately raise the quality of the teachers. Policy guidelines provided by the National Curriculum Framework for Teacher Education 2010 that adequately interprets the problems and laws are needed to bring about the necessary changes to successfully and effectively implement the changes.

This chapter highlights the status of and issues facing the teaching profession and teacher education programmes in India. Numerous reports have highlighted the challenges facing teacher education and its provision of professional development for teachers.

NATIONAL COUNCIL FOR TEACHER EDUCATION

The National Council for Teacher Education is a statutory body set up under the National Council for Teacher Education Act, 1993 to facilitate planned and coordinated development of the teacher education system in the country, and for regulation and proper maintenance of norms and standards in the teacher education system. The mandate given to the NCTE is very broad and covers the whole gamut of teacher education programmes including research and training of persons to equip them to teach at pre-primary, primary, secondary and senior secondary stages in schools, and non-formal education, part-time education, adult education and distance (correspondence) education courses. The Council, under Section 12, is responsible for the following activities and functions:

1. To coordinate and monitor teacher education and its development in the country.
2. To lay down guidelines in respect of minimum qualifications for a person to be employed as a teacher.
3. To lay down norms for any specified category of courses or trainings in teacher education.
4. To lay down guidelines for compliance by recognised institutions for starting new courses or training.
5. To lay down standards in respect of examinations, leading to teacher education qualifications.
6. To examine and review periodically the implementation of the norms, guidelines and standards laid down by the Council.

The Council is empowered to grant recognition of institutions offering courses or training in teacher education (like B.Ed., M.Ed. and D.T.Ed.)

NCTE website provides details of institutions recognised by NCTE including courses recognised by it. There is a summary Fact Sheet about the institution with details of the Courses (www.ncte-india.org).

STRENGTHS OF TEACHER PROFESSIONAL DEVELOPMENT IN INDIA

The infrastructure to impart teacher training already exists throughout the country. What is required is the upgradation of these facilities as per the changing needs and the redressing of the teaching programmes. The government is aware and acknowledges the importance of effective teacher training as a vital part of lifting the education standard of the country. The NCFTE 2010 is a great policy document, which is in the process of implementation.

The proposed mandatory NAAC accreditation of all teacher training institutions in the country by April 2012 is a giant step in the right direction. All spurious teacher training institutions will either close down or set up suitable infrastructure by this time.

The setting up of Tamil Nadu Teacher Education University focusing only on teacher education in all its dimensions is a welcome move. It has helped focus on the need and requirements of teacher education as a discipline as well as help in catering to the needs of the state in teacher recruitment.

NATIONAL CURRICULUM FRAMEWORK—CONCERNS ON TEACHER EDUCATION

The NCF has described the current concerns of teacher education as follows:

1. Experiences in the practice of teacher education indicate that knowledge is treated as 'given', embedded in the curriculum and accepted without question; there is no engagement with the curriculum. Curriculum, syllabi and textbooks are never critically examined by the student teacher or the regular teacher.
2. Language proficiency of the teacher needs to be enhanced, but existing programmes do not recognise the centrality of language in the curriculum.
3. Teacher education programmes provide little scope for student teachers to reflect on their experiences.
4. Disciplinary knowledge is viewed as independent of professional training in pedagogy.
5. Repeated 'practice' in the teaching of a specified number of isolated lessons is considered a sufficient condition for professional development.
6. It is assumed that links between learning theories and models and teaching methods are automatically formed in the understanding developed by student teachers.
7. There is no opportunity for teachers to examine their own biases and beliefs and reflect on their own experiences as part of classroom discourse and enquiry.
8. Theory courses have no clear link with practical work and ground realities.

The evaluation system followed in teacher education programmes is too information-oriented, excessively quantitative and lacks comprehensiveness.

Apart from conceptual and pedagogical aspects, existing programmes need to develop certain attitudes, dispositions, habits and interests in a teacher. The present evaluation protocol has no place for evaluating these aspects.

KEY ISSUES AND PROBLEMS RELATED TO TEACHER EDUCATION

The proliferation of sub-standard private teacher education institutions and the current state of teacher education programmes are both serious impediments to fulfilling the objectives of the NCF and the Right to Free and Compulsory Education. The programmes have come under severe criticism for not addressing the needs of contemporary Indian schools and not preparing teachers who can impart quality education in schools. Their design/practice is based on certain assumptions which impede the progress of ideas and professional and personal growth of the teacher. They train teachers to adjust to a system in which education is seen as transmission of information. They take the school curriculum and textbooks as 'given' and train teachers to adjust to the needs of the existing school system through fastidious planning of lessons in standardised formats and fulfilling the ritual of delivering the required number of lessons (NCERT, 2005).

Lack of Standards—Improving Quality

The improvement of quality refers to initiatives taken by all stakeholders of the education system to raise the standards and meet global standards. Competency standards can enlighten the work of curriculum development as well as serve as a means through which good teaching can be identified, practised, and rewarded. In Australia, the National Framework for Professional Standards in Teaching describes four career dimensions for teachers. These include graduation, competence, accomplishment and leadership. Each of these dimensions is defined through four professional components of teachers' work, which are professional knowledge, professional practice, professional values, and professional relationships (Furniss 2005). In general, there are three types of teacher education standards, including standards for teachers, teacher education units and teacher education programmes and subject areas (Levy, 2004).

Professional standards constitute the 'critical knowledge, skills and attitudes needed to perform a particular role effectively'. They describe the primary components of performance rather than provide a comprehensive list of responsibilities. In addition, they serve to specify what performance and/or behaviours a school is particularly looking for. The extent to which professional standards have been met can be assessed via performance indicators. They can be transformed into measures of performance that are meaningful to schools without restricting roles to a series of mechanistic tasks.

A lack of standards for education in India has resulted in the challenge of harmonisation of school education with teacher education as the required competencies of teachers have not been defined. There is a mismatch between teacher education curriculum and the school curriculum. However, the Sarva Shikshya Abhyan and the Rastriya Shikshya Abhyan with their aggressive training schedules in most states of India are doing a great job filling the gap. The introduction of ALM methodology in all training colleges in pre-service education as part of the regular training is a step in the right direction.

Licensing and Accreditation

Accreditation, licensing and certification are separate but complementary processes in order to ensure quality teaching. They constitute three distinct points along a continuum of teacher preparation.

Accreditation is an evaluation process that determines the quality of an institution or programme using predetermined standards. Accreditation, say, by NAAC is normally carried out on a peer review basis by competent, nongovernmental agencies such as national, regional, and/or local associations. It is, in essence, a collegial activity conducted by institutions that have voluntarily organised to form and to support an accrediting association.

Licensing is the process by which a governmental agency grants a license—or permission—to an individual who has met specified requirements. These requirements are usually minimal. Their purpose is to assure the public that the licensed individual will do no harm to the student learner. In the case of licensing teachers, the intent is to prevent individuals from doing harm in the classroom.

Certification is the process by which a non-governmental agency or association bestows professional recognition to an individual who has met certain predetermined qualifications specified by that agency or association.

Improving Access

Higher education in general, and teacher education in particular, must be accessible to all. This can be done by:

1. Increasing the number of institutions offering courses, B.Ed. and D.T.Ed. courses, relevant to the needs of the students as well as meeting national goals.

2. Reducing cost.
3. Availability of easy loans facilitating payment of fees for poor students.

Organising Practice Teaching

It seems to be necessary to integrate practice coherently into all models of teacher education. In integrating practice and the other components of teacher education into specific programmes prominent factors will include:

1. The development of a strong, mutually beneficial, partnership with schools.
2. Differentiation and understanding of the division of work and responsibilities between the partners.
3. High quality teachers specially educated to fulfil the demanding tasks of cooperating supervisors, mentors and partners.

Research and Development

As in all other (and not only academic) professions, a close relationship between (educational) research and development, and the (teaching) profession seems to be indispensable. An increasing recognition of the high relevance of research for high quality education in general and high quality teacher education in particular, has led to a certain expansion and cultivation of research and development related to, and relevant for, teacher education. However,

1. Most institutions of teacher education and their staff as well as student teachers and teachers have, until recently, been separated from research and development.
2. Many institutions of teacher education do not have a clear responsibility to take part in, or adequate resources for, research and development.
3. Initial teacher education as well as in-service teacher education needs to find a clear profile in regard to research and development, and an active involvement of teachers in it.
4. A development in this direction implies that all institutions and/or departments involved in teacher education programmes must themselves be actively involved in research and in doctoral programmes specifically related to teacher education, teaching and teacher work.

> Reform of teacher education to move forward on a sound footing demands dedicated research in the area of foundations of education in the Indian context by universities, preferably in independently established departments. The research in such departments would help develop the teacher education programmes on a more sound theoretical basis. The existing departments of education have hardly been able to engage themselves in this long-pending need for their pre-occupation in conducting routine teacher training and research programmes
>
> —NCFTE 2010

In-service Education and Professional Development

There is a dire need for:

1. Improving the quality of training programmes and training institutions.
2. Expanding training facilities.
3. Making adequate provision for the continuing professional education of all teachers.
4. Creating appropriate agencies, both at the Centre and in the States, for the maintenance of standards in teacher education.

Problems in regard to in-service education of teachers are as follows:

1. Continuous professional development and in-service education have yet to be perceived as integral parts of the professional responsibilities and the work load of teachers neither by employers nor by some members of the teaching force. Making high quality education a reality calls for the recognition of continuous professional development and in-service education as integral parts of teacher work and of teacher education.
2. Issues relating to whether in-service education ought to be voluntary or compulsory must be sorted out.
3. Formal in-service education is frequently subject to control by the school administration. Issues of evaluation and quality control of in-service education have to be resolved.

Removing the Isolation of Training Institutions

Removing the isolation of training institutions by bringing them into the mainstream of the academic life of the universities and by building up closer relations with the schools and between the training institutions preparing teachers for different levels is necessary. The Tamil Nadu Teacher Education University has done a commendable job in bringing all training colleges in Tamil Nadu under one umbrella. This has reduced the isolation of teacher education colleges from schools, university and one other. This isolation takes the following three forms:

1. **Isolation from university life:** The professional education of primary teachers is not looked upon as a concern of the universities. The professional education of secondary teachers is with the universities, no doubt, but it has become separated from other intellectual disciplines in the university. Education should be brought into the mainstream of the academic life of the universities. In India, the general trend has been to identify education with pedagogy. It has been taught mostly in training institutions and is studied only by those who decide to enter the teaching profession, after such a decision has been made. In the educationally advanced countries, however, education has developed considerably as a social science and a separate academic discipline.
2. **Isolation from schools:** Teacher education, both at the primary and secondary levels, has become isolated from schools and current developments in school education.
3. **Isolation from one another:** The different types of teacher-training institutions are isolated from one another and do not form an integrated community.

The ultimate objective should be to bring all teacher education under the universities in such a manner that it continues to function in close collaboration with state departments of education and teachers' organisations.

Recommended steps to reduce the three-fold isolation are:

1. Conducting courses in professional education for different categories of teachers-pre-primary, primary and secondary.
2. Providing extension services to a few institutions of teacher education at all levels and to assist them to grow.
3. Organising summer institutes and in-service programmes in subject content as well as in professional education.
4. Working in close collaboration with a few schools of all types with a view to developing research and evolving better curricula and techniques of teaching.
5. Promoting research in education, especially with an interdisciplinary approach.
6. Adopting a practice of appointing eminent professors in different disciplines as part time professors in the schools of education, to explain new developments in their fields and the manner in which they will affect education at the school stage
7. Introducing courses in undergraduate education giving an orientation in three broad areas—sociological, philosophical and psychological foundations of education.

8. Guiding neighbourhood schools and their staff in planning their work and in using improved methods of teaching. Such extension work is needed as much for the improvement of schools as for the improvement of the training programme itself.
9. Promotion of effective alumni associations which would periodically bring together old students from far and near to discuss problems of common interest with the college staff.
10. Making student-teaching a comprehensive internship in which trainees are able to observe the entire work of the school and to participate actively in all the important professional activities of a teacher, both in and out of the classroom. This will be possible only when there is a systematic collaboration and cooperation between the schools and the training institutions and when student-teaching is regarded as the joint responsibility of the producers (i.e. the training institutions) and the users (i.e. the schools and state departments).
11. The training college staff itself, which will find a fruitful field of research in educational methods and practices opened up to them through their collaboration with schools, will benefit considerably if they can do some continuous teaching in the cooperating schools.

Pre-service Education

The `input' stage in the teacher preparation process is comparable to recruitment into the profession. Candidates to the teaching programme, whether B.Ed. or D.T.Ed., should be selected based on a set of criteria which includes content knowledge, formal and informal education accomplishments related to technology, and a disposition for organising and sharing knowledge and competencies with children. Admission to the course should be highly competitive and should involve interviewing as well as competence testing. A teacher-needs analysis within the target region should be done to rationalise the setting up of teacher training colleges by the NCTE and also to justify the recruitment process from year to year. By examining the entire teacher development process from recruitment, through pre-service preparation, to the first two years of teaching, continuity from the beginning teacher's perspective, is enhanced, and programme excellence is fostered.

INCLUSIVE EDUCATION

Two kinds of exclusion exist in schools, largely because of an inadequate preparation of teachers to address diversity in the classroom.

1. The exclusion of the *children with disabilities of different kinds and learning difficulties*. Neither does the teacher understand their needs nor what she can do to make learning possible for

them. The Persons with Disabilities (PWD) (Equal Opportunities, Protection and Full Participation) Act, 1996 (amended in 2016) provides for free and compulsory education up to the age of 18 years for all children with disabilities which are listed (21 disabilities) in the Act. To enable the implementation of this Act, teacher education institutions will need to reframe their programme courses to include the perspective, concept and strategies of inclusive education.

2. The *social exclusion of children who come from socially and economically deprived backgrounds, Scheduled Castes (SCs), Scheduled Tribes (STs), minority and other communities, girls and children with diverse learning needs.* There is a dire need to equip teachers to overcome their biases in this regard and to develop professional capacities to address these challenges. The education of socially and economically disadvantaged groups, especially the SCs/STs and minorities, has remained a primary national concern of education for several years.

Inclusive education refers to a philosophical position as well as an arrangement of institutional facilities and processes. This is to ensure access to and conditions of success in education for everybody, including those in the margins, either with learning difficulties because of physical or mental disabilities or because of their social position. The aim of inclusive education is to create an integrated school setting, providing equal opportunities to children with special abilities, varied social backgrounds and diverse learning needs.

Teachers need to be quipped to sensitively bring and include girls in the classroom transaction. It is necessary that teachers who teach and manage the classroom are sensitised and made aware of the philosophy of inclusive education and oriented to the different kinds of adjustments that schools have to make in terms of infrastructure, curriculum, teaching methods and other school practices to relate teaching to the needs of all learners.

EQUITABLE AND SUSTAINABLE DEVELOPMENT

To promote equitable and sustainable development for all sections of society and respect for all, it is necessary that they be educated through perspectives of gender equity, the perspectives that develop values for peace, respect the rights of all, and respect and value work. Education has a crucial role to play in promoting values of peace based on equal respect of self and others. The NCF and subsequent development of syllabi and materials provide a direction in this regard. For this, teachers need to be equipped to understand these issues and incorporate them in their teaching. The new teacher education curriculum framework will need to integrate these perspectives in its formulation.

ROLE OF COMMUNITY KNOWLEDGE IN EDUCATION

It is important for the development of concepts in children as well as the application of school knowledge in real life that formal school knowledge is linked with community knowledge. This increases the relevance of education as well as the quality of learning. Teachers should be trained in identifying entry points in the curriculum and textual materials in the context of the local situation. These contextual references may include community knowledge about technology, local occupations both farm and non-farm, local folk culture including songs, festivals, fairs and games. As teachers develop curriculum materials and learning experiences, informed by the perspectives enunciated above (gender, peace, sustainable development), they will also learn, through actual participation, the skills to identify and process the specifics for the purposes of meaningful curriculum transaction.

ICT IN SCHOOLS AND e-LEARNING

With the onset and proliferation of Information and Communication Technology (ICT), there is a growing demand that it be included in school education. Teacher education needs to orient and sensitise the teacher to distinguish between critically useful, developmentally appropriate and the detrimental use of ICT. In a way, ICT can be imaginatively drawn upon for professional development and academic support of the pre-service and in-service teachers.

Figure 17.1 shows the adapted version of the "21st Century Skills" model, developed by The Partnership for 21st Century Skills,

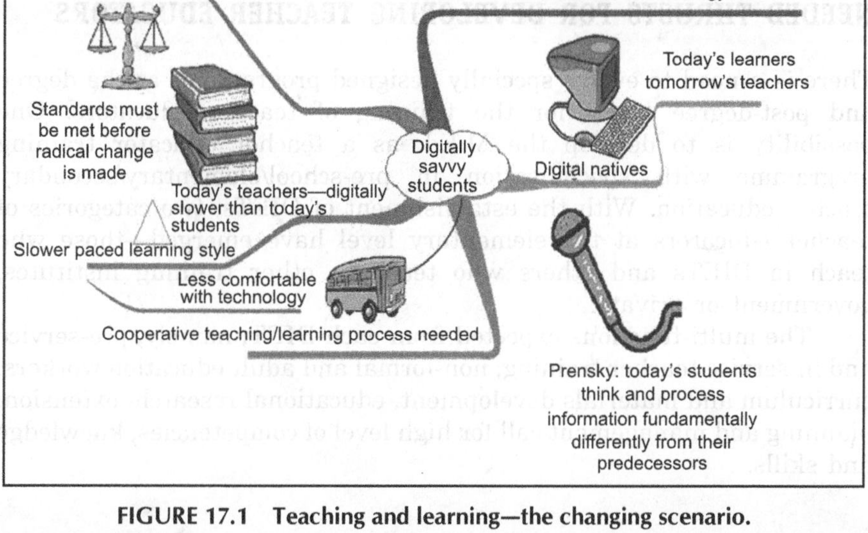

FIGURE 17.1 Teaching and learning—the changing scenario.

in education. The vast majority of teachers are entering the profession without basic technology skills to implement in their classrooms. Fresh out of teacher education programmes, they know less about technology than their students, and yet they are expected to teach digital savvy students how to think creatively using skills that are still evolving with technologies they are not adept with to solve future problems not yet identified. This graphic demonstrates the fundamental disconnect between teachers and students in today's average classroom.

PREPARING TEACHER EDUCATORS

It is obvious that the education and training of a prospective teacher will be effective to the extent that it has been delivered by teacher educators who are competent and professionally equipped for the job.

This necessarily means that in addition to revamping the existing M.Ed. programme, a fresh discourse has to be initiated in teacher education to arrive at tangible understandings of the implications of aspects such as:

1. Creating multilateral entry points for the study of educational studies as a pursuit in higher education.
2. Broad basing the profile of teacher educators by infusion of persons who have knowledge of disciplines generic to teacher education so that the discipline of education grows into specialisation requiring persons to be well-versed in cognate disciplines outside education.
3. Working out possibilities to pursue educational study at the post-graduate level through the route to teacher education involving bridge courses, wherever required and considered necessary.

NEEDED THRUSTS FOR DEVELOPING TEACHER EDUCATORS

There is a need to evolve specially designed programmes at the degree and post-degree levels for the training of teacher educators. One possibility is to develop the M.Ed. as a teacher educator training programme with specialisation in pre-school/elementary/secondary teacher education. With the establishment of DIETs, two categories of teacher educators at the elementary level have emerged—those who teach in DIETs and others who teach in other training institutes, government or private.

The multi-functions expected from each DIET, namely, pre-service and in-service teacher training, non-formal and adult education workers, curriculum and materials development, educational research, extension, planning and management call for high level of competencies, knowledge and skills.

The B.Ed. programme is offered in colleges of education and university departments of education. The programme is also offered through centres of distance education/open universities. There has been a proliferation of private colleges offering the B.Ed. over the past number of years. Triggered by market factors, their total number, as on March 2009, is 14,428 in 11,861 institutions with an approved intake of 10,96,673 candidates.

With the mushrooming of teacher education institutions over the years, the situation has become critical as the supply of teacher educators has not kept up with the increasing demand for faculty, and institutions have compromised faculty requirements with reference both to qualifications and number.

ENHANCING THE STATUS OF EDUCATIONAL STUDIES AND PROFESSIONAL DEVELOPMENT OF TEACHER EDUCATORS

Isolation of education as a discipline from the system of higher education is identified as one main cause for the continued low status of educational studies. The NCF has also suggested that undergraduate students be provided with a variety of routes to pursue studies in education like four-year integrated courses in elementary and secondary education, electives in educational studies in undergraduate programmes of general education, followed by a range of postgraduate studies in education, social sciences, sciences, humanities, mathematics, language studies and the liberal arts. Such diverse routes are likely to tap talented and motivated young people to enter into education and pursue options such as teacher education, research, curriculum and pedagogy.

The recommendations of NCFTE 2010 include the following:

- Setting up of Schools of Education in selected (30) university departments including the RIEs for breaking the isolation of elementary and secondary teacher education from the mainstream and integrating it with higher education. The Schools will have Centres for pre-service teacher education, curriculum research policy and educational development, learning and pedagogic studies, assessment and evaluation, professional development of teacher educators and teacher education curricula and teacher resource and academic support.
- Setting up one Inter-University Centre at the national level functioning under the UGC to coordinate the Schools in terms of academic content: redesigning teacher education curricula, developing curriculum materials, commissioning of materials in regional languages, setting up of web portals on curriculum and pedagogic materials for teacher education. The mandate for Centre would be to provide an integrated focus on elementary and secondary levels of school education.

- Instituting Specialised Centres of Education in lead national level institutions like IISc, Homi Bhabha Centre, TIFR to offer sandwiched postgraduate courses of 3 years' duration (B.Ed. for 2 years or M.Ed. for 3 years) towards developing a specialised cadre of Senior Secondary school teachers and teacher educators.
- Establishing four Regional Centres of Educational Management in the IIMs and NUEPA to provide a postgraduate degree in educational management for Heads of DIETs, SCERTs.
- The Centre for Professional Development of Teacher Educators will offer Master's programme in elementary education/secondary education with specialisation in curriculum and pedagogic studies in mathematics/science/social science education and assessment.
- Reorientation of select secondary school teachers for elementary school teaching through Advance Diploma in elementary education; focused programmes of professional development for DIET/SCERT faculty including curriculum and pedagogic studies and disciplinary knowledge base.
- Special emphasis for professional renewal of existing teacher educators through Refresher Courses for all teacher educators including elementary school teachers in the proposed University Schools of Education and special subject refresher courses by university departments.
- Institute teacher educator fellowships to undertake research with provision for mentoring. About 200 or more Fellowships for teacher educators working in government and aided institutions of teacher education. The Fellowships will offer opportunities for attachment to institutions of higher learning to pursue teaching and research for a period of 2 years.
- Periodic academic enrichment activities—public lectures, film and book discussion sessions, need-based issues, short-term orientation courses on teaching-learning skills, meta-learning strategies related to different curricular areas and child development, pedagogical aspects related to reading, writing, thinking and instructional design theories for curriculum developers.
- The Centre for Teacher Resource and Academic Support: provision of teacher resources, children's literature, variety of school curricula, textbooks, multimedia materials, internet access; platform for teacher interaction, faculty exchange, seminars, study sessions, academic support, face-to-face as well as through ICT; development of learning and teaching materials for use in schools and sharing across schools.

PREPARATION OF TEACHER EDUCATORS—FUTURE DIRECTIONS AND POSSIBILITIES

The education of teacher educators is a major issue in teacher education. Presently, the education of teacher educators takes place mainly through the well-entrenched one-year M.Ed. Table 17.1 gives the key recommendations of the NCFTE 2010. Further advancement is available through M.Phil. and Ph.D. routes. However, these are not specifically designed to prepare a teacher educator, although they all provide knowledge related to some aspects of teacher education.

The NCFTE 2010 gives the following recommendations in this context:

- Mechanisms need to be evolved to promote the entry of talent in teacher education programmes.
- Vertical linkages for postgraduate studies in education, including research programmes for students from a variety of science and social science disciplines need to be provided.
- Integrated models of teacher education of four or five years' duration could comprise of core components that would be common to all teacher education programmes (pre-primary, elementary, secondary and senior secondary) followed by specialisation of professional development, specific to the stage of education.
- Specialisation at the postgraduation level in science education, language education, social sciences education and mathematics education need to be developed.
- The distinction between education as a liberal study and education as a professional preparation needs to be appreciated and postgraduate programme design should take this into consideration.

TABLE 17.1 In general-key recommendations

For collaboration between institutions of colleges and institutes of education and the school community

Institutions of teacher education and school districts that are involved with partnerships for teacher education should—working together—establish a comprehensive, integrated system of recruiting and advising people who are interested in teaching as a profession.

For the teacher education community

1. Teaching departments in colleges and universities should assume greater responsibility for offering college-level courses that provide teachers with strong exposure to appropriate content and that model the kinds of pedagogical approaches appropriate for teaching that content.
2. Autonomous colleges and universities should re-examine and re-design introductory college-level courses in all subjects to better accommodate the needs of practicing and future teachers.
3. Universities whose primary mission includes education research should set as a priority the development and execution of peer-reviewed research studies that focus on ways to improve teacher education, the art of teaching, and learning for people of all ages. New research that focuses broadly on synthesising data across studies and linking it to school practice in a wide variety of school settings would be especially helpful to the improvement of teacher education and professional development for both prospective and experienced teachers. The results of this research should be collated and disseminated through a national electronic database or library.

The National Vision Mission will definitely nurture innovations as evident through the emergence of National Curriculum for Teacher Education (NCTE, 2009) and Teacher Education: Reflections Towards Policy Formulation (NCTE, 2009).

There are proposals for Integrated Innovative Teacher Education Programmes (Navrachna University, Vadodara, 2009, Carolex University, Ahmedabad, 2009). A Bill is through on The Indian Institute of Teacher Education, Gujarat (Bill 4, 2010) which envisages to establish a Centre of Excellence in Teacher Education for Research, Training & Development, Extension Capacity Building to Exhilarate and Enthuse Educators and Institutions. There is Research for Holistic Education. Even the general streams of Science and Arts have realised the importance of Teacher Education (Gandhigram Rural University, Dindigul). Attempts are being made for enhancement of professional competencies of teachers through ICT mediated Constructivist Approach.

Changing the Approach to Teacher Education

Artificial intelligence (AI), robotics, automation—as well as disasters such as pandemics—mean the way the future generations are studying and working will look very different to how it is today. According, to the World Economic Forum Future of Jobs report 2023, there will be a greater need for strong cognitive skills to solve more complex problems. As a result, their research lists the top five 'skills on the rise' as:

- Creative thinking
- Analytical thinking
- Technological literacy
- Curiosity and lifelong learning
- Resilience, flexibility, and agility

The NEP2020 envisions that by 2030, the minimum degree qualifications for teaching will be a 4-year integrated B.Ed. degree. Major changes carried out in higher education including teacher education so far are:

- Upgradation of Curriculum-Pre-Service Education
- UGC Credit transfer-for online courses from 20% to 40%
- Use of MOOC (Massive Open Online Courses) platforms, edX sites, Swayam courses have been increased
- Upskilling with rapid digital innovations in Teacher Education, more so due to the pandemic
- In-service teacher training especially in digital literacy, of all teachers and teacher-educators

CONCLUSION

In an evolving society,forward looking attitudes towards education needs to evolve, too. No longer will it be the norm for a learner to spend the first twenty or so years of life in formal education before employment, where frequent on-the-job training on an ad-hoc basis is needed. Education is today a lifelong endeavor, and online learning will play a big part in this.

Teacher education needs to keep pace with the societal needs and modern trends of changing times.

REFERENCES

Annual Report (2008–2009), *National Council for Teacher Education (NCTE)*, New Delhi.

Batra, Poonam (2005), Voice and Agency of Teachers: The Missing Link in the National Curriculum Framework, 2005, EPW, October 1–7.

Curriculum Framework for Teacher Education, draft 2006, National Council for Teacher Education (NCTE), New Delhi.

Furniss, Elaine (2005), *Report of a Needs Assessment of Government Colleges for Elementary Teachers*, Punjab Province, Pakistan, 2005, Government of Pakistan-UNICEF Programme of Cooperation.

Government of India NEP1986. *National Education Policy*, Ministry of Human Resource Development, New Delhi.

Government of India (2009), *National Curriculum Frameworks on Teacher*, National Council for Teacher Education (NCTE), New Delhi.

Levy, Jack (2004), *Teacher Education Standards and Their Role in Education Reform*, Presentation made at the National Teacher Training Conference, Academy for Educational Development.

Mohan, Radha, Myint Swe Khine (Editor), and Yang Liu (Editor), (2022) and "Reshaping Teacher Education for the 21st Century-An Indian Perspective" in Handbook of Research on Teacher Education: Innovations and Practices in Asia, Springer, Singapore, https://doi.org/10.1007/978-981-16-9785-2_25.

Myint Swe Khine (Editor), and Yang Liu (Editor) (2022), Handbook of Research on Teacher Education: Innovations and Practices in Asia, Springer, Singapore, 1st ed.

National Knowledge Commission Report, (2007), Government of India, New Delhi.

Position Paper of the National Focus Group on Peace Education, NCERT, 2006.

Right of Children to Free and Compulsory Education Act, 2009, *The Gazette of India*, August 27, 2009, New Delhi, p. 9.

Working Group Report on Elementary Education and Literacy, XI Five Year Plan, January 2007, pp. 187–190.

Web References

Government of India NPE2020.Final National Education Policy 2020 (PDF) (Report). Ministry of Human Resource Development. https://niepid.nic.in/nep_2020.pdf.

World Economic Forum https://www.weforum.org/agenda.

Index